THE GOLDEN MIDDLE AGE

THE
GOLDEN MIDDLE AGE

BY
ROGER LLOYD

Essay Index Reprint Series

 BOOKS FOR LIBRARIES PRESS
FREEPORT, NEW YORK

First Published 1939
Reprinted 1969

STANDARD BOOK NUMBER:
8369-1208-X

LIBRARY OF CONGRESS CATALOG CARD NUMBER:
75-90654

PRINTED IN THE UNITED STATES OF AMERICA

To Helen Waddell
in Admiration

INTRODUCTION

THE wrath of the expert when the amateur goes clodhopping in the midst of his carefully tilled gardens is a fearsome thing, and no one can publish a book like this without being uneasily conscious of it. That this is the book of an amateur no one knows better than its author, but he will hope that to the term "amateur" the correct meaning may be attached. The word "amateur", says the *Oxford Dictionary*, means, "One who is fond of; one who cultivates a thing as a pastime". That is exactly the position. This book has been written for love, as an expression of an odd fondness of many years' standing for reading about the various aspects of the scholar's life in the twelfth century, and of the effects of the twelfth-century Renaissance on the social life of Europe as a whole. Thus the book is really a holiday task. As such it is limited to those sides of twelfth-century life which I happen to find interesting, and is very far from being either an exhaustive or comprehensive examination of the life of the century as a whole. Thus but little is said of the monastic revival, and nothing of the growing power of Pope and Emperor which came to their respective climaxes at the end of the century in Innocent III and Frederick II. The Crusades, which absorbed so much of the creative thought and action of the time, are hardly mentioned. The gaps are tremendous, but to draw a truly proportioned picture of the history of Europe during those hundred vital years would occupy nothing less than the lifetime of a great scholar: the more modest

INTRODUCTION

holiday task of an amateur must make no such claim. He must be content to glean where others have sown and reaped, but, because he is an amateur, he has the privilege of gleaning only in those parts of the whole field which he personally happens to find attractive.

Half the attraction of writing history lies in the arrangement, the architecture. I have tried to find a *via media* between the view of Carlyle that the hero makes history, and the more fashionable view of the Marxists that the hunger of the anonymous masses is history's differentiating term. The twelfth-century achievement is essentially that of the anonymous host of the wandering scholars, so that to approach it from Carlyle's point of view would inevitably result in serious distortion. On the other hand, every building must have a corner-stone; and the corner-stone of even a social history has to be personal, for otherwise it could be neither definite nor strong. Happily, the Muse of History generally comes herself to the rescue of the historians; and from this dilemma she delivers them by providing in most generations some articulate figure, who "goes everywhere and knows everyone", who lives among the giants but is not himself so giant-like or heroic as to lose touch with the broad masses of the people. Pepys is of course the crowning example. Any history of England in the time of Charles II is inevitably written around Pepys, and largely rests upon his diary. Mr. Creevey rather less creditably performs the same office for the historians of a later generation.

In the twelfth century there is John of Salisbury. He was immersed in the life of Europe at every creative point, and he wrote down his impressions in his grave and pure classical Latin. Every historian of the century rises up and calls him blessed. To find a character who can with equal facility

INTRODUCTION

illuminate from his own articulate experience fields so diverse as the teaching curricula and staff at Chartres and Paris, the ecclesiastical administration of England, and the work of the chancery clerks in the Roman *Curia*, and who is in himself intensely individual and sympathetic, is better luck than the historian can reasonably expect. This book rests so fully on John of Salisbury and so constantly calls his writings as evidence that it might almost bear the sub-title *John of Salisbury and His Circle*. It does not bear it because such a sub-title might be misleading, for this book is in no sense a biography, but a more composite portrait of an epoch and only incidentally of some of the famous men who lived in it, and guided its fortunes.

For something like ten years this study has been the companion of my leisure. Its completion has had continually to be postponed in order to meet the pressure of more immediate and topical writing. But although no one could claim topicality for a work like this, yet it may not be altogether without an indirect relevance to the essential task of our own generation. For the real task of John of Salisbury and his generation was exactly that of our own, to build up a civilization; and although their methods cannot now be ours, yet we still build upon the foundations they laid and use the instruments of higher education which they founded. Were they alive to-day they would still have a function to perform in the building and perfecting of our civilization, and the record of their failures and successes is still worth our attention.

R.L.

Winchester.

INTRODUCTION

Note

A few of the paragraphs in this book are taken, though in a rearranged form, from articles of mine in the following periodicals, the *Quarterly Review*, the *Fortnightly*, the *Church Quarterly Review*, and *Chambers's Journal*. I am grateful to the editors for their ready permission to make further use of this material. One or two further paragraphs are taken from my earlier biography of Abelard, *The Stricken Lute*, which has long been out of print. My friend and colleague, Canon Edward Moor, was kind enough to read through the proofs of the book for me, and his vigilance detected and saved me from many errors.

CONTENTS

		PAGE
INTRODUCTION		vii

CHAPTER

I. THE TWELFTH-CENTURY EFFORT . . . 1

II. FROM CHARLEMAGNE TO ABELARD
   1. Prologue: St. Boniface . . . 10
   2. Carolus Magnus 12
   3. The Line of the Scholastic Succession . 20
   4. Trade and Transport . . . 32

III. THE SCHOOLS AND THE SCHOLARS
   1. Preparatory School 44
   2. Paris 49
   3. In Statu Pupillari 59
   4. The Teaching Scene 67
   5. Cornificius 92
   6. Out into the World 102

IV. THE UNIVERSITIES AND THE EUROPEAN MIND
   1. The Rudiments of Medievalism . . 115
   2. The Civilized Society: Canterbury . . 119
   3. The Instruments of Authorship . . 129
   4. Historians and Poets 141
   5. The Battle for Freedom of Thought . 159

CONTENTS

CHAPTER		PAGE
V.	THE SOCIAL BACKGROUND	
	1. The Village	179
	2. The Town	187
	3. The English at Home	199
	4. The Struggle for Civilization	203
VI.	THE CHURCH OF GOD	
	1. Rome and the *Curia*	214
	2. The State of Religion in England	229
INDEX		253

CHAPTER I

THE TWELFTH-CENTURY EFFORT

IN his introduction to *The Chronicle of Jocelyn of Brakelond* Carlyle thought it necessary to remind his readers that Abbot Samson of St. Edmundsbury, the hero of the chronicle, lived in a real world of historic actuality, "and not in a void infinite of grey haze with phantasms swimming in it."[1] He wrote in 1843; and he set a fashion for writers of medieval history. Few books on this theme have since appeared which have not begun by administering a caution to the reader. Sometimes it is a caution to beware of falling victim to the romantic falsifiers of medieval history who flourished forty years ago, and were apt to draw pictures of society which always exhibited the liturgically correct outlines of an Age of Faith, with Tilt Yards, Trade Guilds, and Maypoles well in evidence. The contrary warning against supposing that the whole of Europe for a thousand years of its history was an organized expression of brutality, superstition, and general beastliness is no less frequently given. Nor does it cease to be necessary in days when the adjective 'medieval' is regularly applied by those who should know better to all that is low and brutish, and passes without comment as an adequate and just term to describe impartially the twentieth-century slum, the concentration camp, and the torture chamber. Finally,

---

[1] *The Chronicle of Jocelyn of Brakelond.* Ed. Cardinal Gasquet. (Chatto and Windus), p. 13.

THE GOLDEN MIDDLE AGE

there are those writers who seek to persuade their readers into some sort of sympathetic regard for the distant world they are about to explore by reminding them how like to ourselves are its inhabitants—in religion, the same compromise with the World; in social life, the same stark and agonizing inequalities between rich and poor; in life in general, the same concentration for most upon keeping one's head above water, and only for the few on the art of living richly and with grace.

Such cautions may be necessary, but if they are taken too seriously they darken counsel. For incontestably the Muse of History frowns on comparisons and analogies drawn between the centuries; and some historians, as jealous for their art as for the accuracy of their facts, set themselves a rule never to refer to any person or document unknown for chronological reasons to the generation about which they are writing. This may perhaps be an exaggerated integrity, but it is a good fault. At least they are delivered from that profound falsity of interpretation which suggests that one age is best understood in the light of a later one, and draws the totally mistaken conclusion that because the Middle Ages and the Twentieth Century were both populated by human beings, therefore at bottom they must be very like each other. Medieval people were certainly human, but they were quick with a humanity very different from that of either the ancient or the modern world. It is indeed by the very reality of their contrast to either that they link both together. Not "How Like to Ourselves," nor "How Different from Ourselves," but "How True to Themselves," is the promising exclamation of the modern student who seeks to come to an understanding of medieval Europe in any of its phases.

Profoundly conscious though he was of the ties which

THE TWELFTH-CENTURY EFFORT

bound him to classical Greece and Rome, and by no means unforgetful of posterity, the medieval man was busily engaged in building up a civilization, and a social structure to contain and express it, which should be characteristically his own. This ambition was certainly the most gigantic, and perhaps the most heroic, which human beings have ever entertained. The dream was born in the mighty intellect of St. Augustine, and set out in his *City of God*. The backbone of the whole enterprise was to find the harmony, or the creative level of tension, between the religions and secular interests of life, and to create the functional structure of society which alone could provide a truly satisfying background for men and women far more conscious of their relationship to God than of their relationship to their own space-time world. In politics, this involved the efforts to make theocracy practical—always the most difficult feat known to political science. The medieval man was always an extremist, who thought and saw in two shades only, black and white; and thus his idealism was headlong, and his vision of opportunities clearer by far than his view of difficulties. So he failed; but his failure was more glorious than many successes in less profoundly difficult enterprises. The dream lived on—the dream of a single, united, continental civilization of Western Europe, bound into a harmony by Christian devotion, and transcending in its daily life all barriers of race, culture, and economics—a dream powerful still.

To unite Christendom and to make it a settled, theocratic reality of peace and freedom, the medieval thinkers relied on the three great formative instruments, cited by one of their own writers as *sacerdotium, imperium, studium*,[1] the Church, the

[1] Hastings Rashdall. *The Medieval Universities.* Ed. Powicke and Emden. (Oxford University Press), Vol. I, p. 2.

THE GOLDEN MIDDLE AGE

Empire, and the whole range of Education, culminating as it did in the *studium generale* or University. Everything turned on the harmonious co-operation of these three instruments of civilization, and at the centre of the medieval ideal lay always the vision of this full and unimpaired harmony. The great periods are those in which the harmony comes somewhere near to full existence. The dark centuries are those in which it breaks down. Throughout the thousand years of medieval history the fortunes of the great ideal wax and wane, flag and revive. Twice it comes within sight of a real fulfilment, first in the ninth century under Charlemagne, and then again in the twelfth and thirteenth centuries under the impetus of the universal passion for learning. The Carolingian renaissance was broken in its brief childhood by the inability of Charlemagne's squalid little descendants to sustain the mighty vision of a united and purified Church and Empire, which, in some degree, he had actually achieved. The twelfth-century renaissance was finally betrayed by many agents, and chief among them the greed, the tyranny, and the fatal secular success of the Roman *Curia*. Its failure to achieve its more distant and absolute aims set in motion the stream of cause and event which, in the supreme revolution of the Reformation, finally destroyed, once and for all, the vision of the ordered, civilized, Christian society, building its life on the medieval synthesis. Yet though the Middle Ages ultimately failed in that which was their supreme ideal, the ten centuries of confused, flagging, but still heroic struggle to achieve it, bequeathed a rich subsidiary legacy. There were the cathedrals, the guild system of industry and the institution of the Just Price, the Papacy, the scholastic philosophy, the urban communes with their self-government by mayor and cor-

THE TWELFTH-CENTURY EFFORT

poration, the germs of democracy in the infant parliamentary system, and finally there was the university. Each of these institutions and ideas has always played a great part in subsequent history, and all are active and influential still. But the greatest and the most enduring part has been played by the most characteristically medieval institution of them all, the University, the real gift of the Middle Ages to the world, and of the twelfth century to the Middle Ages.

The twelfth century forms an era all its own. Some historians call it the Golden Middle Age. It was charged with a vitality so abundant that there was no single field of medieval self-expression into which the surging, restless blood of creative experiment was not poured. Whatever might be said of some of the shadier sides of twelfth-century life in Western Europe —the Papal Schism of its middle years, for example—it cannot be denied that here, if anywhere, history provides a glowing picture of an age which had life and had it abundantly, peopled by men and women who looked upon their world new every morning, and saw that it was good.

The century knows no phantasms swimming in grey haze. In every ecclesiastical centre architects are busy designing new cathedrals; and they are new in more senses than one, for the old conventional romanesque is dead at last, and the new ornamented Gothic, so rich in symbolic meaning, holds the field. Chartres, Noyon, Notre Dame, Canterbury, Lincoln, Rheims, and many others, are all being built together. As the masons finish their task, the sculptors succeed them. They too are in full revolt against the old stiffness and austerity, and they chip and chisel their stone with an enormous zest, as they create a passionate riot of vivid, youthful statuary—no longer single figures, but whole Last Judgments, Apocalypses, crowded with detail and carved with an artist's mastery over his own endlessly inventive spirit. To this century belongs such a glory of sculpture as the Royal Portal at Chartres. As the sculptors gather their tools and depart to start on the next job, the painters succeed them, decorate the grey walls with broad bands of colour, scarlet, blue, and gold. Then they go off to some nobleman's house, perhaps in the Strand, and paint the walls green, and spangle gilded stars in a blue firmament all over the ceiling.

In quieter cells and rooms, men are experimenting with handwriting. Vellum and parchment are at last fairly cheap, and there is no longer as much need to save the precious material by contracting every other word, and writing a poem in between the lines of a Bible. Handwriting suffers a double change. For books destined to be looked at, and even read, but certainly not to be generally circulated, the Gothic script becomes the normal type; while for students' texts and books for which the author hoped a wide circulation, Caroline Minuscule is invented, the first form of handwriting which is both easily legible, and able to serve the purpose of a writer whose pen must stay the pace as he unpacks his heart with words. Far south, in Saracen Spain, mills are being set up to manufacture a curious white, smooth, but perishable substance called paper, which has come to them by a journey from China, by way of Turkestan, Samarkand, Baghdad, Damascus, Egypt, and Morocco, and taking three hundred years on the way: clearly, one of the more romantic journeys of the world. But the new paper will have to wait for another three hundred years before it is much used in Europe.

In the great professions of arms, law, and medicine, conditions are passing through profound changes. The feudal

THE TWELFTH-CENTURY EFFORT

warlord goes on crusade: his motives are as mixed as his achievements, but he creates, almost by accident, a new art of war. The lawyers find it a great century: the people of every village are far more ready to "go to law" than they have ever been, a state of affairs profitable both to pocket and to prestige. The doctors find their ranks doubled and even trebled, and the first, faint signs of regarding the art of healing from a scientific point of view are to be discerned in the classrooms of Montpellier, and even at the bedside of the sick cottager. The cities are fairly humming with trade and with life. Runaway serfs claiming freedom through citizenship are constantly increasing both their population and their power, and one city after another wins the rights of a commune, and full exemption from feudal, and limited exemption even from royal authority. At Clairvaux is the centre of gravity of another vital section of medieval society, the cloister; and both there, and at Chartreuse a little later, heroic efforts are being made to revivify the dream of St. Benedict, and the two greatest of all the medieval Orders are born, and come almost at once to swift maturity. In Rome, the Papacy grows from strength to strength until with Innocent III at the end of the century it comes to the very apex of its power.

But none of these holds the centre of the European stage, and the future is not with them. Every road in Europe, from the Orkneys to Sicily, from Lisbon to Vienna, is dotted with small, trudging figures. In ones and twos they make their slow and painful way, shabby, poor, but young and ardent. From all over Europe they come, breathing eagerly an air quick with philosophic surmise. They tramp to the school and master of their choice, whose sound has gone out into all the world, and his words to the ends of the earth. There they will put themselves painfully to school with him. Then, some of them will find that admiration has somehow changed to criticism, and one fine day they will put all their movable property on their backs and renew their journey in search of the whereabouts of another great *magister*, of whose fame they have heard tell. It is such figures, young, unknown, shabby, disrespectful, who made the Golden Middle Age. For they are the wandering scholars, and the University is their contribution to the immemorial effort of men to create the fully civilized society.

It was in the twelfth century they did it; the thirteenth but developed what the twelfth had created. But it is not possible to be too nicely pedantic about dates. The first renaissance was not precisely born in A.D. 1100. The century may, however, be stretched at both ends, and still remain the twelfth. In one rather limited sense it was born when Berengar made his famous assault on the citadel of Theology in the name of Reason; and Berengar was born in 990. Rashdall suggests the date 1000 as the turn of the tide, but in a firm footnote guards himself against being accused of the superstition of choosing it because it was the millenary year, when, in the confident expectation of most of Europe, the world was to come to an end.[1] Or it has been suggested that the "rawness went from the air" in 1053. For Guibert de Nogent, who was born in that year, and himself became one of the secondary lights in the early days of the twin rebirths of letters and religion, wrote a biography, suggesting the 'fifties as the date of the coming of the dayspring: "Shortly before that time was so great a dearth of grammarians that almost none could be found in the towns and scarce any in the cities, and if it befell

[1] op cit., I, pp. 31, 32.

THE TWELFTH-CENTURY EFFORT

that any were found, their learning was so slender that it could hardly equal that of a wandering clerk in modern times."[1] Sixteen years later Abelard was born in Brittany, and it might well be maintained that he who did so much to shape the new age heralded it in his first infant cries.

But in truth one can no more isolate the birth of the spirit which makes the century memorable than one can name the date when the harsh, freezing winds of winter give place to spring showers and breezes, and the thrushes begin to sing again. Its origins are hidden deep in antiquity. For four hundred years at least they slowly grow to maturity, and then, in the fulness of time, "Europe emerges from the Dark Age into that splendid twilight which a large proportion of civilized humanity still prize more highly than the morning light of the Renaissance or the mingled storm and sunshine of the Reformation."[2]

[1] Helen Waddell. *The Wandering Scholars* (Constable), p. 91.
[2] H. W. C. Davis. *England Under the Angevins and Normans.*

CHAPTER II

FROM CHARLEMAGNE TO ABELARD

1. *Prologue: St. Boniface*

IT is not merely English pride which causes the story of the approach to the twelfth-century renaissance to begin with one so distant from it both in time and in spirit as the English St. Boniface, the greatest figure of the eighth century. For he more than anyone was responsible for the alliance between the Franks and the Papacy, which made it possible for Charlemagne to set European history in motion down a new path on Christmas Day 800. Boniface himself never knew Charlemagne, for in 752 he crowned a glorious life of great-hearted obedience by the martyr's death he had always coveted. In the text books the title "The Apostle to the Germans" has become firmly fastened to his name. But it was an administrative rather than a missionary apostolate which really placed him among the small band of the heroes who have caused history to take place. He was the devotee of uniformity and centralization in an age when the Church lay in great danger of becoming chronically fissiparous; and how real the danger was can be seen in the fact that he, an authoritarian to his finger-tips, should think it both necessary and reasonable formally to bind himself to be a loyal son of the Pope, and to follow the Roman practices of worship. Thereupon, in 722, he was consecrated Bishop of Thuringia and Hesse, and began his great work of reforming the distant and rudimentary Frankish Christian communities. Carloman, the king, knew greatness when he saw it. He made Boniface first Chief Bishop, then Primate; and soon it became a settled condition of Frankish social life that Boniface ruled through the king.

The times might have been made for such a one as Boniface, and the very difficulties of contemporary political circumstance did but work together to give him his chance to make of his genius for obedience and diplomacy the ground of creative advance in the next generation in every European field of expression. Christendom was in the thick of the Iconoclastic Controversy. The Papacy was between the devil of an heretical emperor in Byzantium, to whom the Pope owed a legal suzerainty, and the deep sea of the raiding proclivities of the Lombard Luidprand, who, with suspicious speed, became suddenly more righteous than they all, and proceeded to overrun the domains of the Emperor in Italy and to threaten Rome herself in the guise of the Protector of the One True Faith as against the heresy of the Emperor and the supposed compliance of his nominal subject the Pope. Nor did the Roman citizens help matters by dropping into their invariable habit of raising a series of riots to tie the hands and embarrass the efforts of the papal leaders, whose cause was in fact their own. Vicious circles can be broken only from without, and the circle within which Pope Gregory II was hemmed was vicious indeed. But north of the Alps was a catholic monarch, Carloman of the Franks. He had but recently proved both his power to aid and his devotional attachment to the Christian cause by flinging back the advancing wave of Mohammedans from Spain at Poitiers. And with him was Boniface, by far the ablest bishop of the day, and a resolutely devoted son of the

THE GOLDEN MIDDLE AGE

Roman See. Gregory sent forth his call. It was answered by Carloman's son, Pepin, whom Boniface had appointed and crowned. A compact was made. Pepin twice crossed the Alps, twice drove the Lombards from Rome, bestowed on the Papacy the lands of the iconoclastic Byzantine Power which he had conquered. After that, the alliance between the Franks and Rome could not easily be disturbed.

Yet all the time Boniface had hungered for the work of a missionary. He petitioned the Pope in 738 to be allowed to go to the heathen darkness of Saxony. But the answer was "No," and so it remained until after he had crowned Pepin as king in Carloman's stead. Then at last the longed-for permission came, for his real work was done, and he was allowed to set out for Frisia, where a martyr's death soon became his. But if his death made heroism, his life of obedience made history. He it was who alone made possible—even inevitable—the traditional function of the Carolingian house to protect the whole Church of God. In a very real sense both the Holy Roman Empire and the University owe the genesis of their being to Crediton, where Boniface was born; and to Nursling, near Winchester, where the monks taught him the creative powers of heroic obedience.

2. *Carolus Magnus*

Charlemagne is one of the deathless names of history. At the fires of his memory men warmed themselves for five hundred years; and the story of his paladins "riding proudly to their death at Roncesvaux" thrills the blood still. All students of history come early to the knowledge of his greatness, for it is defined in one of the most splendid passages of

FROM CHARLEMAGNE TO ABELARD

a masterpiece which is placed in the hands of every student of every university who sets out on the quest for a degree in the Honours School of History. The masterpiece is Bryce's *Holy Roman Empire*, a book æsthetically exciting from end to end, but rising to the very height of grave eloquence when its author comes to describe that event in which was contained the climax of his story, the coronation of Charlemagne as Emperor on Christmas Day, 800.

At length the Frankish host entered Rome. . . . Charles remained in the city for some weeks; and on Christmas Day, A.D. 800, he heard mass in the basilica of St. Peter. On the spot where now the gigantic dome of Bramante and Michael Angelo towers over the buildings of the modern city, the spot which tradition had hallowed as that of the Apostle's martyrdom, Constantine the Great had erected the oldest and stateliest temple of Christian Rome. . . . Out of the transept a flight of steps led up to the high altar underneath and just beyond the great arch, the arch of triumph as it was called: behind in the semi-circular apse sat the clergy, rising tier above tier around its walls; in the midst, high above the rest, and looking down past the altar over the multitude, was placed the bishop's throne, itself the curule chair of some forgotten magistrate. From that chair the Pope now rose, as the reading of the Gospel ended, advanced to where Charles, who had exchanged his simple Frankish dress for the sandals and the chlamys of a Roman patrician, knelt in prayer by the high altar, and as in the sight of all he placed on the brow of the barbarian chieftain the diadem of the Cæsars, then bent in obeisance before him, the church rang to the shout of the multitude, again free, again the lords and centre of the world, "To Charles Augustus, crowned by God, the Great and peace-giving Emperor, be life and victory." In that shout, echoed by the Franks without, was pronounced the union, so long in preparation, so mighty in its consequences, of the

THE GOLDEN MIDDLE AGE

Roman and the Teuton, of the memories of the South with the fresh energy of the North, and from that moment modern history begins.[1]

Who does not remember the thrill with which, as a young undergraduate or perhaps in the sixth form at school, he first read this passage?

The Holy Roman Empire had been born, and with it a new age. But in a far more personal sense than this Charlemagne stands out as the Father of the Middle Ages, the only begetter of the characteristically medieval civilization at its best. Three hundred long years were to pass before the full flowering, but the seed was sown by him. How true this is may be seen by anyone who reads one of the composite surveys of the various aspects of the medieval civilization, such a book, for example, as *The Legacy of the Middle Ages*. There various scholars describe what that legacy was in each separate field, Religion, Law, Education, Philosophy, Architecture, Sculpture, Handicrafts, Handwriting, and all the rest. Each essay devotes most of its space to the twelfth and thirteenth centuries, but, almost without exception, the introductory survey begins with Charlemagne. To read the book straight through is to be brought back time after time, by each writer in turn, to the same point of departure; and one is left with the irresistible impression that Charlemagne is among the tiny company of giants who really turned the stream of history and forced it into a new course.

He owed it to his profoundly theocratic mind, for the nature of medievalism was such that only the mould of a theocracy could contain and nourish it. For the theocrat the word Secular has no meaning. In God lies his universal

[1] Viscount Bryce. *Holy Roman Empire* (Macmillan), pp. 48, 49.

FROM CHARLEMAGNE TO ABELARD

principle of interpretation, and his conception of God is such that neither the trivial act nor the epoch-making event can be thought of as being irrelevant to the Majesty of the Universe. The joy of God becomes the fundamental aim and purpose of the whole social organism; the divine principles of God become the criteria by which all kinds of social structure, and the laws which hold them together, are tested. Medievalism was consciously, profoundly, and ruthlessly theocratic; and the institution of the Holy Roman Empire may be an object of mirth to the secular historian of to-day, and was then a constant scandal to the medieval thinker, but it did hold society together both as an actuality in one sense, and as a dream in another. Charlemagne was in a sense the founder of this historic institution, and from the first he laid the weight of his stress on the first of the three epithets. He had a strongly imperial sense, and Rome to him was a name charged with glamour, but, over and above these, he thought of himself as the Lord's Anointed, the King David of Western Europe. He even desired his intimate friends to call him David. It was, of course, the innovation of his house. The Carolingian succeeded the Merovingian dynasty, and the whole social emphasis of the Merovings had been profoundly secular. But both Charles Martel and Pepin had been drawn by events, and by Boniface, into the orbit of Rome, and the change had brought about a new and deeper realization of the divine basis of power and of the spiritual purpose for which all earthly government exists. Thus to the solution of his overwhelmingly vast problem Charlemagne was able to bring the great asset of a unifying point of view and principle of interpretation. He faced a heterogeneous chaos, but his own mind was a synthesis. A spiritual synthesis of experience and of ambition, harnessed

THE GOLDEN MIDDLE AGE

to the power to set its implications in motion, was the one thing needful if Western Europe was ever to be rescued from the anarchic squalor of the Dark Ages, and to bring to birth a culture, a civilization, and a social structure of its own. Charlemagne was that synthesis in his own person.

"Lord and Father, King and Priest, the Leader and Guide of all Christians"—such was Charlemagne's claims for his office, stated in a letter to Pope Leo III.[1] He had no doubt at all of the majestic awe surrounding his office, and he expected popes no less than his own military paladins to hearken to it. "It is the king's business," he continued in his letter, "to defend the Holy Church of God outwardly with arms and inwardly to maintain the Catholic Faith, and it is the business of the Holy Father to support the royal work with his prayers."[2] He caused a new oath of allegiance to be taken by all his subjects. They were to be first instructed that, "it binds those who swear it to live, each and everyone of them, according to his strength and knowledge in the holy service of God."[3] He sent out his emissaries bearing letters of Credence in a new form: "We have been sent here by our lord, the Emperor Charles, for your eternal salvation, and we charge you to live virtuously according to the law of God, and justly according to the law of the world."[4] His letters and enactments have the spirit of Deuteronomy and Leviticus behind them. Their detail is as varied and as elaborate as the Mosaic code of law. He enforces the payment of tithes. He reforms the capitular constitutions of monasteries. He lays down the duties of the Cathedral Chapter. He hears that certain nuns have been

[1] Christopher Dawson. *The Making of Europe* (Sheed & Ward), p. 219.
[2] J. W. Thompson and E. N. Johnson. *An Introduction to Medieval Europe* (Allen & Unwin), p. 341.
[3] Bryce, p. 66.   [4] Dawson, p. 218.

FROM CHARLEMAGNE TO ABELARD

receiving "valentines"—love poems written in the vernacular—and he forbids them. He orders that a letter be sent to every parish priest in Europe asking what is his method of administering Holy Baptism, and he personally inspects the answers. He is interested in the consecration of an obscure Irish bishop, and he sends a personal subscription towards the expenses of the ceremony: Alcuin, the Yorkshireman, his aide-de-camp and minister of education, sends the money for him and adds to it, on his own account, a flask of the proper oil of consecration, which is easier come by in Germany than in Ireland.

Charlemagne's educational reforms also had the same theocratic motive behind them, for they were originally undertaken in order to ensure a supply of reasonably educated secular and monastic priests to work among the Frankish tribes. But in this field he was building upon traditions as ancient as they were varied. Rhetoric counted for at least as much as theology in his court, and Charlemagne was the last potentate in the world to regard himself as slavishly bound by the ancient tradition of ascetic Christendom that one must keep oneself unspotted from the classics and the poets if one would save one's soul alive. The young exquisites of the court who showed no proper care for poetry were bidden to sit down, reach for their tablets, and produce a tolerable poem at once and on the spot. None the less, the general trend of Charlemagne's passion for the things of the mind was theocratic at least in this, that the Church was inevitably the instrument on which he relied. Monasteries and cathedrals were given the central place in his educational programme. Monasteries he expected to provide him with teachers, and cathedrals were to provide the teachers with schools and the necessary tools of their trade. Among monasteries, Fulda was pre-eminent: with the tremendous exception of Alcuin, all the greatest scholars of Charlemagne's time had been either monks or pupils there.

Charlemagne had, in a word, raised the position of *magister* to one of the highest honour, an achievement which Europe had hardly seen since the days of Plato. In spite of the fact that he himself never learned to write, though he tried hard enough, his own court was a school of letters, and none was held in greater esteem there than the scholars of many nations who were attached to his service. Among his own Carolingian schools were many names, Tours and St.-Gall, Rheims and Chartres, which were to be doubly famous in the twelfth century; and it was to one of these schools, Corbie, and to Charlemagne's personal encouragement, that the world of scholarship owed the superseding of the old illegible scripts by the Caroline Minuscule, a form of handwriting which provided the intellectual revival of the twelfth century with a universally intelligible medium of communication.

Charlemagne's political empire broke in pieces after his death, and the security which he had won was again drenched in anarchy. But not even the brutalities of the tenth century were able wholly to destroy the mechanism of scholarship which Charlemagne had created. And, what is still more important, Charlemagne had, perhaps by accident, perhaps by design, placed the centre of gravity of his educational system not in Italy but in the northern provinces of France. When the twelfth-century revival of learning came, it was a movement which hinged on Chartres, Paris and Rheims. Nor is Charlemagne's achievement irrelevant even to twentieth-century politics. Still the dream of the United States of

FROM CHARLEMAGNE TO ABELARD

Europe fills many minds, and, significantly, its advocates are generally French statesmen. For France must lie at the centre of the fulfilment of any such ideal, as in the Middle Ages it always did. It is a geographical as well as a cultural necessity. Charlemagne hardly saw even as a dream the civilizing unit of the United States of Western Europe, but by making both Italy and Germany culturally dependent upon France he created it; and the primary condition of its re-creation to-day is still the same.

In 814 Charlemagne died, and his son Lewis reigned in his stead. Within three years Lewis made several divisions of his dominions among his sons. They quarrelled over the spoil of which they had thus early gained control. The floodgates were opened to anarchy, and the barbarian hosts began to pour in. The Saracens invaded and looted Rome, and the Northmen devastated Flanders, Normandy, and the valleys of the Seine and the Loire. The Hungarians wreaked their will upon Bavaria. The clock of Europe was put back for two centuries at least. But it did not wholly stop, nor was Charlemagne's work ever completely undone. The tenth century deserves all the hard things said of it by the historians, but it was at least less universally grim than the seventh. The seeds Charlemagne had sown had first to be tested by an icy winter covering, but they did not die, and when at last the wind blew soft and genial in the middle of the eleventh century, they at once burst into flower.

Charlemagne's court at Aachen is joined to the University of Paris by a thin red line, wavering and far from straight, but none the less distinct. A true succession of the Apostolate of scholarship and culture unites them, and to trace these links this narrative now turns.

THE GOLDEN MIDDLE AGE

3. *The Line of the Scholastic Succession*

The keys of the future were held by the cathedrals, the institutions upon which Charlemagne had lavished so much loving care. He had made them the essential administrative centres of the Church, and had prescribed for them a definitely intellectual function as well. For every cathedral its school and its canons was the Carolingian principle, and in order to ensure the continuance of the cathedral school in cathedrals where it might happen that not one of the canons was competent to teach, provision was made to allow them to engage some wandering scholar. The bishop was ordered to see that this was duly performed, and was encouraged to link the whole of his diocesan work to the cathedral by using the services of members of the capitular body. The modern custom, so often denounced, of using residentiary canonries to provide specialists of one kind or another, and suffragan bishops for the diocese is in reality not modern at all, but at least eleven hundred years old. But at the same time Charlemagne ordered that the members of a capitular body, diocesan servants though they might be, must maintain a community life of their own, and cement it not only by praying and worshipping, but also by working together. Their work, he said, must be in part intellectual and literary, and one special task in this field laid upon them was the writing of Chronicles or more local sets of annals in every cathedral.

It was due to the rigidity and many-sidedness of these enactments that the cathedrals were better placed than the monasteries not only to stand firm as islands of culture and reason in an ocean of chaos and bloodshed, but also to preserve intact the form of organization and emphasis of interest which provided

FROM CHARLEMAGNE TO ABELARD

the great scholars of the twelfth-century renaissance with the ground on which they stood. Charlemagne had, of course, shown an almost equal care for monasteries; and they too were to survive the long testing of the tenth century, and to become islands of security within it because they were a completely essential part of the whole social structure. But in each and all of their functions they were as old as the hills, tied to their great past, and bound to the ideals contained in the Rule of St. Benedict. The Cathedral, on the other hand, was venerable only in so far as it was a building: its function as the centre of the whole life of a diocese, as the corner-stone of its intellectual interest, and as the executive arm of the ruling bishop, was new, a Carolingian invention.

The debt of the world of scholarship to the monastery cannot be too frequently acknowledged, but it can be, and it commonly is exaggerated. Scholarship was not its function, and though such a one as Cassiodorus might remind monks that it was their function to fight the devil by pen and ink just as by prayer and worship, the facts seem to show that his was a lone voice, finding but little support either in the Rule or in the actual practice of the average abbey. The Rule laid its chief stresses on the daily chanting of the services for the Seven Canonical Hours, on works of mercy, on the need of manual labour, but not on the need to gather or spread any learning except what could be called strictly devotional. The practice of the tenth-century abbey maintained the same order of emphasis. The maintenance of schools, except in the sense of schools for novices, was quite exceptional. Even the copying of books was not enjoined by St. Benedict, though in this many, probably most, abbeys did far more than supply themselves with texts of Bible, Liturgy, and Fathers. The Rule set

THE GOLDEN MIDDLE AGE

aside hours for daily reading of holy books; but it is only laid down that each monk should be given one book at the beginning of Lent, and be required to show he had read it properly after twelve months' time, and it is clear that even in the twelfth century this was the limit of the monk's private reading in many monasteries of the older foundation. A special study of one such monastery, Troarn in Normandy, shows that in all its history it gave birth to only one writer, that its library was meagre and composed wholly of devotional books, and that as late as 1169, it only maintained a school for its novices, and thought but little of that.[1] This, of course, is but to say that monasteries showed a perfectly natural inclination to plough in their own fields, and restrict themselves to their proper functions, for as one of the greatest of Modern Benedictines has said, "All the services of the Benedictines to civilization, education, and letters have been but by-products."[2] Yet this restriction of functions barred them from winning the position of becoming the really creative force of the medieval Church. Some of them felt this keenly. As the years passed by, and the tenth century drew to its inglorious close, a number of the monasteries were shaken out of their obscurantist views of the place of education in the Christian life by the competition of the cathedral establishments. They, too, set to work to provide opportunities for young men to learn the *Trivium*. But they were too late. By this time the cathedrals had the future well in their keeping, and were even then experiencing the early birth pangs of their tremendous child, the University.

[1] C. H. Haskins. *The Renaissance of the Twelfth Century* (Harvard University Press), p. 36.
[2] Dom Butler. Quoted in Haskins, op. cit., p. 33.

FROM CHARLEMAGNE TO ABELARD

No single cathedral establishment can show an unbroken line of scholastic descent from Charlemagne to Abelard. Rheims and Chartres were the two which most nearly achieved full continuity. The annals which Charlemagne had ordered to be written in every cathedral were continued uninterruptedly at Rheims until 966; and by 980 Gerbert of Aurillac was teaching there.

Gerbert is one of the great names in the history of scholarship. Alive he was Stupor Mundi, and in death a whole cycle of legend. He became Pope, but his personality was too terrific to be lost in the official name of Sylvester II. Around such as he legend gathers fast, and most of the legend was preserved for posterity by William of Malmesbury. As became a historian whose soul, as well as his body, was in the cloister, William did not look any too kindly on Gerbert, for he held that not even a Pope could be excused the supreme sin of absconding from a monastery in his youth. Being Pope, indeed, did but aggravate the offence, since it was notorious that he held communion with devils and familiar spirits, and that their malign influence, not the Holy Spirit's, was responsible for his election. Which same was proved in the sight of all men by his impious conduct in searching for, and finding, the buried treasures of the Cæsars in the underworld. He was unable to bring them away, for the outrage was too much for the divine powers who mightily intervened, which clearly shows there is a limit to what even demons can do. Yet Gerbert's demon had been powerful beyond the ordinary. It belonged to Toledo, and Toledo was as famous for demons as for swords, and a city much loved of Gerbert, for it had received him when a fugitive from his abbey at Fleury. This demon of Toledo, said William, made Gerbert what he was.

THE GOLDEN MIDDLE AGE

By its necromantic aid he did things not lawful for a man to do. He made a water organ. He delved into the nature of steam, and came close to discovering the latent force contained in it. In a furnace he forged a brazen head, and this head solved all his mathematical problems for him with an unfailing accuracy not to be looked for except in those possessed of a devil. Moreover, his mathematical technique cast over what now seems to us an extremely rudimentary knowledge of the science which stretched no farther than the more elementary propositions of Euclid and geometry, and the discoveries of Bede in astronomy, the mantle of a high and exotic mysticism. He revived the use of the Roman counting machine, or abacus, but he re-christened its counters by using a mystical terminology all his own. So much, and more beside, has legend added to the historic achievements of Gerbert—as though in themselves they were not enough to make him one of the giants which tower above the Middle Ages.

He anticipated by more than a century the typical mental attitude of the twelfth-century scholar. His intellectual curiosity was insatiable, he turned his knowledge into compressed power, and this power he liked to test and display by an extreme eagerness for public debate. Thus his scholarship was fundamentally competitive in spirit, and of this he gave evidence in the famous debate which he staged with a certain Otric, to be held at Ravenna before the Emperor Otto II himself. Logical Palestrics formed the apple of discord, and to the unhappy Emperor the apple was a dry, Dead Sea fruit. Early in the morning the boy Emperor—he was only nineteen—took his seat on the throne, and opened the proceedings with the blameless remark, "Meditation and

FROM CHARLEMAGNE TO ABELARD

discussion, as I think make for the betterment of human knowledge, and questions from the wise arouse our thoughtfulness."[1] Then the contest began, and it went on and on and on until at last the evening shadows fell, and a nod from the Emperor brought an end and a release to the weary audience, "fatigued with prolix and unbroken disputation."[2] The twelfth-century student would have shown greater staying power, for such scenes as these, acted in the midst of terrific and unflagging enthusiasm, were of the very stuff of the infant universities of Paris and Orleans, and took place every day. It was by way of constant battles of just such verbiage, undertaken day by day for years on end with one teacher after another, that the great Abelard came to his place in history.

Yet the Ravenna disputation was a gesture only, undertaken by Gerbert to show that he could do that sort of thing as well as anyone and better than most if he wanted. Actually he probably knew but little about Logical Palestrics, for he was a natural rather than a formal philosopher. Pure thought for its own sweet sake was not his line—he was too practical. The marriage of learning with thought, undertaken for the purpose of the procreation of power, was his aim. Thus, as the cool and lucid authority of Lane Poole judges, Gerbert must be regarded as "the ready accumulator and diffuser of what was actually within the range of any well-read student of his day."[3] But if his mind was a filter, power and greatness were sucked from the waters which fed it, and only dry dust left behind. His aim was to use knowledge to live the full life. "I have

[1] Taylor. *The Medieval Mind* (Macmillan), Vol. I, p. 291.
[2] Taylor. op. cit., Vol. I, p. 293.
[3] R. Lane Poole. *Illustrations of the History of Medieval Thought and Learning* (S.P.C.K.), p. 77.

THE GOLDEN MIDDLE AGE

always," he wrote to a friend, "joined the study of speaking well to the study of living well."[1] One condition of living the full life is not to waste time, and not even William of Malmesbury accused him of that. He was probably the most concise and least prolix writer of the whole of the Middle Ages, a stylist with an ever-present sense of classical form and discipline.

Not in scholarship only but also in politics he laid the foundations and created the conditions which issued in process of time in the Golden Middle Age. He was raised to the Papacy by his own pupil, the Emperor Otto III, and he prevented the real danger both of the present and the future, the isolation of Rome from Western Europe and her absorption in the orbit of Byzantium. This would have deprived the West of its spiritual centre, and made the dream of the United States of Europe for ever impossible. Yet the demand of the north-west for independence of Roman spiritual jurisdiction was natural and not unreasonable. The Papacy had for long been held by so profligate and wanton a succession of Popes that in 991 all the bishops of France met in solemn conclave and protested against the Roman primacy. "Is it to such monsters, swollen with their ignominy, and devoid of all knowledge, human and divine, that the innumerable priests of God throughout the world should lawfully be submitted?"[2] asked Arnoul, Bishop of Orleans, writing in all their names. Gerbert's great achievement, as Pope Sylvester II, was to capture this northern movement of reform, and apply it to the betterment rather than the repudiation of the Papacy. For it was Gerbert's learning which had taught the Emperor Otto

---

[1] Taylor. op. cit., Vol. I, p. 287.
[2] Christopher Dawson. op. cit., p. 278.

FROM CHARLEMAGNE TO ABELARD

III that the Roman tradition Otto so passionately ached to revive was a Western and not an Eastern growth. "Let it not be thought in Italy," wrote Gerbert to Otto, "that Greece alone can boast of the Roman power and of the philosophy of its Emperor. Ours, yea ours, is the Roman Empire. Its strength rests on fruitful Italy and populous Gaul and Germany, and the valiant kingdoms of the Scythians."[1] Both Otto and Gerbert were in their several ways ill-fated, but between them they saved the Papacy from becoming an appendage of Byzantium, and in so doing made possible the later intellectual quickening of Europe. To keep the Pope tied to Europe was to create one of the essential political conditions of the twelfth century.

But it was as the Gerbert who was the greatest *magister* of his day that his influence on the centuries was most decisive and profound. At Rheims he had not only the Emperor Otto III as his pupil—himself a scholar and patron of scholarship of such eminence that German historians will write of the Ottonian Renaissance to this day—but also Robert Capet, the future humanist monarch of France, and patron of letters in his kingdom. He also taught Abbo, who in 986 became abbot of Fleury, and founded there the distinctive literary traditions which come to their fullness in Orleans in the twelfth century. Above all he taught Fulbert, and with Fulbert the movement is well under way, for there was hardly a great scholar of that generation in Europe who had not Fulbert as a master. An archbishop of the time—Guitmund of Aversa—who sadly wagged his head and lamented "at that time the liberal arts had all but become extinct in the land,"[2] was sadly

[1] Christopher Dawson. op. cit., pp. 280, 281.
[2] R. Lane Poole. op. cit., p. 76.

THE GOLDEN MIDDLE AGE

wrong in his facts. Gerbert, Otto, Capet, Abbo, Fulbert—were all flourishing together. They are not many names, but of sufficient stature to be a host in themselves.

The tale moves now from Rheims to Chartres as Fulbert succeeds Gerbert. Chartres was no more than one cathedral school among many, and in no way more distinguished than any of the others, when Fulbert came to preside over it in 990. He made its name and that name is immortal.

Few characters in all the Middle Ages are as attractive as he, and none was more passionately revered and loved by his own generation. "Almost every man of letters in that age in France had him as master," said the admiring Odericus Vitalis. He had absorbed all his master Gerbert's learning, but he imitated none of his uncertain and flashing brilliance. When Fulbert died no legend gathered round him. There was no need for it. His monument was the school he left, and those he had taught there. "Do you remember," wrote one of his pupils to another, "the evening talks he used to have with us, our venerable Socrates, in the garden beside the chapel, entreating us with tears that now and then would break out in the midst of his talk not to be turned aside, not to slip into a new and deceptive way."[1] He was as great a teacher as his own master had been, and a saint and a sage as well. He had the scholar's innate conservatism, and, being above all else a classicist, the principles of order and authority in education naturally commended themselves to him. "We ought to walk," he would say, "in the familiar and often trodden ways of the Fathers, to bear their memory in mind, and to have their example before our eyes." His best remark has a pleasantly oriental ring, and it exactly describes every-

[1] Helen Waddell. op. cit., p. 88.

FROM CHARLEMAGNE TO ABELARD

thing for which he made his school famous, "Let us beware of gnawing the bone of contention with the tooth of temerarious cavilling."[1] Before his death, he became Bishop of Chartres, but still he lived in his school and among his pupils as he had done before. Humble minded always, he so admired St. Odilo and condemned himself that he wrote to the saint asking him to teach him how to live a saintly life. But the saint replied by bowing to the sage, "whose learning shines like a bright star in the sky."

When that star was put out by death, in 1029, it seemed to Odilo's biographer as though "the study of philosophy in France decayed, and the glory of her priesthood well-nigh perished."[2] In truth, however, his work did not perish nor his memory fail. None of those he had taught forgot their venerable Socrates, "as they delighted to call him. There was gentleness in his ways. He would come slowly into the lecture room, cover his face with his hood, and stand there silent and still, in deep meditation upon the eternal verities lying behind what he had to say. Then he would turn to his pupils, speaking to them in a still, almost a dreamy voice. A modern scholar, Dr. Lane Poole, whose own writing is a living example of the grave beauty of scholarship which Fulbert spent his life to propagate, has given us a brief but eloquent picture of Fulbert with his pupils. "He was wont of an evening to take his disciples apart in the little garden beside the chapel, and discourse to them on the prime duty of life, to prepare for the eternal fatherland hereafter."[3]

The pupils whom Fulbert thus taught and guided were very numerous. One of them, Adelman, afterwards Bishop of

---
[1] Glunz. *The Vulgate in England* (Cambridge University Press), p. 153.
[2] R. Lane Poole. op. cit., p. 99.   [3] ibid.

Brescia, writing to his old friend and fellow-student, gives a list of the distinguished pupils of Chartres whom they both had known. This list includes two masters and a chancellor of Chartres, masters at Paris, Orleans, and Tours, a famous pilgrim to the Holy Sepulchre, a great mathematician of Cologne, and almost the whole staff of masters at Liége. The greatest of all Fulbert's pupils, Berengar, was the recipient of this letter and list, which was very far from exhausting the full tale of the pupils of Chartres in Fulbert's time who had won distinction in the wider world. A great Christian and scholar, an artist, a poet of more than ordinary merit, a magnificent teacher, and, with it all, a holy and humble man of heart, it was inevitable that the name of Fulbert should be honoured with absolute veneration by all of his generation who had the least care for the things of the mind, and that he should leave behind him the secured foundations of one of the greatest schools in human history as his gift to Christian civilization. His death in 1029 left a gap. The school went on, but we know nothing of his immediate successors. Later, Ivo, a great canonist and Bishop of Chartres, who died in 1115, *fecit scholas*,[1] whatever that may mean. It need not mean more than that he had something to do with the school, and perhaps bore the same relationship to it as the chancellor does to a modern university. It can hardly mean that he personally taught in the schools, for if he had, history would surely have furnished some other reference. As it is, these two words furnish the only clue to Ivo's wearing of Fulbert's mantle. Ivo was a great lawyer, but his influence on the true genius of Chartres, which was predominantly a literary foundation, was negligible.

[1] In *Martyrologium Ecclesiae Carnotensis*, affixed to Ivo's letters.

FROM CHARLEMAGNE TO ABELARD

Not Ivo, but Berengar of Tours stands next to Fulbert in the great line of succession, and there is a sense in which he brings it to an end, the last holder of the torch which in his hands was thrust into the pyre, and set alight this greater beacon fire which for two hundred years lit a continent. Berengar was born in 990, and Fulbert taught him. But the master's spirit of calm wisdom was not reproduced in his pupil, for Berengar was the vehement champion of Reason, the rebel against authority, the spit and image of the twelfth-century dialectician. In his pride and self-confidence, he was wont to ask, "Why err with everyone if everyone errs?" and answered his own question by openly despising all the hearthold gods of the earlier medieval scholasticism, the Fathers, Priscian, and even Boethius; which was only a shade less temerarious than his careful investigation of the miracle of the Real Presence in the Blessed Sacrament, new every morning, and his loudly expressed dubiety of the authority which lay behind, and guaranteed, the change in the substance of the bread and wine. He preferred the more dangerous and heretical literary company of Erigena, who had written combustible philosophy in *The Body and Blood of Christ*. To Berengar it was given to fight the opening skirmishes of the great battle between Dialectics and Theology, which was the very breath of twelfth-century scholasticism. "It is the part of courage to have recourse to dialectic in all things, for recourse to dialectic is recourse to reason, and he who does not avail himself of reason in all things abandons his chief honour, since by virtue of reason he was made in the image of God." Berengar, the pupil of Fulbert, the pupil of Gerbert of Aurillac, wrote it; but it might well have been Peter Abelard, or Gilbert Porée, or Peter Lombard, for this is also their authentic voice. With these words, the twelfth-century renaissance had begun. It remained only to create the conditions of political and economic security for the isolated glories of Chartres and Rheims to become the commonplace of Western Europe, and almost universal within it.

4. *Trade and Transport*

"Order and peace, leisure and security are the most indispensable conditions of intellectual activity."[1] Of universities they are the *sine qua non*. Tiny schools in scattered centres are possible enough, however anarchical conditions may be, but before the little school of Rheims when Gerbert was master there, and a very few scholars—and they the very elect—brave the real dangers of the journey to go to hear him, can become such centres as Paris or Orleans in their great days with thousands of students standing where only tens had stood three generations earlier, the ideals of security and peace must be brought to some sort of actuality. The tenth century knew neither and the twelfth knew both, and the external conditions which brought about so notable a change in the atmosphere of Europe must plainly find their place in a chapter which seeks to set out some of the causes of the twelfth-century renaissance.

In this story the road has pride of place. The first of all the needs of a university is that its students should have a reasonable chance of getting there safely, not let or hindered, and with their money, their books, and their clothes intact.

The medieval road has found its historian in M. Jusserand

[1] Rashdall. op. cit., Vol. I, p. 33.

FROM CHARLEMAGNE TO ABEL

D in his *English Wayfaring Life in the Middle Ages* and its epic romance in Charles Reade's *The Cloister and the Hearth*. Those who have given themselves the intense pleasure of reading either work are delivered from making the common mistake of supposing that throughout the Middle Ages travel was rare, expensive, dangerous, and fraught with hardships—an adventure undertaken only by armies, kings' messengers, couriers, bishops, and archdeacons with their portentous trains. Such a picture is wildly false in the twelfth century, and it had never been true even in the worst and most hopelessly chaotic centuries. In 550 anarchy was rampant, but at that time the traffic of Irish scholars to the mainland of Europe was such that it almost seems as though there were a regular service of boats from Cork to the Loire outward bound, and returning to Bangor with cargoes of Europeans who wished to study in Ireland, home of the most famous schools in Europe. They came in companies of fifty at a time, regularly taking three days on the journey.[1] Later, but still centuries before a settled order reigned, the possibilities of travel were far wider and more exotic. King Offa of Mercia issued a new series of coins: they were copies of an Arab dinar minted in 774. In that century and the next the route from Arabia to Germany and France must have been populous with travellers. How else account for the minute knowledge of Arabs and their ways in the *Songs of Roland*? The Franks were fully aware—and Roland's songs were meaningless without this awareness—of the medley of races in the Near East, the Caliphs and Emirs who ruled them; and they roared applause as they heard tell of all the exotic treasures of Solomon's kingdom, jewels, ivory, peacocks, camels, sung still by their own harper. It is the mental

[1] See Helen Waddell. op cit., p. 29.

THE GOLDEN MIDDLE AGE

outlook of Elizabethan London eight centuries before its time, and four centuries before the Crusades made the lure of the East, and the experience of its exotic mysteries the commonplace of multitudes from the West.

As the centuries draw on the commerce of ideas between different parts of the world becomes still more varied and extensive, and people travel more swiftly. John of Salisbury, who should know for he did the journey ten times, five of them in successive years, used to reckon seven weeks as the proper time of the journey from London to Rome, and if one was in a hurry, travelled light, and killed one's horses, it could be done in four weeks. Naples to Cologne took six weeks, and the news of the Emperor Frederick Barbarossa's death in Asia Minor reached Germany in four months. The hagiographical literature of Thomas Becket, written in England, was being read in an Icelandic translation within three years of the martyr's death. Henry II of England entertained a Norwegian archbishop who then passed on to stay with the Abbot of St. Edmund's in Suffolk. A Greek book of animal lore, called *The Kiranides*, is found in no less than six Latin translations scattered widely over Europe. An Englishman, Thomas Brown, acts as a Sicilian judge, passes thence into Arabia where he gets the title of Kaid Brun, and comes back to end his days as an official at Henry II's court. Matthew Paris at St. Albans has detailed information about the Tartars. One of the most famous chronicles is begun by an Irishman, Marianus Scotus, in Mainz; continued in Worcester by Florence, a monk there, and ended at Gembloux by Sigebert. A monk of Canterbury travels to Constantinople and Jerusalem, and does it safely and in style. Already London was the great clearinghouse of Europe, Hamburg alone competing:

FROM CHARLEMAGNE TO ABELARD

It was the terminal point in the trade route from Constantinople, by the Danube and Regensburg, to the Rhine and the narrow seas. The trade was controlled by the men of Lower Lorraine, subjects of the Emperor. They brought to London goldsmiths' work, precious stones, cloth from Constantinople and Regensburg, fine linen and coats of mail from Mainz.[1]

Norwegian merchants might stay in London for a year and even merchants from distant Novgorod were not uncommon visitors. And the humbler folk too were constantly on the move. A savage law was enacted in 1157 against Rhemish weavers, "men of the lowest class who move frequently from place to place and change their names as they go."[2] These, however, were notoriously addicted to heresy.

From about 1050 onwards, moreover, there was always a very strong probability that all these travellers would arrive at their journey's end unharassed and in peace. For the trend of the times was everywhere towards more centralized and more bureaucratic authority. The age of great national monarchies, such as those of Philip the Fair in France and Henry II in England, was beginning; and already the Norman rulers in the North and in Sicily had developed the germs of a police force and a civil service. The romantic merits of bureaucracy give a constant theme to the court historian of the twelfth century, perhaps the one and the only time in history when bureaucracy has found an artist to praise it. The great barons, with their profoundly anarchic instincts, were not of course everywhere tamed or held in check. Let the recently established authority loose the reins but for a moment, and such a cruel chaos as the England of King Stephen swiftly

[1] F. M. Stenton. *Norman London* (Bell), p. 19.
[2] C. H. Haskins. *Medieval Culture* (Oxford University Press), p. 202.

resulted. But their day was inexorably passing, and even such a chaos as this could be more quickly ended than would have been possible for centuries past. For the general tendency of manorial as well as of national and civic government was likewise towards the concentration of power into fewer, stronger, and far more competent hands. It remained feudal, for that was the Manor's *raison d'être*, but it became orderly.

The importance of the barony as a feudal state in miniature has been appreciated more slowly because of a long-prevailing tendency to associate legal authority and order only with centralized government. The twelfth century, however, did not regard feudal decentralization as necessarily synonymous with anarchy. Consequently, to obtain a more complete understanding of feudal society at its apogee it is essential first to rid ourselves of the modern prejudice that the king alone stood for order and security.[1]

This is the general conclusion of a most careful and thorough investigation of one such barony, Bayeux, and it holds good as a general principle. It all meant that travellers were safer than they had been for centuries.

Whether soldiers or traders first cause roads to be made is a moot point, but if, with the memory of the Roman Legions in mind, we award the palm to soldiers, it is certainly traders who most use them, and in whose interest the great trade routes are kept open. In the Middle Ages these roads are not many but they bear a notable company of travellers, and upon them the Cathedral School and the University were dependent. From Bruges to Marseilles, from Hamburg to Venice and Genoa ran the two great land routes, north and south, of

[1] S. E. Gleason. *An Ecclesiastical Barony in the Middle Ages* (Harvard University Press), p. 3.

FROM CHARLEMAGNE TO ABELARD

Western Europe. They were crossed by another running from Lyons to Venice, while Basle and Cologne were the great junctions whence smaller routes spread out fanwise. For traders, Hamburg was perhaps the most notable of all centres. There came the land-borne traffic from Italy and southern France, and the sea-borne goods from London and Kings Lynn. Thence you went by sea to Dantzig and Riga; and Riga was the sea-gate of the great caravans passing by way of Novgorod, down the Volga to Asov, across the Black Sea to Trebizond, or to Constantinople, where you set out again to Aleppo and Baghdad. Change there for the sea-route to India, or go on to face the hardest, most romantic journey in the world to Merv, Samarkand, Tashkent, and all the way to China, or to India *via* the Himalayas, Kashmir, and Peshawar.

The sight of Western traders in Eastern cities whose very names are poems, Trebizond, Samarkand, Tashkent, was no doubt unknown before the Crusades, and a rarity for centuries afterwards, though they became regular trading outposts before the Middle Ages finally closed with the fall of Constantinople. But long before the twelfth century dawned Constantinople was bound to the trading cities of the north in ties of commerce and diplomacy. The Christian reconquest of northern Spain, a wave which reached Toledo in 1085 and Saragossa in 1118, opened another door whereby translations from Arabic of the forgotten works of Aristotle, and the philosophy of such Arabic scholars as Averrhoes, could pass the Pyrenees and feed the insatiable appetites of the Paris masters. Still another door was opened by the Norman conquest of Sicily and southern Italy, through which a westward flow of Greek manuscripts first trickled, and then poured.

But magic memories of "the Golden Road to Samarkand"

THE GOLDEN MIDDLE AGE

run away with the text, for we are not concerned here with the strings of laden camels plodding along under the burning sun. It is the network of the great roads of Europe joining France to Germany, to Italy, and to Austria, which lie at the centre of our picture, for along them the wandering scholars passed and repassed on their way. The inn was its nerve-centre. There, night by night, a new vernacular literature was in the making. The great Middle-French Epic was made in the twelfth-century inn by clerks and wandering scholars who sang for their supper, and wove into their songs the stories of local shrines, local ruins, local fairs for the delectation of their travelling patrons. To such inns, every night, came traders on their way to some famous fair, pilgrims seeking a shrine, the purveyors of faked relics, the scholars making their way towards some famous master. The scholars never knew their debt to merchants, and would have been furious to hear it suggested, for their attitude towards those that bought and sold was that of Aristotle before them, who, in reply to his friend's question, "shall we condescend to legislate at all on these vulgar commercial matters?" murmured, "No, it is not worth while." But they owed to merchants the fact that they had roads to walk on, that these roads were comparatively safe. They even owed a part of the vital equipment of scholarship to trade. Late in the eleventh century, for example, Italy enjoyed a great trade revival. It cheapened vellum, it released more money for the purchase of books and manuscripts, and it greatly accelerated the rise to power of the cities of Italy and Western Europe, making possible in the next century the achievement of so many of them in winning the semi-independence of the Commune.

For, of course, trade involves the making of towns as well

as roads; and scholarship is an urban growth. It can be kept alive in a purely agricultural atmosphere; it can eke out a bare existence in nomadic surroundings; but it grows and expands on the pavements of a city, not on the grass of the field. "In Aquitaine there is no learning," said Benedict of Clusa with his customary tact to an audience of the various bishops of Aquitaine. "They are rustics all: and if anyone in Aquitaine has learnt any grammar, he straightway thinks himself Virgil." He went on to tell them that once his uncle had died he would be the Abbot of Clusa, since he was already chosen in advance, and if he was not as yet consecrated, that was due to "the malice of some evil monks who care for nothing but hypocrisy and rusticity."[1] Hypocrisy, Rusticity, Ignorance—an unholy trinity, but evidently, in his eyes, a true three in one. Not many scholars were so senseless, but few would have denied that rusticity and learning went ill together. Even the Great Abelard, when multitudes flocked to him in the wilderness near Troyes, importunately demanding learning at his hands, swiftly abandoned the improvised buildings they put up, and led his new following back to Paris, to the school on the side of St. Geneviève.

For a century past towns had been growing up at a great pace, especially on the rivers in Germany, and in Lombardy and Tuscany. They were all trading centres, with a fast-growing population, constantly recruited by runaway serfs from the countryside, who could claim freedom from their feudal lords if they could establish citizenship in any city with the privileges of a commune. Already, by 1050, such towns as Cologne and Nurnberg stood in no awe of lords, feudal or ecclesiastical, and Italian cities such as Brescia were a by-word for asserting with

[1] Helen Waddell. op. cit., p. 83.

THE GOLDEN MIDDLE AGE

truculence their civic independence and authority. Some were not content with mere assertion. Laon, for example, plundered the bishop's palace, found his lordship hiding in a wine barrel and cut his throat. This, of course, was not commendable, but as a form of direct action when more reasonable counsels had failed, it did not stand alone. Even in Spain, always a generation or two behind the rest of Europe, the civic communes won their right in the twelfth century to be represented in the Cortes on equal terms with nobles and bishops, and they had the special privileges of voting the King's taxes and of demanding that he should make new or repeal existing laws. The importance of London was such that every contemporary historian was forced to refer to it and to "illustrate the importance of the city and the political interest of its citizens."[1] In King Stephen's anarchy the citizens even claimed a supposed right to say who should be king. The whole social trend of the second half of the eleventh century was to assert the supremacy of town over country, and to drive the ambitious townwards. Nor could the Church stand aside. Bishops, with their great administrative responsibilities, were forced to spend more and more time in the central towns of their dioceses, and an edict given in London in 1075 bade bishops move from "villages and unimportant places to towns", which brought Bishop Herman from Sherborne to Salisbury.[2] The making of towns, and their rise to power is all-important among the causes of the twelfth-century renaissance, and its instrument the University. They could house multitudes of scholars and masters, and they could protect them against irresponsible tyranny and exactions on the part of feudal magnates. For in

---

[1] F. M. Stenton. op. cit., p. 5.
[2] Dora H. Robertson. *Sarum Close* (Cape), p. 23.

FROM CHARLEMAGNE TO ABELARD

the town neither the law of scot and lot nor the law of their strong right arm ran. And towns then most commonly asserted their new-born civic pride in two ways, by violently defying any of great feudal position who sought to lord it over them, and by struggling to persuade a body of masters and scholars to settle within their walls and under their protection, and to give them the highest pride of a commune, their very own university.

But the day of the University as such was not yet. The Paris citizen of 1100, even of 1150, had not heard the word, and would not have understood it if he had. What he had seen was the sudden passion for learning which swept over the youth of every country in Western Europe from Norway to Sicily, from Britain to Austria, and which brought them in their thousands into his streets, and into the streets of Orleans, Laon, Bologna, Chartres, and many other towns, any town in fact which could boast one of the small and ancient cathedral schools, and a master of fire and magnetism teaching there.

Thither they came in huge numbers. Nothing like it had ever been seen before, and no teacher in the past, not even Plato, had enjoyed in his own time the tumultuous enthusiasm and the far-flung fame of an Abelard or an Anselm of Laon. The slow gestation of the centuries had woven together into a creative unity the many different threads of social life, trade, the roads, civic consciousness, bureaucracy in palace and manor house, which made it all possible. They constituted the external conditions which could hold the new world of twelfth-century Europe together—the world in which, for a full century and a half, scholars and not potentates were the heroes, the classroom and not the tented field was the scene, and the essential conflict of the drama was played out not

THE GOLDEN MIDDLE AGE

between Pope and Emperor, or monarch and monarch, but between two ideals of philosophic speculation, and two views of the means and ends of education. For the first, and as yet the last century in history, Europe enjoyed a just standard of values, and placed in the centre of her interest the things which really did matter most. She entered upon a golden age, still in the opinion of many the greatest century of her history, in which creative activity in all the things of the mind and the spirit was everywhere alive and in tumultuous motion.

It all happened quite suddenly. The intellect impalpably quickened, and the air changed, became charged with the atmosphere of philosophic surmise. This change came almost overnight. It is as though men woke up one fine morning

> Look'd at each other with a wild surmise—
> Silent—

The historian can trace the external conditions of society which made it possible. But that is all he can do. They did not cause it. Search history as we may for the causes of this awakening, we do no more than pick up a few threads here and there. These we weave together, but the cord we weave will not bear the weight which must be hung upon it. "No one quite knows how it happened," said Rashdall himself, and he would know if anyone could. He can say no more than "it is a great spiritual movement" and admit that "for the most part it is the conditions only, and not the originating causes of great spiritual movements which admit of analysis at the hands of the historians."[1] We are thrown back on Miracle, and all the historian's patient research does but bring him to the point where he must say, "A miracle happened," and

[1] Rashdall. op. cit., Vol. I, p. 33.

FROM CHARLEMAGNE TO ABELARD

thus excuse himself from further analysis. No one can say more than Sir Arthur Quiller-Couch. The universality of the passion to learn, the fame of the great teacher, "spreads almost as pollen is wafted on the wind: but spreads, alights, and fertilizes."[1] But How? or Why? The questions cannot be answered. They are hidden in the mind of God who does not generally vouchsafe us with an explanation of the miracles He performs.

[1] *Studies in Literature* (Cambridge University Press), Vol. I, p. 18.

CHAPTER III

THE SCHOOLS AND THE SCHOLARS

1. *Preparatory School*

"A FATHER I had who was to no small extent imbued with letters before he girded on himself the soldier's belt. Whence at a later time, he was seized with so great a love of letters that whatever sons he had he was disposed to instruct in letters rather than in arms."[1] It is Abelard writing. He received his early training in his father's house at Palais. But his family stood among the higher ranks of the feudal hierarchy, and the rudiments of learning were easily come by at home. It was not so with the more ordinary student who set out to trudge to Paris or Orleans. He probably belonged to what would now be called the Lower Middle Class, which, translated into medieval social terms, meant that he was born on the farm, and that no one at home could either read or write. Where did he learn these necessary accomplishments? Who taught him sufficient Latin to understand it when he heard it spoken? How did he pick up the rudiments of the technical language of dialectical philosophy? Without these, it would be useless to go to Paris for his learning; and later on, when the organization of the university had effectively strangled the fresh, free life of the cathedral school from which it grew, he would not have been admitted to studentship until the authorities were satisfied that he had received this ground-

[1] *Historia Calamitatum: Letters.* Ed. Scott Moncrieff, p. 3.

THE SCHOOLS AND THE SCHOLARS

ing, until he could show his ability to understand, to speak, and to write Latin.

To point to the parochial system of the Church is to give one part of the answer. The parish priest in every generation has an eye for a likely lad, and gives a good deal of his spare time to helping him onward. John of Salisbury, for example, in pure scholarship the finest flower of the twelfth century, and perhaps of the whole Middle Ages, had his elementary schooling at the hands of the parish priest of Old Sarum about the year 1130. He also had other things less desirable than the rudiments of Latin grammar. This particular priest beguiled his loneliness by practising necromancy and the blacker arts. Crystal-gazing was his hobby, and the essential condition of success was that the scrying should be done by an innocent youth. John was therefore shown the crystal globe, but could see no chirping and muttering spirits in it. He tells the tale himself in his famous fragment of autobiography:

It happened that he made me and a boy somewhat bigger than I, after some unholy preliminaries, sit at his feet and apply ourselves to this sacrilegious business of scrying, so that what he sought to know might by our means be revealed to him, either in nails smeared with some consecrated oil or chrism, or in the smooth polished body of a basin. When then, some names having been invoked, which, child as I was, I judged from the horror I felt at hearing them to be names of evil spirits, and certain adjurations having been uttered by way of preface, my comrade had intimated that he saw some shapes, though but dim and misty, I for my part proved myself so blind a scryer that I could see nothing there but the nails or basin. So I was after this considered useless for this sort of employment.[1]

[1] *Policraticus II:* 28. Tr. Clement Webb. *John of Salisbury* (Methuen), pp. 3, 4.

THE GOLDEN MIDDLE AGE

But this sort of lesson was no doubt the exception; and here at least we see one tiny village with an unofficial school kept by the parish priest, consisting of at least two, and probably more boys. The same thing must have been happening in thousands of villages in Europe.

Such a school as this was called unofficial in the previous paragraph. It owed its being to the private initiative of the parish priest, and not to the settled educational policy of the Church. The medieval equivalent of the "Elementary" or the "Preparatory" School—actually it was a cross between the two—was lavishly provided. One twelfth-century writer, Theobaldus Stampensis, says that there was such a school in every town and village in England—a wild exaggeration of an approximate truth. Every town and every great ecclesiastical centre certainly maintained such a school. Gerald of Wales,[1] the one really lovable archdeacon of the twelfth century, began his education at the school of the Abbey of St. Peter at Gloucester, under "that most learned scholar Master Haimon, then wearing the Cluniac habit, and very well fleshed both in face and body".[2] The famous Abbot Samson of St. Edmundsbury went first to the school at Diss in Norfolk. Years later, almost his first task as abbot was to buy stone houses for the school of St. Edmund's, that "the poor clerks might there be for ever free of paying rent for houses".[3] Two centuries later, Oxford was maintaining Grammar Schools,

---

[1] Gerald of Wales, that is Giraldus Cambrensis, as he is called in all the books. I can never understand why he, alone among twelfth-century worthies, is thus latinized: we should never think of calling John of Salisbury Johannis Sarisberiensis. In this book Gerald will be called by his British name and not the latinized form of it. R.L.

[2] *Autobiography*. Ed. H. E. Butler (Cape), p. 79.

[3] *Jocelyn of Brakelond*, p. 72.

THE SCHOOLS AND THE SCHOLARS

intended to be used as a training ground and a qualifying centre for a career in the university. There young boys were received for fivepence a term; board was eightpence a week; and if the services of a visiting teacher in writing were required, the cost was twopence a week. London, which throughout the Middle Ages never possessed a school which could remotely be described as a university, or even the germ of one, offered ample scholastic facilities for young boys to be prepared for the higher education of Paris. In the twelfth century there were three such schools, attached to St. Paul's Cathedral, and to the parish churches of Holy Trinity and St. Martin. In each of them, boys were given a thorough training in the principles of dialectical disputation as well as in the rudiments of the Latin tongue.

Boys left such schools as these and passed on to a university at what seems to us an incredibly early age. Few were out of their teens when they said farewell to their parents, pocketed their usually scanty journey money, and set out in twos and threes to trudge all the way to the school of their choice. The journey was still not without its dangers. Journey money always burns a hole in the pocket, and there were many taverns by the way to charm it forth. Nor were all roads rid of bandits. An Italian scholar, richer than most, was passing over the Alps on his way to Bologna. Bandits ambushed him and deprived him of clothing, horses, books, and money. Naked he sought refuge in the nearest monastery, and thence wrote sadly home to announce his state. Another band of robbers disguised themselves as clerks, ingratiated themselves with a scholar tramping to Paris, and then stripped him, leaving him helplessly bound by the roadside. Bandits were the most real and frequent danger, for though the average wandering scholar was not worth the trouble of robbing, there was always the chance that the gang might happen to light upon some nobleman's son. Some of the wealthier parents provided escorts for their sons, and there seems even to have grown up a new profession of providing a cart to carry and an armed guard to protect a body of young scholars to the schools. The scholars themselves might well be armed, for the regulations forbidding the carriage of weapons by private travellers was often expressly relaxed for scholars travelling to a university or home from it.

Politics could be a source of danger to the travelling clerk no less real than bandits, and far less predictable. At the time of the Papal Schism in the middle of the century, for example, an English clerk was travelling in Italy, when

all clerks bearing letters of Pope Alexander were seized, some of them being imprisoned and others hanged, and others, after having their noses and their lips cut off, were sent back to the Pope to his shame and confusion.

But this clerk had a ready wit.

I pretended that I was a Scot, and put on Scottish dress, and adopted the manners of a Scot. And I often shook my staff as they shake a weapon which they call a gaveloc at those who mocked me, shouting threatening words in the manner of the Scots. To those who met me and asked me who I was, I answered nothing except, "Ride, ride Rome, turne Cantwereberei."[1]

This device succeeded well until at last the ingenious traveller was captured by the retainers of a suspicious baron, who called him a spy. He escaped with his life, but not with his

[1] *Jocelyn of Brakelond*, p. 77.

THE SCHOOLS AND THE SCHOLARS

money. The perils of the journey, in fact, were still real enough to make it exciting, but few enough to provide a good deal more than a reasonable chance of a safe arrival, especially in northern France and Germany. Scholars who were molested and hindered by the way were wholly exceptional.

2. Paris

When St. Thomas Aquinas, a young, unknown monk, first came to the Schools of Paris, his friends took him to dine at the King's table. A large company was gathered in the hall, and no one took much notice of Aquinas. This was a relief to him, not an affront, for he was always a silent man. He could sit in a corner and think, and everybody would forget about him. And this they did until the noise of talk and laughter was broken by a sudden crash, coming from a corner of the room, which made the cups and goblets dance. It was Aquinas. His hand had banged the table as though roughly demanding silence; and then his voice was heard crying "like a man in a dream": 'And that will settle the Manichees'." The King, St. Louis of France, was in no way disturbed. Instead of having the young man thrown out for his behaviour, he at once turned to a secretary, bade him take his tablet over to the absent-minded thinker and take down the heads of his argument: "It must be a very good one and he might forget it".[1]

It is a thirteenth-century story, but it illustrates the general attitude towards the things of the mind of a century earlier. The universities were made by the conviction that nothing matters quite so much as learning, and that to get learning was

[1] G. K. Chesterton. *St. Thomas Aquinas* (Hodder & Stoughton), p. 117.

THE GOLDEN MIDDLE AGE

well worth any amount of inconvenience, effort, discomfort, and even suffering. Everything which the writers of the Old Testament Apocrypha had to say about Wisdom, her price and her rewards, and the composers of the Elizabethan lyric were moved to write about Anthea, Celia, or Damaris, the twelfth-century student said about learning. He was as passionate and as prodigal as they, and much more pertinacious. And, in this regard, the student is not merely the wandering scholar: he is the whole of articulate European society, from the Pope downwards. Such an attitude was quite new in history. There had been many eras in the past which had valued learning, but there had been none in which the tributes had been paid by every articulate section of the community. Not even Athens in her fifty most dazzling years had seen anything like this. In it was essentially a movement, a conviction of the people, not of the nobility. It was the then equivalent of the Lower Middle Class which filled the schools, which valued learning enough to get it at a great cost, "keeping vigil till dawn, working by candlelight, and joining night to day."[1] It was one of the very few movements of the mind which has sprung spontaneously from the broad masses of the people. They kindled the blaze at which others caught fire.

"The next year after that the glorious king of the English, Henry the Lion of Righteousness, departed from human things." John of Salisbury "went into Gaul for the cause of study."[2] To go to the schools had become the Grand Tour of the day, the darling ambition of every spirited youth from Norway to Sicily; and the journey was no snail's progress, unwillingly enterprised. "In those first days when youth in

[1] Gerald of Wales. *Autobiography*, p. 122.
[2] *Metalogicus*, Vol. II, p. 10.

THE SCHOOLS AND THE SCHOLARS

me was happy and life was swift in doing, and I wandering in the divers sweet cities of France, for the desire that I had of learning, gave all my might to letters," said an Irish scholar, and he spoke for all his tumultuous brethren.[1] ."The divers sweet cities of France"—it might be Angers, Rheims, Chartres, Orleans, or many others, but almost certainly Paris would be included in the itinerary of ambition, and it would come first on the list. Paris was the Athens of twelfth-century Europe, for on the island of the Seine it possessed the Episcopal cathedral school of Notre Dame, and none other possessed a tithe of its far-flung fame. It was this magnet which above all others lured most of the ambitious scholars of Europe from their homes. The city had external advantages over many of its competitors. Its climate was healthy, which is an unusual thing to be able to claim of a university town, and also so pleasant that "medieval writers exhaust the resources of their vocabulary in praise of the climate of Paris."[2] It was also politically important, for the Counts of Paris were soon to become the reigning kings of France, and therefore it offered the security which scholarship needs, a boon which not all university towns could confer.

But these are external reasons only. The fame of Paris was not primarily due to them. It rested on the place it held in the hearts and the passions of the scholars who had studied there. There is no limit to the passionate admiration and love which the twelfth-century scholar had for Paris. It was "an *aurora borealis*, a sunrise in the north." The words are G. K. Chesterton's,[3] but they are staid and colourless when set beside

---
[1] Helen Waddell. op. cit., p. 111.
[2] Rashdall. op. cit., Vol. III, p. 8.
[3] In *St. Thomas Aquinas*, p. 114.

THE GOLDEN MIDDLE AGE

the authentic and contemporary praises of the scholars. "Paris, queen among cities, moon among stars. On that island hath Philosophy her royal and ancient seat: who alone, with Study, her sole comrade, holding the eternal citadel of light and immortality, hath set fast the victorious foot on the withering flower of the fast ageing world."[1] That is the lyrical norm of praise and declamation with which the name of Paris was greeted. This enthusiasm affected also temperamentally cautious folk not in the least given to uncritical exaggerations, and the idea of Paris as a praise and a sweet song in the memory never departed from them when they grew old and were immersed in the business of the world. "Verily the Lord is in this place and I knew it not," said John of Salisbury, when he came back again in later years after a long absence. On another occasion John had been stranded at Paris on his way from Rome to Canterbury. He was helped out of the difficulty by his lifelong friend, Peter, Abbot of Celle. He wrote to thank Peter for the help given, which had saved him from what had seemed like perpetual exile. "Perpetual exile?" replied Peter, in mock reproof. How could John bring himself to call a forced stay in Paris exile? "It is the city of all delights."

"O Holy God of gods in Sion," burst forth Richard de Bury, the great Bishop of Durham, "what a mighty stream of pleasure made glad our hearts whenever we had leisure to visit Paris, the Paradise of the world, and to linger there;where the days seemed ever few for the greatness of our love."[2] The tribute continues in an unchecked torrent of declamation, amid a perfect riot of classical allusion. There is passion, even

[1] Guido de la Bazoches in 1175—Tr. Helen Waddell. op. cit., p. 112.
[2] *Philobiblon* (Chatto & Windus), p. 56.

THE SCHOOLS AND THE SCHOLARS

extravagance in it, but the twelfth century would have hailed the one, and not even noticed the other.

The Paris to which these scholars came was still a walled city, very small by modern standards. It stood architecturally at the beginning of the transitional period when stone was everywhere replacing timber as building material. Like London in the same period, new buildings were being erected in every street. Most of the houses were still wooden erections of two or three storeys, each jutting out above the other, and darkening the narrow cobbled pavement in the alley below. While there is no need to exaggerate the dirt of the streets, and speak of them as a modern American does as "bottomless quagmires in rain and thick with dust in dry weather" (for if this were wholly true the students must continually have suffered from disease, whereas actually they were as healthy as their modern descendants) yet still they were both dark and dirty. The full measure of the distance separating twelfth- from twentieth-century Paris is perhaps indicated by the fact that in specially hard winters people had to watch carefully over their young children, for marauding packs of wolves would force their way in, and there would be exciting wolf hunts in the streets.

To such a city the scholars came in their hundreds. They revitalized it beyond belief, and it surged and heaved with tumultuous life. It was, of course, extremely crowded. It is impossible to do more than guess at the figures. But beyond doubt they would be at least double the Oxford figures throughout the twelfth century, and by 1209 there were at least 3,000 students and masters at Oxford. In 1192 complaints were made that the students of Oxford were so many that the resources of the city could hardly feed them. To suggest therefore that about 5,000 students formed the average undergraduate population of Paris would be an error on the cautious side. A permanent addition of 5,000 to the population of any city, few or none of whom ever become householders, most being always out of funds, and given to rowdiness, would create a municipal problem in any century. The wonder was not that there were so many Town and Gown riots, but that there were not many more. There is no contempt like that of the clerk for the commoner, and no type was less able to conceal it than the average medieval student. This sudden eruption of thousands of young scholars did not merely create the obvious problems of feeding, housing and controlling them. In addition, they gave a new impetus and direction to the economic life of the city. Landladies and taverners assumed a new importance in the scheme of things, and after the still extant tradition of their trade, not slow to profit withal, prospered and exceedingly increased. Many new trades were created, and the streets were thronged not by students and their masters only, but by the professional writers of model or form letters—chiefly for begging purposes—by copyists, by booksellers and the proprietors of lending-libraries, and by the inevitable mass of servants of all kinds, without whom no great school or university could long exist.

Twelfth-century Paris was perhaps the most truly international city which has yet existed. We still have evidence that in John of Salisbury's time scholars had come not only from Brittany, Normandy, Germany, Italy and England, but from Sweden and Hungary as well. The masterships of the schools were also thoroughly international. A Paris mastership was almost the highest dream of scholastic ambition, and she therefore drew her masters from an area no less wide than the whole of Western Europe. Thirteen are named in a

THE SCHOOLS AND THE SCHOLARS

contemporary document, *Metamorphosis Goliae Episcopi*, five of them were Bretons, and not at this date technically French, three were English, and one a Lombard. John of Salisbury made another list, adding several whose names are not found in the other document, his additions being one German, two Normans—no more French than Bretons—and but one Frenchman.

The intellectual standards of a master were in that day very high, as we can tell by looking at the names John gives of his own Paris teachers. First there was Abelard, and though he then lectured in the days of his wretchedness, and with the sword of a great fear, St. Bernard's wrath, hanging suspended by a hair over his head, his voice seems to have lost none of its charm, nor his logical arguments their power to enthral. Then there was Robert of Melun, an Englishman in spite of his title. He was an eminent theologian, grave, precise, caustic in speech, and very highly orthodox, as became a friend of St. Bernard, and later, one of the advocates of the prosecution of Gilbert Porée for heresy. "There is most certainly nothing heretical in *his* teaching," emphatically commented a contemporary, John of Cornwall. Yet he was very soon to stand out fearlessly as one of Abelard's defenders, after the final condemnation at the Synod of Sens. Finally, there was the mysterious Alberic, who cannot be exactly identified. Between him and Robert, John drew a comparison, which tells us much about both.

The one was in questions subtle and large, the other in responses lucid, short, and agreeable. They were in some sort counter-parts of one another; if the analytical faculty of Alberic had been combined in one person with Robert's clear decision, our age could not have shown an equal in debate.

THE GOLDEN MIDDLE AGE

For they were both men of sharp intellect, and in study unconquerable. Thus much for the time that I was conversant with them: for afterwards the one went to Bologna and unlearned that which he had taught; yea, and returned and untaught the same; whether for the better or no, let them judge who heard him before and since. Moreover, the other went on to the study of divine letters, and aspired to the glory of a nobler philosophy and a more illustrious name.

No one seems to have thought it worthy of specially vehement comment that in the school of Paris, the capital of France, and a city very conscious of the sense of nationalism, there were twelve foreigners teaching as opposed to one native. It is a curious fact, for which it is not easy to account, since to say that members of a great cosmopolitan school shed their nationalistic prejudices as soon as they arrived there is emphatically not true. In all medieval schools there was endless trouble between the students of one nation and another. The French and the Germans were particularly troublesome. Nationality was a concept wholly undefined and hardly realized with any consciousness. But the French and German students loathed each other on sight, and what is more, for exactly the same reasons as they do now. But though the national hatred of French and Germans may have been specially virulent, they did not stand alone. Each nation had its unseemly qualities, and, says Jacques de Vitry, none was backward in pointing out that

the English were drunkards and had tails; that the sons of France were proud, effeminate, and carefully adorned like women. They said that the Germans were furious and obscene at their feasts; the Normans vain and boastful; the Poitevins traitors and adventurers. The Burgundians they consider vulgar and stupid. The Bretons were reputed to be fickle and

THE SCHOOLS AND THE SCHOLARS

changeable, ... the Lombards avaricious, vicious and cowardly; the Romans seditious, turbulent, and slanderous; the Sicilians tyrannical and cruel; the men of Brabant bloody, incendiaries, brigands, and ravishers; the Flemish, fickle, prodigal, gluttonous, yielding as butter, and slothful.[1]

After that, he comments, "they often came to blows." It was not surprising that riots between nation and nation were frequent. They always ended in bloodshed and sometimes in death. It was to deal with precisely this difficulty that Paris was divided into areas, and the students of each nation were forbidden to lodge outside their allotted area, and proctors were appointed over each nation to maintain order.

This piece of organization made safer the life of citizen and student alike. But it was never intended, and it would in any case have been utterly impossible, to place restriction on the daylight intercourse of the nations. For Paris was a gossipy city, and the talk, when not scandalous, was dialectical in pattern, and of the high matters of philosophy and theology. There was no knotty question which Paris could not unravel, said one of her greater sons, Peter of Blois. Day in and day out groups of scholars endlessly paced the left bank of the river, the stretch near the Little Bridge, a walk consecrated to the talkers' parade. There young logicians disputed as they walked, endlessly dissecting the indivisible Trinity, eternally debating the subtleties of Nominalism and Realism.

The street scene was even more garrulous, and, fortunately, can be reproduced with some exactness. For one scholar, John of Garland, had the happy idea of compiling a dictionary on a novel plan, a dictionary of the Paris street, giving a description of all the objects which were to be seen therein. Shops

[1] Nathan Schachner. *The Medieval Universities* (Allen & Unwin), p. 78.

THE GOLDEN MIDDLE AGE

selling various kinds of food were naturally most numerous of all. The pastry-makers specialized in cakes for students, a tart stuffed with eggs and cheese, a pie with pork, eels, and chicken, highly seasoned. The eggs were famous—for being generally bad. They were particularly odorous in Paris, much more so than in Cologne, as a student testified who had left Cologne for Paris, and been ill there; but now "I am fully wont to eat our eggs, more corrupt and fewer in quantity than the eggs which are supplied to our brethren in Cologne."[1] The Paris egg continued to be specially infamous throughout the Middle Ages, and Erasmus had bitter remarks to make about it. There were many cooked-meat shops for the scholars, who at dinner-time sent a servant to fetch home a roast bird, freshly turned on the spit and all hot. For poorer scholars, and those who liked to try their own hand at cooking—an accomplishment most common in universities then and now—they sold all kinds of meat, uncooked but well seasoned with garlic in advance, for to impregnate mutton with garlic might be deemed beyond the powers of an amateur. A tray of tripe and sausage was kept ready for the poorest of all. But if such shops as these, being most indispensable, were most numerous, there was no lack of others to supply every kind of luxury dear to the undergraduate heart from bows and arrows to wine. The wine shops were not merely taverns. They sold wine at anything from fourpence to twelvepence a measure, to be consumed not on the premises. The trades congregated in quarters; the bookstalls around Notre Dame, next door to the school; goldsmiths and jewellers on the Grand Pont; and sellers of desks, paper, quills, and pigments for

[1] G. G. Coulton. *Life in the Middle Ages* (Cambridge University Press), Vol. I, p. 141.

illuminating not far away. By day the streets were noisy with the cries of travelling fruit-sellers. They came in from the farms outside, and their reputation for honest dealing was not high. Their skill in hiding all the bad fruit at the bottom of the basket was famous. At night, the place of the fruit-sellers was taken by the wandering pastrymen, with their immense trays holding covered baskets of shortbreads and rissoles. These baskets were a favourite stake at dicing, and the winner used to hang them outside his window as trophies.

All this, and more besides, was carefully noted and preserved by John of Garland. Clearly, his dictionary was entertaining beyond the ordinary. One imagines there was a ready sale for it as a gift to fathers and uncles, so aptly would it serve to rekindle the fires of their own youthful memories of the Paris schools.

3. *In Statu Pupillari*

As for the students themselves who trod these streets, and the streets in many other towns beside from Chartres and Orleans to Palermo and Bologna, not even the mould of seven centuries has cast oblivion over them. It may be true that to-day we know the names and lives only of the exceptional among them, but it is also true that the phrase "Twelfth-Century Scholar" is one to which we are able to attach a quite definite and characteristic meaning. For the impact which their vitality made upon the imagination of their own generation was overwhelming, and many of the imaginations thus stimulated expressed themselves not merely in speech, but in writings which we still possess.

Very much of this evidence is a complaint. The students

as a class were rowdy and undisciplined—a characteristic made inevitable by the common use of dialectic as the primary educational method. Thus they annoyed their teachers. They could, and often did turn the streets and market-places of the university city into a riotous bear garden, thus earning the dislike of municipal authority and unenviable mentions in civic records. Richard de Bury echoed the general opinion of their more decorous and sober elders when he thundered:

The race of scholars is commonly badly brought up, and unless they are bridled in by the rules of their elders they indulge in infinite puerilities. They behave with petulance, and are puffed up with presumption, judging of everything as though they were certain, though they are altogether inexperienced.[1]

It is firm language, but then sundry specimens of the student world had just been infuriating the mighty lover of books, by letting their noses dribble dewdrops on to the pages of books borrowed from him, marking a passage by scratching filthy nail grooves along the margin, and using damp straws to keep the place. Furthermore, they were, even the best of them, even so sober a person as John of Salisbury, incurable wanderers, thus drawing upon themselves as a class the suspicious regard of the Church, which thought that people generally, and clerks certainly, ought to go where they were sent and stop there, unless and until authority moved them again.

The moralists and preachers found in the students a fit theme for eloquent and interminable discourse, mostly in condemnation. "The student's heart is in the mire, fixed on prebends and things temporal," thundered a preacher. It is

[1] *Philobiblon*, p. 105.

THE SCHOOLS AND THE SCHOLARS

the note of all the Paris Sermon Books; but few of the sermons seem to have been of much avail. After all, St. Bernard himself experienced one of the very few failures of his life when he went to preach a course of sermons at Paris. "Some," he said, "wish to know that they may know, and this is curiosity; some that they may be known, and this is vanity; some that they may be enriched, and this is covetousness."[1] But the chief ground of clerical criticism was that many of the scholars were tonsured clerks, sent there by the Church, and at the expense of the faithful laity, in order to staff the various benefices with an educated clergy. The Church was not without just cause of complaint. The schools were intended to educate people to do the work of the Church, but unless a student could edge himself into a comfortable benefice or prebend immediately on completing his course, he very often preferred to go gallivanting about Europe rather than to serve a less exciting apprenticeship to preferment at home. The Church regularly granted leave of absence to parochial and cathedral clergy, who had not been to the schools, to go there and return better fitted for their work. They went—but many never returned. The pulpits of university towns were constant in denunciation, but though the preachers went the wrong way to gain their end, those ends in themselves were certainly right. Many of the students were unquestionably guilty of breach of an unwritten but real contract.

Gambling and drinking were the dominant evils of university life in its earliest days, and Robert de Sourbon's complaint about the average student's proficiency with the dice is abundantly justified by the numerous stories of queer dicing

[1] R. F. Bennett. *The Early Dominicans* (Cambridge University Press), p. 59.

matches which still exist. Drunkenness was no less common. The Proctors' Book of the English "nation" at Paris shows that in the small area of the city reserved for the accommodation of English students were no less than sixty taverns. These evils, however sadly they mitigated against a student's later life, were fruits rather than roots of an antecedent evil which caused their prevalence.

The seat of the trouble was the poverty, and the quite wretched living conditions of the majority of students. John of Salisbury in a list of the Six Keys of Learning, included Poverty and Exile among Humbleness of Heart, Love of Enquiry, Peacefulness, and Meditation. There is hardly any student, who afterwards became so famous that we still possess the narrative of his life, who did not have to face both poverty and exile at some time or other. Nobody, and least of all John, imagines that being poor possessed in itself any subtle alchemy of learning, but, in that day, it was an almost inescapable condition which had to be fulfilled. "A student's first song is a demand for money, and there will never be a letter which does not ask for cash," wrote a weary father. To judge by the students' letters which have come down to us, and by the ready sale which model begging letters had, this father did not complain unjustly.

Well-beloved father, I have not a penny, nor can I get any save through you, for all things at the University are so dear: nor can I study in my Code or my Digest, for they are all tattered. Moreover I owe ten crowns in dues to the Provost, and can find no man to lend them to me; I send you word of greetings and of money. . . .

Dear father, deign to help me! I fear to be excommunicated; already I have been cited, and there is not even a dry bone in my larder. If I find not the money before this feast of Easter

THE SCHOOLS AND THE SCHOLARS

the church door will be shut in my face: wherefore grant my supplication, for I send you word or greetings and money.[1]

Such is the plaint of an Orleans scholar. Here is another, from Chartres:

> Have pity, dear father, have pity! Stretch out your hand to your son, who is very hard up. Let your mind be filled with fatherly feelings, and do not let the mood of paternal affection evaporate. Do please try to send me straight away by the bedesmen four silver marks to Chartres, where I am living under the tuition of Master Bernard. Next Easter I shall make an effort to come home again fully instructed in those famous *sentences*.

It is good to know that this father duly sent the money his son asked. These are but two examples out of many scores which could be given, nor are they by any means the most heartrending. The chronic poverty of the medieval student, and his unabashed fertility in discovering highly original methods of begging, can be seen by a multitude of letters and stories given in Helen Waddell's *The Wandering Scholars*, and in C. H. Haskins's *Studies in Medieval Culture*.

The glimpses of poverty, stealing down the centuries, are many. One youth had begged his way from the Netherlands, and, being unskilful at the art of begging, had never got more than crusts of bread. Undismayed, he beguiled his way and kept up his spirits by composing a lengthy and philosophic dissertation on the differing stalenesses of the crusts he had been grudgingly given. That MS. still exists, but has not been translated. And there is the Oliver Goldsmith of twelfth-century Paris, who had frequented the dicing-houses and gambled away all his money and every stitch of clothing, and

[1] G. G. Coulton. op. cit., Vol. III, p. 113.

had left only a dirty patchwork quilt. Naked, he must needs stay under the quilt, and when his friends came to succour him they found him incorrigibly gambling still, but academically, by making the many fleas race down the quilt, with his toe, stuck through a hole, as the winning-post.

The effect of such examples and of translations of the begging letters is no doubt to cast the mantle of comedy over the students' poverty. But it was not always comic in actuality. To leave home so full of hope and confidence, to trudge in faith for miles day after day, to arrive at last at the haven where one would be, to find, with a sudden shock, that one's store of money was hopelessly insufficient to meet one's needs, to be reduced to begging from door to door "crying, 'O Good Masters,' and receiving nothing save a few scraps of refuse"[1]—there are the elements of bitter tragedy here. "We have made little glosses: we owe money"[2] was the picture of Chartres burnt into the brain of two students. "The poor scholar," wrote John of Garland, who had known himself what being a poor scholar meant,

is overcome by study, not deprived of virtue: moreover, the rich man, who does not study and who lives in tall houses, scoffs at poor scholars and even strikes them. I eat sparingly in my little room, not high up in a castle; I have no silver money, nor do the Fates give me estates. Beet, beans, and peas are here looked on as fine dishes, and we joke about meat which is not on our menu for a very good reason.[3]

In any stage of the world's history, past or present, and in any class of society, debt follows poverty with inexorable swift-

---

[1] Haskins. *Studies in Medieval Culture*, p. 13.
[2] Haskins. *Twelfth Century Renaissance*, p. 114.
[3] Schachner. op. cit., p. 332.

THE SCHOOLS AND THE SCHOLARS

ness. Gerald of Wales, for example, left Paris hopelessly in debt. But he went to hear Mass in a chapel of St. Thomas of Canterbury and "straightway received from heaven the reward of his devoutness"; whether in cash or in kind he does not tell us, but we are certainly meant to infer that a miracle had been worked for him. Any university town is notoriously prone to encourage debt, and twelfth-century Paris, or Chartres, or Orleans, or Bologna were not exceptions. At Bologna the authorities licensed four pawnbrokers to act as moneylenders to the students, and bestowed on them a monopoly. At Oxford, the amount a moneylender could loan to a student was fixed by statute, as also was the value and the nature of the pledge the student must deposit for it. But, despite all legislation and all care, many students became insolvent beyond all hope of rescue by any but a really rich relation. One of the effects of really hopeless debt on the debtor is to encourage him in wild gambling on horses yesterday and on the turn of the dice to-day, in the hope that, by a lucky stroke, he may extricate himself from the net. Then, as now, success in such an enterprise was a rarity.

For the corresponding plague of drinking mere conviviality and good spirits were mostly responsible, but other causes existed. There was also the drowning of sorrows, and the need to forget living conditions which would have been bad in any age. The students lodged as they could, some with landladies, but most with masters in hostels. Only the well-to-do could be sure of even a candle, much less a desk and a chair. A master would take four or five to board. At night they all slept together, he in a large bed, and they in small ones, which, by day, were pushed out of sight under his. There were some still more luckless, who slept on damp straw pallets in a garret, and without bedclothes. But the chief physical discomfort was the cold of winter. No one will understand the incessant harping by the old poets on the glories of spring and summer who does not also realize the extreme discomforts of a medieval winter for all but the rich. One student writes home to say that he has been very ill with the cold, another that the cold is so intense that he simply cannot study at nights. A fire in a room was a rarity. Vivid descriptions of students writing up their lecture notes in a room where the only warmth is one guttering candle and their fingers get so numbed that they cannot hold their pens still exist. A picture comes drifting down the ages of one such unfortunate blowing on his numb fingers, and grousing that it "is two years since he has tasted wine, washed his face, or trimmed his beard."[1] One famous wit and scholar—the Archpoet—perished of consumption; many more died of the same plague who left no memorial. Ale comforts a cold body more cheaply than a fire, and taverners are more apt to give credit than landladies.

Faith and hope proverbially give place to love, the quality greater than either. In the twelfth-century school faith and hope were weapons which often broke in the student's hand, but love never deserted him. *Alma mater* was for him a phrase grounded not in sentimentality but in genuine passion, expressing a real, dominant, and lifelong emotion. The average student, anonymous, turbulent, unstable, with his passion for learning, and his romantic devotion to the Schools, became the norm of a whole civilization. It is pleasant to reflect that the supreme gift of the Middle Ages to the world, the University, was bequeathed not by warriors or potentates, and not primarily by the creative magic of illustrious names, but by the

[1] Haskins. *Studies in Medieval Culture*, p. 13.

THE SCHOOLS AND THE SCHOLARS

anonymous host of the wandering scholars, gathered from every nation in Europe to seek learning and escape from tedium.

4. *The Teaching Scene*

Up to the present in this study the words School and University have been used as though they were virtually synonymous. "I go to the Schools," said the twelfth-century boy, as he kissed his mother good-bye and trudged down the road which led to Paris, If he said it before 1160, or thereabouts, he meant the Cathedral School: if he began his journey after that date, he meant the *studium generale* or University. That is to say, he meant it if he sought Paris or Bologna or Orleans: but if Chartres was the goal of his journey, he would mean by it a Cathedral School throughout the century, for Chartres, though by far the greatest house of learning of them all, never became a university.

Universities were never precisely founded. They evolved gradually out of the Cathedral School, the most elastic of all the earlier medieval instruments of education. The process is a story with three phases. In the earliest phase there is a master, appointed by the bishop or the chapter, with one or two assistants, and a body of perhaps a hundred students. There is but little organization, for none is needed; and it occurs to neither master nor students to get their rights and privileges defined and guaranteed. They stand in need neither of protection nor assertion. Then there comes the sudden passion for learning, for which, as has already been said, the historian is bound to postulate a miracle. At first it is tied to the magic of famous names, a William of Champeau, an Anselm of

THE GOLDEN MIDDLE AGE

Laon, or a Peter Abelard. Where they teach, the old schools at once burst their bounds. Their customary numbers are multiplied suddenly by ten, by twenty, or even more. At once problems arise. The most immediately pressing are problems of discipline, for the students of one nation constantly quarrel with the students of another. So they are divided into *nationes*, they lodge in different sections of the city, and each nation has its proctor to keep order. When this has been done, the first step towards turning a Cathedral School into a University has been taken. But in other respects, soon to be rigidly regimented, all is still free and easy. The great master still sets up his school where he chooses and asks no man's leave to teach. Abelard, for example, sets up his horn —a phrase fitting *rhinocerus indomitus* which was his nickname —on Mount St. Geneviève in Paris, and asks no man's permission. He is sought out in his wilderness retreat near Troyes by hordes of importunate students, and he and they together immediately build with their own bare hands a new school. They give it an ornately carved gateway and call it the School of the Paraclete, and for both actions they get into trouble with the straiter brethren among the clergy, but this is because the carving suggests heresy and the dedication is an innovation. Later the buildings become the Abbey of the Paraclete, and Heloise is the first abbess. From the rooms in which Abelard once taught are sent out the most famous love letters in the history of the world, which even to-day profoundly move all but the insensitive. The school, in fact, still attaches to the master: wherever he happens to be, there the school is. As yet, he asks no man's leave to teach, and he craves protection and security from no guild. There is but one exception, and significantly, it is in theology. At Laon, whilst a student there,

THE SCHOOLS AND THE SCHOLARS

Abelard was dared to lecture on Ezekiel. That he did so, and with enormous success, was counted to him for presumption, and later was introduced as a count in the indictment against him at the Council of Soissons. Abelard was teaching in Paris between 1120 and 1137. In his last days there he taught the young John of Salisbury who came to Paris in 1136. John saw the third phase of the evolution from Cathedral School to University pass in motion during his years *in statu pupillari*. In his time, the rough and ready, disorganized mechanism of scholarship was already changing fast. The master, and the scholar too, must now seek an established school. They must not presume to set up a school of their own free will, nor yet to teach without a licence. From this it is but a step, or a series of steps each involving the others, to the intricate mechanism of a university, degrees, a closed society of masters, disciplinary organizations for students, regular courses of lecturing, and the whole under the direction of a Chancellor or a Rector. "In those first days when youth in me was happy and life was swift in doing, and I wandering in the divers sweet cities of France, for the desire that I had of learning, gave all my might to letters."[1] As long as schools were Cathedral Schools such a spirit was possible. When they became Universities this glorious freedom of the sons of learning was cramped. The change was inevitable but it was not wholly gain.

So far as Paris is concerned, Rashdall dates the change as taking place anywhere within the span of the twenty years 1150 to 1170. During those years John of Celle was "admitted into the fellowship of the elect masters."[2] It is the earliest

---
[1] Helen Waddell, op. cit., p. 111.
[2] Rashdall. op. cit., Vol. I, p. 292.

reference to anything of the sort, and it is not at all clear what the words mean. But they certainly imply the existence of an organized, even of an exclusive, guild; and when the guild system is applied to education the university has begun. Everything which divides modern Cambridge from twelfth-century Paris is then only a matter of time and logical development. The closed corporation, with rules, privileges, strict conditions of entry, undertaken for the purposes of mutual help and protection—this makes the university. It may be a corporation of masters as at Paris, or a corporation of scholars founded as a protection against the greed of landladies and shopkeepers as at Bologna. It does not matter by which route the essential goal is approached. Once the germ of the guild system of trade and industry is applied to any educational centre, it has ceased to be a school and becomes a university.

Too much stress can hardly be laid upon the intoxication, even the magic of the great names which drew the scholars in their thousands in the early days of the century, and so, by sheer weight of numbers, made inevitable the evolution from Cathedral School to University. Movements of thought have always to be expressed in terms of some tremendous personality before the thin trickle becomes the mighty river. Gerbert, Fulbert, Roscelin, and Abelard, they all had personality, and had it abundantly. But the great names of the next generation, John of Salisbury, Gilbert Porée, are less magnetic and meteoric. (Chartres, with the brothers Bernard and Thierry, is significantly an exception.) Yet the multitudes, brought to the scholastic centres by the giants, continue and even increase when the rules and regulations and organization have rather cramped the competitive spirit on which the gianthood of personality depends. This continuance, and even increase, of

THE SCHOOLS AND THE SCHOLARS

numbers in the days when personalities counted for progressively less was due in part to the fact that the medieval Church was the one and the only human society which has ever existed in which a real equality of opportunity was practised. In the far-flung and varied service of the Church lay the ambitious commoner's only chance, and from the twelfth century onwards the School and the University were the only gates of this chance. But the educational method and curricula also played their part in ensuring the continuance of large numbers in the days when the magic of great names had ceased to be.

The educational system was so organized as to be always extremely exciting. Except at Chartres, dullness was systematically excluded from it at every stage, and the salt of competitive and noisy conflict seasoned every lesson and every lecture. The student could therefore be certain that while he might be cold and hungry, he would never be bored; and an educational system which has no moments of boredom is bound to be at least numerically successful. Whether it serves the interests of learning pure and undefiled is another matter. It was all based on the Seven Liberal Arts. These were comprised in the *Trivium*, that is Grammar, Rhetoric, and Dialectic; and in the *Quadrivium*, the four mathematical arts of Arithmetic, Geometry, Astronomy, and Music. It sounds formidable, and so it was, but not in the way we should expect. Music as studied, for example, was actually a mystical inquiry into the rules of plainsong and the doctrine of numbers, thus symbolizing the marriage of music and mathematics which seems so constant down the ages. The *Trivium* was the really formidable course. The book used for teaching Grammar, for example, was always Priscian's *Institutes*, written in the sixth century. It gave all the rules of Latin prose and verse construc-

THE GOLDEN MIDDLE AGE

tion, and exemplified them by quotations from the classics so copious that in the printed edition the book becomes two very thick and heavy volumes. What must have been the mental and physical labour of mastering it when its pages were parchment and its words written in script! There were eighteen volumes of it. When students had worked through them all, they knew at least the more famous quotations from all the classical authors. But still they had mastered only a part of one-seventh of their full course. This, however, did not at all deter them, for their vaulting ambition o'erleaped these barriers, at least in desire, and worried little that the gaiety of their optimism raised barriers yet more formidable. So drunk with the love of learning were they that they entertained scholastic ambitions which most of their teachers thought and denounced as wildly absurd. Many of these teachers added to the *Trivium* the demand of a terrifyingly ample knowledge of the classics, ranging from Virgil to Seneca, and taking in Donatus, Horace, Ovid, Sallust, Tully, by the way, and adding to that Boethius, and all the medieval glosses of Plato and the Christian Fathers. But not content with contemplating so formidable a programme, complained Absolom of St. Victor, the student must needs propose to add to it a thorough mastery of astronomy, botany, biology, geography, physics, and the why and wherefore of the weather. Some teachers, notably Robert de Sourbon, laid down rules as to the method in which the student should address himself to his study. He must learn to concentrate, to take notes skilfully, and to memorize. He must not disdain to talk over his lesson with other scholars, and he must have a fixed time for the study of each subject, resolutely refusing to depart from it. Above all, he must pray, "which availeth much for learning."

THE SCHOOLS AND THE SCHOLARS

The good student should imitate Christ among the doctors, having many masters, always seeking good teachers without regard to their fame or place of birth, and listening as well as asking questions—unlike those who will not wait for the end of a question, but cry out, "I know what you mean." Even when he goes to walk by the Seine, the good student ought to ponder and repeat his lesson.[1]

That is what he should do. But what he actually does, complains the same Robert, is very different.

He is much more familiar with the text of the dice, which he recognizes at once, no matter how rapidly they are thrown, than with the text of the old logic—yet the gloss of the dice he forgets, which is swear, steal, and be hanged.[2]

But if the ambitions of the average student had much to do with making a university education a process exciting as it was exacting, the primary philosophical pre-occupation of the time had still more. The question of questions, which resounded in all the schools, and was eagerly argued in every lecture room in Europe, was one which lent itself to the salt of competitive debate, the controversy of Nominalism and Realism.

As all roads once led to Rome, so in the Paris, and in most other, educational centres of the twelfth century all academic discussions led sooner or later to an eager canvass of the merits of Nominalism and Realism as the philosophic basis of life. The controversy was concerned with the nature of Universals and their relationship to individual units. Is "Humanity" a mere name used for the sake of convenience to denote the totality of human beings? Or is "Humanity"

[1] C. H. Haskins, paraphrasing Robert de Sourbon. op. cit., p. 57.
[2] ibid.

a real essence with a subjective existence all its own? The Realist, leaning on Plato, would say that "Humanity" was no mere class title but a real essence, identical in every man and woman. He would explain their manifest differences by postulating a mere fortuitous concourse of "accidents" to account for them. The Nominalist, however, denied that "Humanity" was anything more than the name given to the general mass of men and women in order to distinguish them from the general mass of dogs or cats. The question was no new academic subtlety. It was, and it is, the problem of problems, which even the mighty intellect of Plato had left unsolved. Beginning in the realm of philosophy, it leads him who wrestles with it into physics, ethics, theology, and even metallurgy, since alchemy—the art of turning base metals into gold—has the postulates of Realism behind it. As Rashdall used to say, "He who suggests a solution has in fact propounded his theory of the universe."

The scantiness of basic knowledge in the early part of the twelfth century made it inevitable that once a general interest in abstract thought began to be taken, this controversy would at once loom large and attract to itself all the eagerness of dialectical attention. Until after 1150, the medieval thinkers possessed only fragments of the works of both Plato and Aristotle. Plato was represented by a Latin translation of part of the *Timæus*, and Aristotle by the *Categories* and the *De Interpretatione*, both of them in Boethius's translation. Meagre remnants indeed! But it happens that in those fragments are contained both Plato's and Aristotle's doctrines of Universals.

The whole question is admirably stated in a single sentence of Porphyry's *Isagoge*. It is, perhaps, a trifle cumbrous and involved. Nor does it yield all the rich possibilities it contains

THE SCHOOLS AND THE SCHOLARS

at the bidding of a single cursory glance. But it has a vital effect on the course of the history of human thought:

Concerning *genera* or species, the question indeed whether they have substantial existence, or whether they consist in bare intellectual concepts only, or whether, if they have a substantial existence they are corporeal or incorporeal, and whether they are separable from the sensible properties of the things (or particulars of sense) or are only in those properties and subsisting about them, I shall forbear to determine.

That sentence does not look epoch-making: it looks extremely dull. But it makes history, and is vital within its course. Rashdall, a philosopher and theologian as well as an historian, who was not given to facile enthusiasms, went so far as to say that outside the pages of the Bible there was no single sentence in all literature with more widespread and permanent effects on life and thought. In every scholastic centre it is debated still.

It is obvious that abstract questions of this kind yield their treasures more kindly to verbal argument, the cut and thrust of impassioned debate, than to written composition. Precisely because this great controversy was the stuff of academic life in the twelfth century, the method of education was always dialectical and argumentative, and hence competitive and exciting. It became far more important for the student to argue than to write well, a bias underlined by the price of writing materials. Dialectical debate, the method of every lecture room outside Chartres, gave an ideal chance for leaping ambition. By his skill in ranging over the troubled waters of Nominalism and Realism on the wings of public argument, the scholar was judged. Let a master stumble over his interpretation of the nature of Universals. Let his pupils harry him by their eager questions, and at once his star had begun to wane. Unless he could recover his ground, and that swiftly, his star set to rise no more. It was by such methods that Abelard came into his fame. But it is perhaps not surprising that a considerable proportion of students really understood nothing of their lectures, and that almost half of them went down without a degree.

"It is the part of courage to have recourse to dialectic in all things," said Berengar. He spoke more prophetically than he knew. In the twelfth century, dialectic, or education by means of public debate became the art of arts, and in consequence it coloured the whole range of academic, and even of professional, life. All through life, and in all departments of life in which learning was required, there was this insistence on the primacy of dialectic. Is he a good dialectician? was the question asked even of candidates for an abbacy. In 1180 the abbot of the great monastery of St. Edmundsbury died, and the monks held long and anxious conclaves to decide who should be elected in his place to rule over them. Jocelyn of Brakelond, then a novice in the abbey, wrote a précis of their conversation in his *Chronicle*: it is one of the liveliest passages in English medieval literature. It is headed, "How the Monks Disputed among Themselves which of them should be Abbot," but as none of them in decency could very well put his own name forward, the discussion quickly turned to answering the question, What qualities should the abbot of St. Edmundsbury possess? One brother was illiterate, but he knew the custom of the Abbey. Another was stupid: let him be abbot "that he may be driven to use our help." The fable of King Log was urged in support of both, but in vain. A brother noted for prudence and eloquence was suggested,

THE SCHOOLS AND THE SCHOLARS

and rejected—"From good clerks deliver us, O Lord, that it may please thee to preserve us from the cheats of Norfolk." Another was a good farmer, and though he had a little learning "it had not made him mad." Another had a positive riot of virtues, kindness, friendliness, amiability, peacefulness, calmness, gravity; yet even these did not avail. Another was "skilled in counsel, strict in the rule, noble in stature." Yes, came the answer, "but he is too scornful, holding monks of no account, and being on familiar terms with secular men." An impediment in speech, "as if he had pastry or draff in his mouth when he should have spoken," disqualified another good candidate. At last, after "many men had said many things," the youngest but the ablest of them all, Jocelyn, got up and said, "I will not consent that any man should be made abbot unless he knows something of dialectic, and how to distinguish the true from the false." It was the one comment of the day which no one rebutted. All agreed that whatever qualities the new abbot possessed, at least proficiency in the art of dialectic must be one.[1]

Disputation, or teaching by means of the give and take of argument, was of course as old as the hills. As an educational method it had the considerable authority of Socrates. Plato and Aristotle had both been trained upon it, and every great teacher from the Hellenistic Age of Greece to the twelfth-century revival of learning had necessarily made great use of it. Indeed, there is not now and there never will be a really good school which does not make a ready use of the *Disputatio*. But John of Cornwall drew a distinction between the old *Lectio*, the formal controversy on a set theme, and the modern *Disputatio*, argumentativeness undisciplined by formalities and

[1] *Chronicle*, pp. 16–20.

THE GOLDEN MIDDLE AGE

running riotously into an empty verbal dexterity. The event which had done more than anything else to change *Lectio* into *Disputatio* was the translation of the full Aristotelian logic by James of Venice in 1128, and its later adoption as a text-book in the schools. It was an event of first-rate importance in the history of thought, and its immediate effect on education was to provide scholars, already argumentatively inclined, with a whole mass of new logical material on which to break their teeth.

The dialectical method had thus set its mark for good or ill on the whole of the medieval educational system, and no school could long flourish which, like Chartres, spurned it. Twelfth-century undergraduates were like all others the world over. A very few had the genuinely scholarly mind, which scorned the glib smattering of a quick wit, pierced through the thin veneer of verbal dexterity, and scornfully withdrew the skirts of their clothing. But the vast majority liked excitement in the schools, a quick and painless passage to the hallmark of a degree, and something to impress the neighbours at the end of it. All of these things dialectics could supply and classics could not: hence dialectical logic was the one thing needful to ensure that popularity without which no cathedral school could hope to become a university.

Before a boy was old enough to travel to Paris or Bologna, his school at home in London had already taught him to think of the formal dispute as vital, and tested his knowledge by his proficiency in argument. Fitzstephen, who wrote near the end of the century, has left a vivid description of the medieval combination of the modern annual examination and speech day as it was then held in London. The masters of the three great schools, St. Paul's, Holy Trinity, and St. Martin,

THE SCHOOLS AND THE SCHOLARS

assembled their boys together on the festivals of each of these three saints, and at the church whose patronal festival it happened to be. It was a great and a most combative occasion. The audience of City Fathers and parents, and masters, anxious that their own aptitude to teach should be reflected in the success of their pupils, assembled, chattered, and hushed. Then the scholars, one after another, stood up, and the battle of words was joined. Fitzstephen must have seen it himself, perhaps taken part in it, for his description has all the liveliness of an eye-witness.

Some "hurtle enthymemes," others with greater skill employ perfect syllogisms. Some are exercised in disputation for the purpose of display, which is but a wrestling bout of wit, but others that they may establish the truth for the sake of perfection. Sophists who produce fictitious arguments are accounted happy in the profusion and deluge of their words; others seek to trick their opponents by the use of fallacies. Some orators from time to time in rhetorical harangues seek to carry persuasion, taking pains to observe the precepts of their art, and to omit naught that appertains thereto. . . . There are others who employ the old wit of the cross roads in epigrams, rhymes and metre; with "Fennescine License" they lacerate their comrades outspokenly, though mentioning no names; they hurl abuse and gibes; they touch the foibles of their comrades, perchance even of their elders with Socratic wit, not to say

"Bite more keenly even than Theon's tooth"
in their "bold dithyrambs." Their hearers
"ready to laugh their fill
With wrinkling nose repeat the loud guffaw."[1]

Fitzstephen's learned editor adds a most necessary footnote to

[1] F. M. Stenton. op. cit., p. 28.

explain what an Enthymeme was: "An argument consisting of a single premise and conclusion as opposed to a Syllogism made up of major and minor premises and conclusion."[1] It is a pity that the totally erroneous assumption should be made that the modern reader of Fitzstephen knows what a "Fennescine License" is. But those boys knew, and they were probably only fourteen. Their Speech Day was spirited far beyond the average run of such functions. Trained thus in early years to regard an adroit and ready tongue as the thing which mattered most of all in education, they passed to Paris and Bologna, or almost anywhere except Chartres, only to find this essentially false impression emphasized. For there too a quick wit and a ready tongue did not merely gain the approval of one's teachers: it was also the road to promotion.

The teaching scene in Paris was no less gay and exhilarating, and any master who did not make it so in these early days of disorganized scholarship ran the risk of finding his lecture room quickly deserted. If he himself became dull and ponderous, his quick-witted and ambitious students provided the thrills of debate for him, and a good time was then had by all—except the lecturer. To catch one's master making a false step in his reasoning, to leap in with the eager question which concealed a trap, to tie him up in verbal but inexorable knots, and to continue the process day after day until both prestige and pupils had fled away, this was the way to a successful mastership of one's own. It kept the master always on the alert, for it was useless to forbid interruption. Either the class kept order, or it was not kept at all.

Abelard had been a past master at this art of publicly pricking the bubble of a false reputation. He came into his own master-

[1] F. M. Stenton. op. cit., p. 28.

THE SCHOOLS AND THE SCHOLARS

ship at Paris by publicly discomfiting William of Champeau so many times that William for very shame could do no other than retire to the refuge of a monastery, and leave his chair open to the occupancy of his impudently successful young rival. The climax came one fine day when William, the champion of the ardent Realists, was lecturing on the problem of problems. Rémusat described the scene in his *Vie d'Abelard*, and the passage is one of the high rewards of those who study twelfth-century scholarship. "Universals," said William, "are real essences and have positive reality. The Universal is one and the same: it resides in each creature, and forms a common foundation for them all. Thus, for instance, 'Humanity' denotes the totality of human beings, but it is much more than a name given to all the individuals of the human race. It is a real essence, common to all, complete in each."

At this point Abelard burst with eager speech, and no one sought to stop him. "If Humanity is the basic essence of every man, then individuality itself is an Accident. Thus, when Plato is at Rome and Socrates at Athens, the aforesaid essence, Humanity, is embodied in its completeness in Plato in Rome, and also in Socrates in Athens. So it seems that the Universal, Humanity, being the essence of the individual, is itself the individual, and it consequently carries the individual about with it wherever it goes. Thus, when Plato is in Rome there too is Socrates; and when Socrates is in Athens, Plato is with him and in him." To this William could find no real answer. He took refuge in distinctions and qualifications, and, when again pressed, lapsed into stuttering unintelligibility.

In the margin of the copy of Rémusat's book in one of our great libraries, some hasty, and perhaps rather weary, student has pencilled the word "Trivial." To many it may seem so essentially academic as to deserve the epithet. But Rémusat has a surer eye. He calls it "Cette question fameuse et redoutée qui avait perdu Roscelin." And now William of Champeau had been added to its victims. He might still intrigue against his successful young rival, but—no one doubted it—he had met his final defeat. After this, as Abelard said, "he was scarcely admitted to be a teacher of dialectic at all."

This of course was a high light of dialectical excitement. Not every day did the goddess of learning bring such rich gifts of drama to the lecture room, and in a few years increasing organization put firmly out of court such methods of winning a mastership. But dialectical proficiency remained the hallmark of learning, and the quick wit and ready tongue continued to count for more than the solid foundation of knowledge gained by sweat and hard labour. Paris became the home of all the arts and sciences which particularly lend themselves to argument, Logic, Theology, and Law. Literature and the slow, painstaking knowledge of the classics, which abstract argument could neither advance nor proclaim fled to other fields.

In particular, they fled to Chartres where they had always been at home. For there the teaching scene was very different. In 1138, when John of Salisbury, its greatest son, went there, the school of Chartres stood at the pinnacle of its greatness. When he died in 1180 its sun was already setting. It never became a university, for it never attracted—it made no attempt to attract—the hordes of scholars. Only the best could hope to pass through the Chartres curriculum, and the school was at all times blandly indifferent to the ever-changing fashions of educational theory. The fatal lure of keeping up-to-date at all costs never constituted a temptation to its masters. It was a school of literary humanism, severely classical, and the natural

THE SCHOOLS AND THE SCHOLARS

European centre of Platonism. Where Paris was tumultuous and hectic, Chartres was serene and quiet. There was little excitement in its streets, and no dialectical combat in its lecture rooms. Its atmosphere was always that of the cool lucidity of the ordered and scholarly life. It offered no short cuts to learning, and it refused to take any part in the scrambling competition for scholars. It attracted only those who were prepared to make themselves worthy to learn there. Nor did it ever make the least attempt to temper the wind of its exacting scholarship. Its masters saw other schools defeating Chartres in the educational competition: but it never seems to have occurred to them to lower their standards in order to compete on level terms. They preferred that the school should cease to exist. In consequence, the school had but two hundred years of greatness. Yet in that time it gave birth to a roll of scholars of the highest order, such as no other school could hope to rival, and it won a name which will never be blotted out.

A hundred and fifty years had passed since the school's reputation was first made by Fulbert, who came to preside over it. He was succeeded by Bishop Ivo, about whose tenure of the office nothing is known. Five years after Ivo's death, however, two great brothers, Bernard and Thierry, came to Chartres, took the school from the position at which Fulbert had left it, and pushed it to a height of greatness it had never yet reached, nor would reach again. Both were canons, and successively, Chancellors of Chartres, Bernard dying in 1130, and handing his charge to his brother Thierry. They were Bretons, and instanced by Otto of Friesingen as an example of the dangerous nimble-wittedness of Bretons. Their orthodoxy was mildly suspect, possibly because they would take no part in the raging controversy of Nominalism and Realism which divided both schools and theologians into passionate camps. Bernard, indeed, though inclining to Realism as became so good a Platonist, sought to wipe away the feud by an attempt to demonstrate the essential harmony between the Platonic and Aristotelian doctrines of ideas. But the attempt was not successful, and the making of it was not counted to him for righteousness by violently orthodox ecclesiastics of the type of William of Champeau or Alberic of Rheims. Thierry composed a treatise on the Six Days of Creation, which shows him to have lingered perilously near to Monism, for the heart of his argument was to say that as all being is God, therefore God must be the form of being of all things. It is probable, though not certain, that it was at these brothers that Abelard was aiming his glancing arrows of satire, when he complained of the heterodox views which could safely be held, if only the holders were of sufficiently high rank. However great the suspicion in which the brothers were held by the rigid and unbending orthodox, Thierry at least was not prevented from being present at two famous trials for heresy, that of Abelard of Soissons, and that of Gilbert Porée at Rheims.

John of Salisbury was still a boy in England when Bernard died. When he came to Chartres he found the spirit and the method of Bernard everywhere about him. He called him "the greatest and most perfect of our Platonists." Another scholar, Herman of Dalmatia, paid much the same compliment to Thierry, dedicating a book to him with the words, "the soul of Plato reincarnate, firm anchor in the tempest-tossed flux of our studies." Both men were classicists before all else, and they had the characteristic patience of the classical scholar, and saw that their pupils had it too. Everything at Chartres

THE SCHOOLS AND THE SCHOLARS

was leisurely, and thorough. "Grammar was the basis of all culture and must be learned slowly, leisurely, thoroughly above all it must be gathered from the classics themselves, and not from all authors alike but from the best authors."[1] Bernard had a famous saying, which John quoted more than once, which exactly describes the spirit and the scope of a Chartres education:

We are as dwarfs mounted on the shoulders of giants, so that we can see more and further than they; yet not by virtue of the keenness of our eyesight, nor through the tallness of our stature, but because we are raised and borne aloft on that giant mass.

Bernard was, of course, a profoundly learned classical scholar, and he had so dwelt with his ancient models that he himself enshrined much of their outlook on life, commending in poem after poem the serenity and peace which come from the ordered, meditative, and studious life. Thierry, though hardly less learned in the classics than his brother, was perhaps a little less unimpressed by the clamour of modernity, and, because of it had not quite Bernard's genius as a teacher. At one time he taught in Paris for a spell, which one cannot imagine Bernard doing, but he was at heart in the Chartres tradition. John called him "a most diligent investigator of the arts". He wrote a summary of the achievements of the liberal spirit in his time, and the two enormous volumes of it can still be seen at Chartres. He wrote also a long commentary on rhetoric.

If nimble-wittedness is one characteristic of Bretons a vehemence, easily becoming quick temper, is another, and both brothers had it in spite of their emphasis on the blessings of the

[1] R. Lane Poole. op. cit., p. 102.

THE GOLDEN MIDDLE AGE

studious life. Thierry was violent in speech. His pupils called him, "The Chartrian doctor with a tongue like a sword." Bernard too was by no means too serenely minded to thrash his pupils soundly when they were troublesome or stupid.

Bernard, "the old man of Chartres," used to tell his pupils that there were six keys of learning. John quoted them, and then added a seventh to the list, "the love of one's teachers." This is a grace which no scholar could commend with greater fitness, for not many have regarded each one of their teachers with so steady and abiding an affection as he. Chartres masters in John's time there became the object of the lifelong and painstaking research of Dr. Lane Poole, who has laid all subsequent students for ever in his debt, for he has done the hardest part of their work for them, and the weight of his learning was such that they can be sure there is probably nothing of importance left to be discovered. But the result of it all is, with one exception—Gilbert Porée—meagre and disappointing, and curiosity must resign itself to the fact that but few of its natural questions can be answered. These teachers of Chartres were plainly men of uncommon force of personality and character besides being profound scholars: the long list of notable characters they trained is enough to show it. But for indications of their separate identities and characters one searches almost in vain. Their scholarship rather than their persons, their theological speculations when they came into conflict with authority rather than their own reactions in life to the Cause of all theology pervade the documents. Of William of Conches, Robert Pullen, and the rest, considered as teachers and thinkers, something can be said, but considered as men, history is almost silent.

Arriving at Chartres in 1138, John "advisedly resorted, by

THE SCHOOLS AND THE SCHOLARS

the good favour of my preceptors, to the Grammarian of Conches." This William of Conches, Norman born, was, as his title "The Grammarian" suggests, in the true line of descent from Fulbert and Bernard. As a classicist he was regarded as being only second to Bernard, but he had the kind of ambitions which the Schoolmen later cherished, to bring classical knowledge and method to the elucidation of the great problems of philosophy and theology, and thus to create a *summa* of knowledge. Having neither the caution nor the serenity of Bernard, and being, in addition, challenging and irascible, it was natural that he should fall foul of the more obscurantist theologians. He was full of interpretations of the Holy Trinity, a dangerous plenitude, for almost everything written on this article of faith can be twisted into heresy if it falls into the hands of those who already bear a grudge against its author. There are a good many parallels between William and Abelard. He adapted the earlier teacher's aphorism by saying, "By the knowledge of the creature we attain to the knowledge of the Creator." He, too, had moments of scepticism as he read the Old Testament, and he did not hesitate to express them. He rejected in tactlessly scornful language the Genesis account of the creation of Eve out of Adam's rib, calling it a piece of unimaginative literalism. Like Abelard, he did not stop to think of the possible consequences of hurling angry abuse at the heads of those who disagreed with him, and regarded his rationalizing theology with alarm.

"These glib smatterers," he wrote, "if they perceive any man to be making search, at once cry out that he is a heretic, presuming more on their habit than trusting in their wisdom. Because they know not the forces of nature, in order that they may have all men comrades in their ignorance, they suffer not that others should search out anything, and would have us believe like rustics, and ask no reason."[1]

His book, *Philosophy*, fell into the hands of William, Abbot of St.-Thierry. This William had written to St. Bernard the famous letter which had brought Abelard's world in ruins about his head. Now he sought to perform a like office for his namesake of Conches. "It is enough," he complained, "to have a new theology to extirpate, without the addition of a new philosophy." But, when thus threatened, William capitulated at once. He retired from the Schools; he withdrew his book, and, writing a new and very much expurgated copy of the earlier edition, he added a preface, begging all who possessed a copy of the earlier edition to join with him in condemning it; and he sought the protection of a powerful noble. In later years, he was tutor to Henry II of England. But all this was in the future, and from 1138 to 1140 John listened eagerly to his lectures, commenting, "nor shall I ever regret that time." For, though timidity robbed him of that opportunity to leave a permanent mark on the history of theological speculation, William of Conches was a great teacher.

At this time John heard also two other masters of Chartres. From the one, Thierry, Bernard's brother, he learned rhetoric, but he found his treatment of the subject meagre, and "scarce understood" it. The other, Richard, was "a man whose training was deficient in almost nothing, who had more heart even than speech, more knowledge than skill, more truth than vanity, more virtue than show." The terms of this catalogue of virtues are carefully chosen to show how unlike Cornificius the good teacher must necessarily be: reverse the opposites in each contrast, and Cornificius plainly emerges. Later, Richard

[1] Tr. R. Lane Poole. op. cit., p. 109.

THE SCHOOLS AND THE SCHOLARS

became the Bishop of Avranches, and is always known as Richard l'Evêque. Throughout life he remained John's constant correspondent, and he died in 1182, the last survivor of the masters of Chartres whom John had known.

The true genius of Chartres, which Fulbert instilled, Bernard and Thierry developed, and John received was literary and classical, and its outlook on life was conservative, and not a little disdainful of successful mediocrity. The normal subjects of the medieval educational curriculum were of course taught there, dialectic, rhetoric, logic, theology—in fact, all of the *Trivium* and the *Quadrivium*. But the classics were the staple, and the primary educational aim of the school was to make Latin something more than a means of communication, to add depth of knowledge to the mere fluency of speech and writing. Grammar in Bernard's view was the basis of all literary understanding; and his successors to the third generation, of which was John, held the supremacy of grammar as firmly as he. "This has the sole privilege of making a man lettered," said John, as, in later life, he contemplated the years he had spent in mastering the full range of the resources of the Latin tongue.

Grammar, in an admirable definition, written three hundred years earlier, was "the knowledge which interprets poets and historians; the correct method of writing and speech; the source and basis of the liberal arts." With it went rhetoric, which might be called grammar in practice, for it was the art of literary expression and included written composition. The third member of the family was dialectic, which was variously interpreted in different schools, and at Chartres was taken to mean a science whereby Greek philosophy and Christian theology might be synthesized. Bernard's methods of teaching grammar were thorough, and were still used in John's day.

Cicero, Virgil, Ovid, Seneca, were the chief Latin authors studied. The students had to make their daily exercise in prose or verse imitations of the best models or of none. Their compositions must observe and repeat meticulously the particular idiosyncrasies of the author they were reading at the time, and which had been carefully explained to them. Ovid and Virgil had to be learned by rote, a practice which John found abundantly fruitful all the days of his life, for no medieval writer had quite his readiness and grace of quotation. The teaching day had three main divisions. In the early evening came the *delinatio*, the solid teaching. It was followed later by the *collatio*, a conference in which the lesson was discussed in a quite free and easy but emphatically not dialectical manner. Then next morning came the *repetitio*, or the calling to mind and committing to writing of the things learned the previous evening.

In the *Metalogicus* John wrote a long and exact description of the educational routine at Chartres, as Bernard had laid it down and he himself had experienced it:

Before those for whom the preliminary exercises of boys in imitating prose or poetry were prescribed, he held up the poets or orators, and bade them follow in their footsteps, pointing out their combinations of words and the elegance of their phrasing. But if anyone had sewed on another's raiment, he detected and exposed the theft, though very often he inflicted no punishment. But if the poorness of the work had so merited, with indulgent mildness he ordered the culprit to embark on the task of fashioning a real likeness of the ancient authors; and he brought it about that he who had imitated his predecessors became worthy of imitation by his successors.

The following matters, too, he taught among the first

rudiments and fixed them in the students' minds: the value of order; what is praiseworthy in embellishment and in the choice of words; where there is tenuity and, as it were, emaciation of speech; where a pleasing abundance; where excess; and where the limit due in all things. History and poetry, too, he taught should be diligently read, without the spur of compulsion; and he insistently required that each pupil should commit something to memory every day; but he taught them to avoid superfluity and be content with what they found in famous writers.

Bernard of Chartres, the most abounding spring of letters in Gaul in modern times, followed this method, and in the reading of authors showed what was simple and fell under the ordinary rules; the figures of grammar, the adornments of rhetoric, the quibbles of sophistries; and where the subject of his own lesson had references to other disciplines, these matters he brought out clearly, yet in such wise that he did not teach everything about each topic, but in proportion to the capacity of his audience dispensed to them in time the due measure of the subject. And because the brilliancy of discourse depends either on propriety (that is, the proper joining of adjectives or verb with the substantive) or on metathesis (that is, the transfer of an expression for a worthy reason to another signification), these were the things he took every opportunity to inculcate in the minds of his hearers.

And since the memory is strengthened and the wits are sharpened by exercise, he urged some by warnings and some by floggings to the constant practice of imitating what they heard. Everyone was required on the day following to reproduce some part of what he had heard the day before, some more, some less, for with them the morrow was the disciple of yesterday. Evening drill, which was called declension, was packed with so much grammar that one who gave a whole year to it would have at his command, unless unusually dull, a method of speaking and writing and could not be ignorant of the meaning of expressions which are in common use. (The material, however, of the evening lesson was chosen for moral and religious edification, closing with the sixth Penitential Psalm and the Lord's Prayer.)[1]

Thus coldly stated, and robbed of the magic of Bernard's voice, it sounds an unexciting curriculum. But those who passed through it did not find it so, and it is interesting to reflect that one result of Bernard's emphasis on the worth of the classics to be ends and not means, was to produce a school which was one of the very few in all the world's history to pursue knowledge for its own pure sake alone. It is no wonder that Chartres was quickly outstripped in the educational race by Paris and Orleans. It was too uncompromisingly fine and delicate an instrument of education to survive in a naughty world.

5. *Cornificius*

Not the thoroughness of Chartres but the glibness of Paris held the keys of the immediate future, and to the chagrin and confusion of the Arts, Dialectics became everywhere victorious. The consequences for scholarship can be seen by providing a miniature biography of a mythical worthy called Cornificius, whom the real scholars of the twelfth century were never tired of abusing and deriding.

Centuries before, Donatus had written a biography of Virgil, which all medieval scholars read as a matter of routine. In the course of it Donatus turned aside to castigate an empty-headed detractor of Virgil called Cornificius. Cornificius in life had been of no importance to anyone but himself; but he gave his name to a numerous and a mighty progeny in the twelfth

---

[1] *Metalogicus I. C. XXIV.* Tr. C. H. Haskins. *The Renaissance of the Twelfth Century*, pp. 135, 136.

century. To abuse his reincarnated person became almost a game—bitter, no doubt, but not wholly unenjoyable—among all twelfth-century writers, who had a real care for the reputation of scholarship, and who held the reputation of letters deep in their hearts.

Abelard began it. "It is one thing," he said, "to inquire into the truth by deliberation, but quite another to make ostentation the end of all disputation." But Abelard was mildness itself as compared with John of Salisbury. To John, Cornificius was a thoroughly bad hat, so foul indeed that polite words were powerless to express him. He turned novices into philosophers in less time than it takes to turn chickens into fledglings; and then they became "bad monks, unscrupulous physicians, dishonest courtiers." True to the training of their master, the Cornificians "deny all possibility of methodical research, declare the results of other teachers to be wrong, and never tire of disparaging what others have recognized as the truth; nor do they admit Holy Writ to be the standard measure of truth." Peter of Blois, who had a taste for sturdy denunciation and a very proper sense of his own capacities, continued the indictment. A young Cornifician named William was reported to him as "of great penetration and ingenious disposition who, without grammar, has mastered the subtleties of logic so as to be esteemed a famous dialectician." Peter fairly snorts with wrath. "These subtleties which you so highly extol, are manifoldly pernicious. . . . What is the use of them—either at home, in the army, at the bar, in the cloister, in the church, or in any position whatever, except, I suppose, the schools."[1] But none of them could match the

[1] Tr. Merryweather. *Bibliomania in the Middle Ages* (Woodstock Press), p. 218.

THE GOLDEN MIDDLE AGE

fluent vituperation of Richard de Bury, Bishop of Durham. He wrote in the fourteenth century, and it seems that Cornificius was a plague still. For three pages he denounces him without once repeating himself, and assembles an array of scornful phrases which compel a reader's admiration still. These Cornificians—they fasten "to their untried arms the Icarian wings of presumption," they "prematurely snatch the master's cap." "Just snatched from the cradle and hastily weaned, they mouth the rules of Priscian and Donatus; while still childish boys they gabble with childish stammering the Categories of *Peri Hermeneias*." Then they pass through their faculties "with baneful haste and harmful diploma" they presume to become even such a one as himself "offering their heads unhonoured by the snows of age, for the mitre of the pontificate." "The pest is greatly encouraged by Papal provisions,"[1] ended the bishop, with a snort of disgust.

Cornificius is nowhere identified in the twelfth century. Lane Poole tentatively suggests that he may be a certain monk Regnold, who has an unenviable mention in the *Metamorphosis Goliae Episcopi*, as a fluent and clamorous arguer who understood nothing of the meaning of his words.[2] But John of Salisbury, who suffered from the pest most of all, came very near drawing and naming a portrait. At one period of his life, when funds were low, he set up as a private tutor in Paris, and there met a competitor, one Adam of the Little Bridge. On the Little Bridge of Paris there lived at this time a small colony of free-lance masters, who lived by taking pupils unofficially. Chief among them was Adam, an Englishman. He was

[1] *Philobiblon*, pp. 68–70.
[2] *Studies in Chronology and History* (Oxford University Press), pp. 241, 244.

thoroughly learned, quick in speech and witty in retort, but very irascible. In him there was no hint or trace of the typically Chartrian attitude of reverence towards scholarship. He attracted pupils by promising quick and showy results. To that end he made his lectures as intricate and obscure as possible, because it upheld his reputation for learning among the unreflecting; and he had a number of clever but absurd syllogisms to prove that whatever is known is unknown, that the greater number is smaller than the less, and that the same statement may be both false and true at the same time. He also taught his students to be immensely fertile in the matter of symbolic meanings. "Hylas was the son of Hercules"— there is an inner meaning—there are five vowels in the two names, and these are the Five Pleas of the Crown. This pose his friends and advocates ascribed to subtlety, and his enemies to the "folly or arrogance of vanity." "He used to say that he would have few hearers or none if he propounded dialectic with that simplicity of terms with which it ought to be taught." His reasons, however, were to be found neither in subtlety nor vanity, but in a very ready sense of the qualities of the bizarre as good advertisement, and his tortuous obscurities attracted quantities of scholars to his school. He was personally attractive none the less, and he really was "a man of exceeding sharp wits, and, whatever others may think, of much learning." "But I was never his disciple, not for one day," adds John, lest his motive for friendship should be mistaken. The two opposites met almost daily, and amid their discussion "upon such topics of discourse as sprang up" a real and deep friendship grew. Perhaps it was the memory of this which prevented John from identifying him with Cornificius, whom he declined to name, "mindful of . . . my brotherly concourse with him in the Lord." But Adam and his like had killed the Paris of Abelard.

It seemed to me pleasant (wrote John of Salisbury) to revisit my old companions on the Mount (the school of St. Geneviève in Paris) whom I had left, and whom dialectic still detained, to confer with them touching old matters of debate: that we might by mutual comparison measure together our several progress. I found them as before, and where they were before; nor did they appear to have reached the goal in unravelling the old questions, nor had they added one jot of a proposition. The aims that once inspired them inspired them still: they had only progressed in one point, they had unlearned moderation, they knew not modesty. One might despair of their recovery.

A higher name than Cornificius awaited Adam. He was to become Bishop of St. Asaph, an office which he accepted, but, perhaps characteristically, never fulfilled. He never went near St. Asaph, but preferred the security of Abingdon, for, as he complained, he really could not stand the Welsh.

But it is probable that neither Cornificius nor Golias ever existed in the flesh of actual personality. Both were class names, the one standing for pretentiousness, the other for gay, peripatetic impudence. But his vices were real enough and they ring through the pages of the authors like counts in a long, formidable indictment read by the Clerk of the Court. Cornificius draws his lectures from books and closets, not from a well-stored mind: he touts for students, and when this unprofessional conduct does not avail, he hires them: to undercut his legitimate competitors, he lectures only on the bizarre and the semi-heretical, and he will actually give lectures on Sundays and Holy Days: he makes life too easy for his pupils, letting them have a "long lie" every morning, and teaching

THE SCHOOLS AND THE SCHOLARS

the bad habits of a *vagans* by allowing them to roam about the streets as they like.

Those who read the Cornifician literature (there would be duller ways of spending an evening) and take it at its face value will suppose that they are spectators of another skirmish in the age-old battle between Logic and Literature. But their assumption will be mistaken. All the writers who turned aside from their normal task to smite Cornificius were logicians themselves, and had been weaned on the dialectical method of education. It was not Logic they disdained, but its parody. What they were fighting was Logic's usurpation of the first and virtually the only place in the whole educational system, whereas it was in fact only one of the whole of the Seven Liberal Arts. But its undue exaltation into the first and foremost of them bade fair to kill all the others. More particularly it was strangling Grammar, or the careful study and imitation of the best Latin authors; and this it was which roused scholars like John of Salisbury to such outbursts of wrath.

To the twelfth-century scholar, Logic meant any study which lent itself to dialectical argument, and the technical terms of which were such mysteries as Syllogisms and Major and Minor Premisses. Now literature, and the arts generally, if they can be "learned" at all, which many deny, certainly cannot be studied by means of argument alone. They require constant and wearisome practice, and only very slowly does one learn to tune and to play on the instruments of any artistic means of self-expression. No short cuts are possible, and no opportunities are afforded to those who by quick wits and ingenuity seek to compensate for ignorance and shallowness. Logic, and its descendants, Theology, Philosophy, and Law, require no doubt an equal thoroughness from those who would excel at them. The full implications of the quarrel between Nominalism and Realism, for example, require a lifetime to master. But a rough idea of what it is all about, and a knowledge of the technical terms in which it has to be discussed, can be acquired in five minutes. Those who would really know Theology, Philosophy, and Law, must sweat blood to learn, and a lifetime does not suffice for the full mastery of even one of them. But each one of them constitutes a field, none the less, in which the clever and glib charlatan can get a footing. From what the twelfth-century student meant by Literature, however, the charlatan is for ever shut out.

This is the background of the crisis through which education passed in the middle years of the century. The ardent renaissance spirit of learning for its own sake was already beginning to pass. The first wandering scholars who had gone out into the world to seek learning had built more than they dreamed, and what they would have most detested. They had built a system, and had made inevitable all the concomitant disadvantages of it, a new platform for ambition, rules and regulations, the inevitable standardization as applied to the things of the mind which flourish to the full only in freedom. They had made Paris the Athens of the West, but they had also made it a paradise for the class of students whom John of Salisbury savagely called Glib Smatterers. That it was inevitable does not make it less melancholy. The commercial spirit was struggling to gain an entry, and to befoul pure learning by making it merely the handmaid of a career. The real scholars were trying to keep it out, and the Cornifician literature was one of the methods they adopted.

But Cornificius merely represented one of the rounds of that titanic engagement which is always called the Battle of

THE SCHOOLS AND THE SCHOLARS

the Arts. It was a battle between curricula and schools. On the one side Grammar, Literature, the Classics, and Poetry were entrenched, and on the other Logic, Theology, and Law. Paris was the stronghold of the one, and Orleans of the other.

> Paris and Orleans are at odds,
> It is a great loss and a great sorrow
> That the two do not agree.
> Do you know the reason for the discord?
> It is because they differ about learning;
> For Logic, who is always wrangling,
> Calls the authors authorlings
> And the students of Orleans mere grammar-boys.

So rhymed Henri d'Andeli,[1] who wrote the saga of the strife. But the Parisians had a better weapon than abuse. They waxed moral. They loudly proclaimed that they were on the side of St. Paul and all the Holy Angels, to say nothing of Plato, in distrusting Literature; and they hunted down isolated scandals in the ranks of the Grammarians, and magnified them for all they were worth. "Alas, how seldom in these days do virtue and learning come together. By some—I know not what—factious bond, lust and literature cling together, a union no less prodigious than pernicious."[2] The Authors were variously denounced as trying to revive paganism, through Venus, and idolatry, through Dagon. They were magicians, mere tellers of stories and inspired thereto by the most repulsive of familiar spirits; they were, in fact, "the offscouring of the human race." It is a method of warfare which has its practitioners still.

The issue, however, was not really decided by polemics such

[1] C. H. Haskins. op. cit., p. 99.
[2] Helen Waddell. op. cit., p. 125.

as these, but by the eternal desire of frail human flesh to make as much money as possible with as little trouble as possible. There was little money in authorship. An author might have a really large circulation, but there was no one to collect his dues and pay out his royalties. The glittering prizes went to the lawyers, and although law became the most expensive of all university courses, no doubt obeying the dictates of the law of supply and demand, there are scores of letters in which a student asks his father to find the extra money to enable him to read law, for "he who maketh his son a lawyer hath fashioned an engine against his enemies, a machine for his friends."[1] But theology was hardly less profitable. In an age when advancement lay for most through the Church, a modicum of theological knowledge was an obvious necessity. The two courses coupled together, led straight to an archdeaconry, and he who held that office need never lack. Parish priests, and sometimes even bishops, might lack and suffer hunger, but never archdeacons. They were invariably fat, well fed, and liking.

As the Battle of the Arts, therefore, dragged out its slow course, the names of the adversaries changed. At first the Scientists challenge the Grammarians, or the Authors. But when the thirteenth century dawns, both Logic and Theology are so strangled by their all-too-successful ally, Law, that they too are found in the camp of the humanists. For Law has so invaded Paris that Theology has to be protected by papal decree, and even Orleans has an infant Law school, which is swiftly to become embarrassingly successful. By the fourteenth century the game is up. Chartres is dead. There is dispute as to why its greatest teachers withdrew from its holy

[1] Helen Waddell. op. cit., p. 132.

THE SCHOOLS AND THE SCHOLARS

places. *Cesserunt*, as John of Salisbury put it. But as Lane Poole points out *Cesserunt* may mean that whereas once these masters had taught well, now they "yielded to the rush of incompetent rivals and followed their example"; or it may mean that "disgusted with the prevalent method of teaching, they withdrew from the field." The context does not help us to clear up the point. Either way, Chartres fell, and Athene was stricken in the house of her friends. A master comes to Orleans to teach Logic: he is not welcomed: "the scholars in arts are few, poor, and superficial."[1] The torch of humanistic learning is held up by Oxford, for Paris is no longer worthy to bear it. The humanists are still fighting, but they no longer denounce Cornificius, the glib logician, as John of Salisbury and his contemporaries had done. Their place is taken by Richard de Bury, the great bishop of Durham, and among the not inconsiderable proportion of the human race which failed to please him, the lawyers, the "Scorpions in Treacle" as he unkindly calls them, are the least pleasing of all. They write unreadable books, which "we have spent but little labour and expense in acquiring." They are dedicated to a sterile trade, for "laws are only human enactments for the regulation of social life, and... refuse to be brought to equity, because they feel that they possess more of arbitrary will than rational judgment." "Wherefore," triumphantly concludes the bishop, "the judgment of the wise for the most part is that the causes of laws are not a fit subject for discussion. In truth, many laws acquire force by mere custom, not by syllogistic necessity, like the arts. For Whatever receives its stability from use alone must necessarily be brought to naught by disuse."[2]

It may be so. The criticism is obviously acute; and it is

[1] Helen Waddell. op. cit., p. 135.   [2] *Philobiblon*, pp. 78–9.

interesting to see times had so changed that an artist can speak with such respect of a syllogism. But the great days of Paris are over:

> We'll to the woods no more,
> The laurels all are cut,
> The bowers are bare of bay
> That once the Muses wore.

6. *Out into the World*

The Battle of the Arts was often described by those who took part in it as though it were high comedy or even knockabout farce. Modern historians, so anxious always to avoid being called Dryasdust, have followed their example and seized the chance they give them to lighten the gravity of their pages. But in truth there was more tragedy than comedy in it, and at least one of the five elements of true tragedy—a fated inevitability—was woven into the whole story of how learning for learning's sake, identified with the classical humanism of Chartres, fell from its high place and became the handmaid of a career. "With much ado," wrote Traherne, "I was corrupted and made to learn the dirty devices of the world"; and then he found, as all must find, that no longer

> The streets were mine, the temple was mine,
> the people were mine, their clothes and gold
> and silver were mine, as much as their
> sparkling eyes, fair skins and ruddy faces.
> The skies were mine, and so were the sun and
> moon and stars; and all the World was mine,
> and I the only spectator and enjoyer of it.

It might be the song of the wandering scholar at any time

THE SCHOOLS AND THE SCHOLARS

in the first thirty years of the century. But inevitably he must earn his living afterwards, and inexorably the educational system must be framed to enable him to do it. The looming spectre of a career, and the need of the student to find his niche in a competitive and naughty world has dirtied the dreams of more than one great educationalist; and these made both the Battle of the Arts, and the triumph of the forces of artistic unrighteousness, a fated inevitability.

Hope, unquenchable and enduring, kindled the scholar's ambition, and sent him out on the toilsome journey to the schools. Hope sustained him when he got there, and only hope could keep his spirits steadfast when he drew near to the end of his course. There was no medieval equivalent of the modern University Appointments Board, and a very large proportion of scholars were doomed either to unemployment or to occupations which their scholastic attainments led them to scorn. Not many enjoyed the career of a John of Salisbury, so varied as to illuminate a whole civilization, and to confer on him the secondary immortality of one whom every subsequent historian is bound to consult and to quote. Fate did not cast him in the dramatic roles of Becket or Henry II, of Adrian IV or Frederick Barbarossa, or Gilbert Porée or St. Bernard. He was rather the ecclesiastical counterpart of Mr. Pepys or Mr. Creevey: he knew everyone, he went everywhere, and he wrote it all down in perfect Latin. He who seeks to master the facts of John's life and to place them against their historic background, who reads his letters and books, studies the work of a long succession of later scholars who have thrown light on John and the civilization which he so notably decorated and expressed, and who so broods over it all that his imagination, quickened and vivified, begins itself to live in the authentic

THE GOLDEN MIDDLE AGE

twelfth-century atmosphere, will find in the end that few features of the life of Western Europe in the years of John's life, 1120 to 1180, have escaped his curiosity.

For twelve years he studied at the two greatest schools in the world, Paris and Chartres, the second of which was, at that time, at the very height of its greatness. There was scarcely any famous master who did not at some time teach him, and few great scholars with whom he was not on intimate terms. He went then to join the Papal *Curia*, and served there in a position which brought him into close touch with two great Popes, Eugenius III and Adrian IV, and which enabled him in later years to write his *Historia Pontificalis*, one of the most important original sources for the history of the period it covers. Returning at last to England, he became an official in the household of Archbishop Theobald of Canterbury, and a member of the famous circle of scholars and sages which revolved round Theobald. In the Archbishop's failing years John became almost his other self, and for a time all the ecclesiastical administration of England passed through his hands. On Theobald's death, John extended the same loyalty to his successor, Thomas Becket, went into exile with him, and acted both as his very outspoken adviser and his ambassador to foreign courts. At the last, he was present in Canterbury Cathedral when Becket was murdered. Finally, by an almost sublime apotheosis, he was appointed bishop of Chartres, the city which had always held his heart in her hands. For Chartres had enabled him to become the greatest classical scholar not merely of his own day but of the whole of the Middle Ages, and had taught him the austere and beautiful use of Latin, which still makes his studies of contemporary statesmanship and scholarship as great a delight to the classicist as they are

THE SCHOOLS AND THE SCHOLARS

mines of valuable information to the historian. Of all the historically important aspects of twelfth-century life, the Crusade is perhaps the only one to remain untouched by such a career. And John, in himself, was no mere characterless but photographic recorder. If there is in him but little which is appropriate to the adjectives picturesque or vivid, still a perfectly definite portrait has come drifting down the ages of a great scholar and churchman, grave, deliberate, a little remote, with a genius for friendship, and still possessing the full magnetic power to charm and absorb those whose imagination delights to project itself into the Europe of his day.

It was as much by way of the classics as of Christianity that John achieved the spiritual poise and balance which all men strive for and few attain. The combination of Roman *gravitas* and Christian love, of Greek understanding and medieval extremism is indeed formidable. John had all four qualities, but they were merged in him as inseparables and not competitors, and by them he was endowed with a perpetual, inexhaustible reserve of power, enabling him always to correct the one-sided waywardness of present circumstances. "The submerged city of the poets is always in John's consciousness: and in the strongest tides of controversy he hears the sound of its bells."[1] But there was also another city he never forgot, the nobler City of God, and he never allowed his clear-sighted view of the present squalid imperfections of the shadow of that City in earth to blind his vision of the splendours of the City that shall be hereafter. It was in the dual consciousness that his strength lay, and from so serene and indivisible a union was generated that in his nature which has made him the one man of his time who has won the unanimous admiration of posterity.

[1] Helen Waddell. op. cit., p. 114.

THE GOLDEN MIDDLE AGE

Such was the career of one great scholar, but it was wholly exceptional in its scope and variety. Another, but also exceptional, was that of Walter Map, a contemporary of John's, and a scholar of Paris. He turns up as a Justice in Gloucester in 1173; in 1176 as a prebend of St. Paul's; in 1183 as the companion and adviser of Henry II; in 1197 as Archdeacon of Oxford; and in 1199 and 1202 attempts were made to procure him as Bishop of Hereford and St. David's respectively. He wrote a good deal, playing a conjectural though certainly a real part in the shaping of the Arthurian Legends, and being stingingly rude on every possible occasion to Jews and Cistercian monks. Curiously enough, it never seems to have occurred to either of these to think of becoming a master in the schools, though this was the first thing which occurred to every other student. By 1150 the path which led to a mastership was no longer easy to tread. In Abelard's time one had simply started to give lectures, and if they were attractive enough one's fame and fortune were made. But before the time of his death such free-and-easy expedients were no longer possible. No one might presume to teach who was not licensed, and the road to a licence was both thorny and expensive. First, examiners had to be satisfied. Then there must be a vacancy on the teaching staff. When a student had successfully jumped over these hurdles there came the inception. In full congregation, the biretta, or master's cap which he must wear to lecture, was placed on his head; he was given a ring, and an open book. Then his hand must dig deep into his pocket to pay for it all —fees to the university, presents of gloves and gowns to its masters, the hiring of students to attend his lectures until he was well enough known to attract in his own right, and the renting of some room to teach in, sometimes no better than the

THE SCHOOLS AND THE SCHOLARS

back room of an inn, or even the waiting-room of the barber's shop. This outlay he hoped to recover from his pupils when his name was made. But in this it was by no means a foregone conclusion that he would be successful. Students had not the reputation of being good payers, and indeed many had nothing to pay with. One master at Bologna used regularly to end a course of lectures with the words:

Since it is the practice that doctors on finishing a book should say something of their plans, I will tell you something, but not much. Next year I expect to give ordinary lectures well and lawfully as I always have, but no extraordinary lectures, for students are not good payers, wishing to learn but not to pay, as the saying is: all desire to know but none to pay the price. I have nothing more to say to you, beyond dismissing you with God's blessing and begging you to attend the Mass.[1]

Bologna was in any case a university to be avoided by the young master. For it was a corporation of scholars, not of masters as at Paris, and the scholars set the rules which the masters must observe.

A professor might not be absent without leave, even a single day, and if he desired to leave the town he had to make a deposit to ensure his return. If he failed to secure an audience of five for a regular lecture, he was fined as if absent—a poor lecture indeed which could not secure five hearers! He must begin with the bell and quit within one minute after the next bell. He was not allowed to skip a chapter in his commentary, or postpone a difficulty to the end of the hour, and he was obliged to cover the ground systematically, so much in each specific term of the year.[2]

[1] C. H. Haskins. op. cit., p. 204.
[2] Haskins. *Rise of Universities*. Quoted by Johnson and Thompson. op. cit., p. 730.

THE GOLDEN MIDDLE AGE

Sometimes, moreover, a master was out of pocket through sheer goodness of heart and generosity. Abbot Samson of St. Edmundsbury, for example, had been allowed to go through the schools at Diss in Norfolk "without terms and of his master's grace, to have an opportunity of learning," which his poverty would have denied him.[1]

The great thing for a young master was to get a following quickly. Unless he could do this he was likely to be doomed, for very few possessed enough capital after their seven years' course as students to maintain them while they lectured to empty benches. There were many devices to gain an audience, most of them some form of bribery or advertisement. A certain young master of Bologna, Buoncompagno by name, gave a famous banquet, and wrote home to his parents triumphantly to tell the tale:

Sing unto the Lord a new song, praise him with stringed instruments and organs, rejoice upon the high-sounding cymbals (Ps. CL. iv, 5) for your son has held a glorious disputation, which was attended by a great number of teachers and scholars. He answered all questions without a mistake, and no one could get the better of him or prevail against his arguments. Moreover, he celebrated a famous banquet, at which both rich and poor were honoured as never before, and he has duly begun to give lectures which are already so popular that other class rooms are deserted and his own are filled.[2]

History does not relate what happened to Buoncompagno afterwards. But if he continued to fulfil the glorious promise of his letter, it is less because of the lavishness of his banquet than the excellence of his inaugural lecture. For on this—the

[1] *Jocelyn of Brakelond*, p. 71.
[2] C. H. Haskins. *Studies in Medieval Culture*, p. 28.

THE SCHOOLS AND THE SCHOLARS

first public lecture—which all young masters must give as a part of their inception ceremonies—most of all depended.

Among the dusty treasures which have come drifting down the centuries is a vivid and amusing account of one such inaugural lecture. It was written by Gerald of Wales, and, needless to say, he is the hero of the piece. The engaging vanity, which has endeared him to generations of historians nowhere shows to better advantage. At Paris he had been the scholar of scholars, having "for many years applied his studious spirit" to each one of the seven liberal arts. His fame had spread, his popularity had, if it were possible, increased. Thus, as he says himself:

When it was known in the city that he desired to discourse, the pleasure of listening to his voice drew such a gathering of almost all the teachers together with their scholars that scarce even the largest hall could contain his audience. For he reasoned on civil and canon law in such lively fashion and so enhanced his exposition with all the persuasion of rhetoric and adorned it with figures and flowers of speech as well as with profound argument, and made such apt use of the sayings of the philosophers and other authors by the wondrous art with which he applied them to appropriate topics, that the more learned and expert his audience, the more eagerly and attentively they applied their ears and minds to drink in his words and fix them in their memory.[1]

Then, in case an impious reader should doubt that any discourse should deservedly win so mighty a torrent of praise from its author, he goes on to give the opening passages of the inaugural lecture. Should a judge give his judgment according to the evidence of the witnesses or according to his own conscience? That was the theme. The opening passage which he

[1] *Autobiography*, pp. 64, 65.

THE GOLDEN MIDDLE AGE

gives occupies a page and a half of print, and in that space he contrives to work in quotations from Seneca, Sidonius, St. Augustine, Pliny, and Horace, without once coming to the point. Posterity is thus bereft of Gerald's enlightenment on what the unfortunate judge should do, but he gives us a careful list of those who congratulated him when it was ended. They were many.

And while we are on the subject of Gerald of Wales and his inaugural lecture, the temptation to step aside for a moment and add the perfect colophon to the story can hardly be resisted. He had been on a journey to Ireland and had written a book *The Topography of Ireland*, in which, among other things, were discussed the resemblances between the Greek of Priscian and the language of the Welsh fairies. Having at last finished the book, which incidentally contains much first-rate geographical information, Gerald very sensibly and characteristically decided not to place "the candle which he had lit under a bushel, but to lift it aloft on a candlestick that it might shine: Matt. v, 15." So he repaired with all speed to Oxford, where "the clergy were most strong and pre-eminent in learning." There he announced that he would read it—all of it—aloud, in the hearing of whosoever might come.

And since his book was divided into three parts, he gave three consecutive days to the reading, a part being read each day. On the first day he hospitably entertained the poor of the whole town whom he gathered together for the purpose; on the morrow he entertained all the doctors of the divers Faculties and those of their scholars who were best known and best spoken of; and on the third day he entertained the remainder of the scholars together with the knights of the town and a number of the citizens. It was a magnificent and a costly achievement, since thereby the ancient and authentic times

THE SCHOOLS AND THE SCHOLARS

of the poets were in some manner revived, nor has the present age seen, nor does any past age bear record of the like.[1]

Such eloquence was beyond the power of most, and in fact only a small proportion of the student host ever became masters. What happened to the others? Most entered the service of the Church, and became parish priests. Others entered the service of kings, and formed the germ of the infant civil service. Others again, laying aside their status of *clericus*, became traders. The student who wished to stay in Paris, who could not bear to leave it, and had not had the luck to gain a mastership, might remain in the capacity of a copyist, and spend his days in the stationer's employ, eternally making fresh copies of the text-books required by the university curriculum. Inn-keeping was another very usual, but hardly orthodox, refuge. Statutes were passed against it, as being a practice derogatory to the dignity of a clerk, which, *ex officio*, all students were. Afterwards, the statutes were relaxed, and clerks were permitted to sell, and presumably to brew beer and wine on condition that there should be no vociferous advertisement, that liquor thus purchased should be consumed off the premises only, and that no jugs or cups be lent to customers.[2]

Of other refuges, medicine was perhaps the most popular, and certainly the most respectable. For that one went to Montpellier. The type of student castigated by Absolom of St. Victor for his overweening ambition found that he had prepared himself wisely if he went on from Paris to Montpellier. For the universal text-book of the medical student, Isadore of Seville's *Etymologies*, though written in the seventh

[1] *Autobiography*, p. 66.
[2] G. G. Coulton. Op. cit. Vol. II, p. 93.

THE GOLDEN MIDDLE AGE

century, still held the field, and prescribed a course of study to which even Absolom of St. Victor's list would have been but an admirable introduction. According to Isadore in the seventh and the Montpellier authorities in the twelfth centuries, the doctor must have a thorough knowledge of grammar, to take in and hand on his reading; rhetoric, to diagnose and define the disease by means of argument; logic, in order to bring the aid of reason to the scrutiny and the cure; arithmetic, to count the hours of a paroxysm; geometry, "on account of the qualities of districts and situation of places"; music, because David once saved Saul from an unclean spirit by the magic of melody; and astronomy, as the human body changes with the procession of the heavens and the alteration of the seasons. With the aid of these the village doctor comes to the house of sickness to give "first a digestive medicine, secondly a purgative, thirdly a sanative."[1] John of Salisbury suggested that most of the students at Montpellier and Salerno were those who had failed to stay the more exacting courses of Paris and Chartres and Orleans. But he was prejudiced against the profession, sourly remarking that doctors had a bad habit of covering their ignorance by resorting to divination and the muttering guidance of familiar spirits. Still, he admitted, there were genuine practitioners, though not very many. "I have too often fallen into their hands, for my sins, to speak ill of them," but, he adds, they would do well to take their fee while the patient is still sick.

Thousands of scholars found no settled employment, and could not again face the monotony of life in their native village when they had once experienced the ever-turning kaleidoscope

[1] G. R. Owst. *Literature and Pulpit in Medieval England* (Cambridge University Press), p. 30.

THE SCHOOLS AND THE SCHOLARS

of the scholar's life. They became the *vagantes*, the Goliards. The worst "wander about naked and lie in bake ovens," the best become court jesters, and the others pass restlessly from the uneasy patronage of one capricious magnate to another.

> Since it is the property
>   Of the sapient
> To sit firm upon a rock,
>   It is evident
> That I am a fool, since I
>   Am a flowing river,
> Never under the same sky,
>   Transient for ever.
>
> Hither, thither, masterless
>   Ship upon the sea,
> Wandering through the ways of air
>   Go the birds like me.
> Bound am I by ne'er a bond,
>   Prisoner to no key,
> Questing go I for my kind,
>   Find depravity.
>
> Down the broad way do I go
>   Young and unregretting,
> Wrap me in my vices up,
>   Virtue all forgetting,
> Greedier for all delight
>   Than heaven to enter in:
> Since the soul in me is dead,
>   Better save the skin.[1]

It is the just epitaph of the *vagans*, written by the greatest of the tribe, the archpoet, Golias himself.

[1] Tr. Helen Waddell. *Medieval Latin Lyrics* (Constable), pp. 171, 173.

THE GOLDEN MIDDLE AGE

"Questing . . . find depravity." Certainly many found it. Forgery, for example, was an opening for an unemployed and hungry scholar. When abbeys might lose all their deeds in a marauder's raid, and then had to face feudal adversaries unarmed by titles, skilled forgers were naturally in demand. Heresy was another depravity—universally regarded as such, —into which the wandering clerk might fall. He rarely had a good opinion of Holy Church and her prelates, and from satirizing dignitaries to contradicting dogmas is never a long step. Cæsarius of Heisterbach tells to his novices the tale of some scholars who were burned in Paris for maintaining "that there is neither Paradise nor Hell, but he who hath the knowledge of God in himself hath Paradise in himself; and he who hath mortal sin hath Hell in himself, as it were a rotten tooth in the mouth."

Such an end as this came the way of an infinitesimal proportion of the scholars; but a success proportionate to their dreams, the career of a John of Salisbury, crowned the student days of almost as few. For the rest there was a greater or less degree of frustration which they must ease as best they could.

CHAPTER IV

THE UNIVERSITIES AND THE EUROPEAN MIND

1. *The Rudiments of Medievalism*

IF, by means of a combination of the Magic Carpet and the Time Machine, the twentieth-century Englishman were enabled to wander at his will through the green fields of medieval Europe, and to see for himself the peaked gables of its towns, he would indeed feel a stranger in a land that is very far off. His subconscious ideas of religion, nationality, culture, and commerce, the very bases of his civilization would meet with neither sympathy nor understanding. Trained in the art of compromise, he would be baffled at every turn by the extremism of remorseless logic. A practical man, he would find the most finely drawn subtleties of thought indulged in for their own sakes. Brought up in the atmosphere of a Christianity subordinated in practice, if not in theory, to the political divisions of nationalism and the ecclesiastical divisions of theology, he would find a Church which was the only supreme political authority, which claimed both infallibility and absolutism, and which upheld its claims with conspicuous success. Having been taught that the art of government consists mainly in combining differing parties within a uniformity which yet respects their cherished individualities, he would find all around him the view that the very conception of unity was one from which all divergent views within itself must be banished.

THE GOLDEN MIDDLE AGE

"Variety in Uniformity" might be his watchword, but he would find that an insistence on Unity in its simplest and extremest form was the watchword of the Europe in which he was travelling.

The political and religious ideas would thus be strange to him, but the ordinary mental habits and processes of the people would be stranger still. It has been said that the main difference between the modern and the medieval character may be explained in terms of colour. The medieval mind loved vivid tones, whether actual or symbolical, and always tended to extremes. The Middle Ages produced the greatest saints and the most appalling villains, and produced them prodigally, and, it seems, impartially. St. Francis of Assisi and Clovis were equally typical of medievalism. The strangely beautiful madness of the Children's Crusade is matched by the highly sordid story of the Fourth Crusade. The treatment meted out to the heretic Albigensians derides the loving care lavished upon the destitute, the incessant exhortations to almsgiving, and the denunciations of usury. The medieval man's white was only white when it possessed the spotless purity of newly fallen snow. His black was of pitch, a defilement to all who approached it.

Carlyle has taught us that clothes reveal character, and certainly the medieval man's revealed his. It has been said that the chief difference between the modern and the medieval character may be explained in terms of colour, and the analogy is indeed capable of an exact application. The medieval man in general, and the twelfth-century Englishman in particular, revelled in gaudy clothes. If he could not afford them himself, he took every chance he had of seeing and admiring the splendid raiment of those more fortunate. Every guild had its own

THE UNIVERSITIES AND THE EUROPEAN MIND

livery, and its members would have been fewer if the livery had been sober. Every festive occasion was marked by processions of great brilliance, and every chance was grasped of organizing such processional displays. The chroniclers always made room for a lengthy report of what the notables wore at any function, and as one reads their ecstasies one wonders idly whether the Lady Betty of the fashion papers has not somehow strayed into the wrong century. A king returns to London:

He came to Eltham, towards London, and the Mayor of London, the aldermen, with the commonalty, rode against him on horseback, the mayor in crimson velvet, a great velvet hat furred, a girdle of gold about his middle, and a bawdzike of gold about his neck, trailing down behind him, his three henchmen on their great coursers, following him, one in suit of red, all spangled in silver; then the aldermen in gowns of scarlet with sanguine hoods, and all the commonalty of the city clothed in white gowns and scarlet hoods, with divers cognisances embroidered on their sleeves.

That, however, was a great occasion. But the everyday clothes and bearing of the wealthy were gaudy and bizarre. "Dress," wrote an observant chronicler, "is a passion, and manners a fine art. A man of fashion carries a fortune on his back. He is gaudy in all the colours of the rainbow. Even his horse is decked with curiously embroidered trappings, and with gold and silver harness." He painted the rooms of his house green, and spangled gilded stars all over the walls. The walls of his churches he decorated with alternate bands of gold and blue and scarlet.

All this is symptomatic of the extremism which was the corner-stone of the medieval character. It had its fruit in tragedy and greatness. It is this extremism, for example, which interprets and illuminates the otherwise incomprehensible quarrel between Henry II and Thomas Becket. Both were thoroughly medieval; therefore neither could compromise, and the climax of that tragedy was inevitable from the moment it opened. There is that in their story which irritates a modern reader almost past bearing, for it seems to him to be merely stupid obstinacy. Yet it was not obstinacy but medievalism. But if extremism often begot bitter tragedy, to it is due very much of the greatness of the medieval achievement. As an extremist, the medieval man preferred to work on the grand, the visionary scale. On July 8th, 1401, the Chapter of Seville solemnly passed this resolution and inscribed it in their minute book, "Let us build so great a church to the glory of God that those who come after us will think us mad even to have attempted it." It was no mere grandiloquent gesture. It was a faithful description of what they accomplished. So it is with many of the great medieval cathedrals and abbeys. When we enter them, and see their vast spaces, their intricate, patient carving, the riot of colour in their windows, it is clear that their builders were endowed with uncommon vision. The craftsmanship of their illuminated manuscripts tells the same tale not only of marvellous patience, but also of the grand conception which lies behind them, and which is one of the fruits of the extremist mind.

But it has other fruits. Its reaction to experience is a violent oscillation, and though it is thus delivered as an easy prey to the gloom and pessimism of adverse circumstances, its reaction when the circumstances change is correspondingly swift and complete. Nothing could be gloomier than the contemporary accounts of Stephen's reign, and no writing could more truly breathe the spirit of pure pessimism. But the change of mood

THE UNIVERSITIES AND THE EUROPEAN MIND

on the accession of Henry II is immediate and dramatic. Stephen's anarchy had done immense harm to English fields and had taken a heavy toll of English lives, but it did no havoc to English characteristics, for England was even more medieval than the Continent at this date in the fullness of its possession of the characteristically medieval armour of the extremist spirit, tough enough to withstand and resilient enough to provide recovery from the psychological effects of nineteen years of anarchy.

2. *The Civilized Society: Canterbury*

It was against such a psychological background as this that the university movement was set. The fundamental psychology of the people who made it was from one point of view crude and elemental, from another, subtle and complicated. The universities did not change these characteristics. They intensified them and they purged them. They enabled the medieval man to play his part in the immemorial effort of humanity to build the civilized city of his dreams; and they made his struggle to create a social structure at once truly civilized and truly medieval come not far short of fulfilment. It failed to achieve either perfection or permanence, as every great civilizing movement in the past and the present has failed, but it left a notable legacy and a long tale of solid gains made for the benefit of those who were to come after.

No true civilization is possible where the things of the mind are not valued at their proper worth, where there is not æsthetic and intellectual awareness. Of the æsthetic awareness of the twelfth century its great cathedrals eloquently testify; of its intellectual awareness the thronged schools and universities

THE GOLDEN MIDDLE AGE

are ample evidence. But intellectual curiosity breaks its heart in vain where there is not a sufficiency of fundamental knowledge to be had, and one part of the legacy of the twelfth century to the general civilizing process of human history lay in the vast increase of the raw materials of scholarship which it made available for the first time for centuries. In 1100 it was quite possible for a very learned man to have mastered the sum total of intellectual knowledge then available. By 1200 such a dream was already almost as wildly absurd as it would be to-day. The century begins with the bare outline of the Seven Liberal Arts, built on fragments of Aristotle and hardly more than memories of Plato. It ends with Roman and Canon Law rediscovered and firmly established. During its course the new Aristotle is brought to Western Europe and becomes the current coinage of the schools. The new Euclid is discovered, and also the Greek achievements in many branches of the physical sciences. Ptolemy comes back to his own: Hermann of Dalmatia translates his *Planisphere* and dedicates it, with a fine sense of what is fitting, to Thierry of Chartres, "the soul of Plato reincarnate." The ample and formidable Arabic philosophy, built on Averrhoes' commentaries on the full Aristotle, crosses the Pyrenees. The Arabic language becomes articulate far beyond the domains of the Prophet, and Peter the Venerable, most lovable of all abbots, travels in Spain and commissions a Latin translation of the Koran. And these discoveries are devoured greedily by the eager questing spirit of Western Europe, purged and re-shaped in its own crucibles, combined with the old civilizing materials and fundamental knowledge which were all its own, and emerge as a new philosophy and a new science. These new coals which fed the burning fiery furnace of twelfth-century

THE UNIVERSITIES AND THE EUROPEAN MIND

creativeness sustain an artistic as well as an intellectual quickening. Not only are the classics everywhere revived again, but a whole generation becomes æsthetically articulate, sedulously practises Latin prose and verse, and creates a new liturgical drama and a new vernacular literature of its own.

The immensity of the change which the century wrought can be gauged by glancing at the typical library of 1099 and 1199. In the 1099 library would be found the Bible, and the Fathers. The Carolingian scholars had commented fairly fully on both, and at least some of these commentaries would be there. Then, of course, there would be the service books of the Church, and certainly some of the Lives of the Saints. Boethius would find a place, and perhaps Priscian, and, more doubtfully, a few of the Latin classics. That is all of which one can feel certain. But by 1199 the same library would be more than doubled. The vast development in the organization of copying would have brought better copies of the older works. In Law, there would be Gratian on Canon Law and the *Corpus Juris Civilis*; in Theology, the shelves would contain books by St. Bernard, Peter Lombard, Anselm, and, very likely, Abelard. History would be well represented by half a dozen composite Chronicles, and by the books of men like Otto of Friesingen and John of Salisbury. Finally, the collection would be rounded off by books unknown a hundred years before on mathematics, astronomy, medicine, and philosophy.

Western Europe comes into its own as a separate and distinct civilizing entity, and lays the foundations for the dreams of its better statesmen ever since of a real United States of Europe. The Continent as a whole had been, and still was, divided into five provinces of culture. There was the Nordic province of North-Western Europe, just becoming Christian, but articulate

THE GOLDEN MIDDLE AGE

with a literature all its own. The Moslem culture, foreign to all the rest but joined to it and influencing it, reigned in Spain and was powerful along all the shores of the Western Mediterranean. The Byzantine Empire represented a quite separate tradition which had outposts in Southern Italy, and in some of the Italian trading-centres. Russia was the province of Slavs and Finns, still pagan and barbarous outside such towns as Novgorod where resident Swedish merchants a little redeemed the barbarity. But the soul of Christendom and of the whole civilizing mission of Europe lay in the West with Northern France as its centre, England, Italy, and Germany as its provinces, and Norway, Bohemia, Austria, and Spain as its frontier countries. From the time of Charlemagne's death this Western European culture had steadily shrunk in the kingdoms both of this world and of the mind and spirit. But from 1100, and throughout the century, it was everywhere expanding. Military weapons, as in Spain, formed one of the instruments of this advance; but the primary instruments were the achievements of Europe's scholars.

Great bursts of civilizing activity have always enshrined themselves in particular centres. The intellectual and artistic ferment which made ancient Greece the glory and the envy of posterity was spread over the whole of the Hellenic world, but inevitably pivoted upon its centre Athens. Similarly, in a later age, Florence was the centre of gravity of the Italian Renaissance. In the twelfth century, the passion for learning expressing itself in the creation of universities, and the rediscovery and the spread of the fundamentals of scholarship brought into strong existence a considerable civilizing movement. At first, it was centred upon Paris. Then the rise to power of Cornificius and his like made of Paris an educational

THE UNIVERSITIES AND THE EUROPEAN MIND

rather than a civilizing centre. Orleans, although for a brief time it became the camp of the humanists, never quite took the place of Paris, perhaps because it *was* a camp, the headquarters of a battle. The palm passed into English keeping, and in the latter half of the century England was the shrine of literature for all the world. In England, too, was the real centre of the conscious struggle for a real civilization, which expressed itself, as all such struggles do, not only in the creation of a general æsthetic awareness, but also in the coming to birth of the idea of the academy, the centre of a body of people, living together in civilized conditions, and stimulating each other, as the citizens of Athens had done in the past, to live a life of reason, grace, culture, and peace. No other European kingdom could boast so long a list of names for ever important in the history of literature, or could point to a comparable library of writings of the first quality. Chronicles, poetry, biography, philosophy, and theology—English writers produced masterpieces in all these fields, and more beside, in Henry II's time.

Henry's own reputation as a man of letters bore no small part of the responsibility and honour. "Your king," wrote Peter of Blois to the Archbishop of Palermo, "is a good scholar, but ours is far better; I know the abilities and accomplishments of both. With the king of England there is school every day, constant conversation with the best scholars, and discussion of questions."[1] Such a monarch naturally attracts scholars to his kingdom. At least twenty books are known to have been dedicated to Henry, by authors as various as Adelard of Bath, under whom he had studied science, William of Conches, Peter of Blois, Robert of Cricklade, and Gerald

[1] Tr. Stubbs. *Seventeen Lectures on Medieval and Modern History* (Oxford University Press), p. 119.

THE GOLDEN MIDDLE AGE

of Wales. Robert of Cricklade, in the dedication of *Defloratio Plinii*, declares it "unfitting that the lord of so large a part of the earth should be ignorant of its different regions."[1] It was not perhaps the most tactful of dedications. Nor was it strictly true. If Henry had not visited all the parts of the world which Robert described, he knew a good deal about many of them, and could speak several of their languages. If Walter Map cheerfully exaggerated when he declared that Henry knew "the world's tongues from the Channel to the Jordan," it is at least evidence that the king was a linguist of no ordinary merit.

Scholarship and civilization have the habits of traders: their practitioners congregate in a few centres, Oxford and Cambridge to-day, and Exeter and Canterbury then, with Lincoln as a possible third. But of these, Canterbury stood easily first, and had no rivals. There Archbishop Theobald had gathered around him a notable company of scholars and sages, including experts, English and foreign, in almost every field of knowledge, so that the boast of one of the company, Peter of Blois, was no more than the truth: "All the knotty questions of the kingdom were referred to us, and when they are discussed in the hearing of all, each of us, without strife or wrangling sharpens his wits to speak on them well."[2] The imaginary traveller coming to Canterbury, wrote Bishop Stubbs, would find himself

in a great literary centre, with teachers and libraries and all appliances that stand to the population and sons of the day in much the same proportion as the literary life of Oxford and Cambridge would at this moment. He would find Gervase,

[1] C. H. Haskins in *Essays in Medieval History presented to T. F. Tout* (Manchester University Press), p. 75 n.
[2] W. H. Hutton. *Thomas Becket* (Cambridge University Press), p. 12.

THE UNIVERSITIES AND THE EUROPEAN MIND

the sacrist, busy over the Chronicles of the Kings and the history of his own time; Nigel writing his verses polishing the great medieval satire, *Burnellus*, or inditing the prose letter in which he castigates the faults of the secular clergy—a monk in a strictish convent, but corresponding with the ministers of a powerful and political court.[1]

Another person whom Bishop Stubbs's traveller would see would be John of Salisbury. He had come there in 1154, and presented to the Archbishop his testimonial from Bernard of Clairvaux. At once he found employment as one of the three or four personal clerks and secretaries whom Theobald kept. At first he appears to have been merely one among his fellows, a secretarial clerk and no more. But the thorough and deep knowledge of the work which the Curia had given him, added to his conspicuous literary abilities and his grave but charming earnestness, quickly raised him to a position of intimacy. He became to Theobald as a son to a father, and in Theobald's failing years he wielded uncommon power in the English Church. For the first time in his life he had money enough and to spare, for he certainly enjoyed the revenue of a canonry of Salisbury, and it is very probable that Theobald also bestowed on him a parish church or a chantry chapel in the city of London. "I am much better off than you and I were at Provins," he wrote cheerfully to his friend, Peter, Abbot of Celle.

If Chartres had a rival in John's heart it was Canterbury. He called it, truly enough, the mother of Church and State alike, and gratefully remembered the calm friendship and peace he had found in that home of learning. When he finished the *Policraticus* he sent it to Becket, at the time in France besieging

[1] Op. cit., p. 145.

Toulouse with the king. But in his letter he adds that when Becket has read it he must send it home again—home to Canterbury, the city of its birth. If only he had not to travel so incessantly all would have been perfect in these few years before his exile. But he was the obvious member of Theobald's household to be entrusted with any Roman business there might be, for not only had he an ample experience of the ways of the Curia, but he was the closest of Adrian IV's personal friends.

But journeys end in homecomings, and at Canterbury there was the benison of the place, the affection of his master, and the stimulation of the members of Theobald's household to enjoy. They were a company which would have been remarkable in any age. There was, for example, Peter of Blois, to whom we are indebted for a warm and vivid description of the circle.

The court in which I live is, I assure you, a camp of God, none other than the house of God and the gate of heaven. In the house of my lord the Archbishop are most scholarly men, with whom is found all the uprightness of justice, all the caution of providence, every form of learning. They, after prayers, and before meals, in reading, in disputing, in the decision of causes, constantly exercise themselves.[1]

It is a remarkable tribute, for Peter, though he had a high opinion of himself—his own writings, he said, would "outlast ruin, and flood, and fire, and the manifold procession of the centuries"—he did not usually entertain a like optimistic opinion of others. "These subtleties which you highly extol are manifoldly pernicious," he wrote to a friend, who had but asked him his opinion of the state of the drama. He grumbled

[1] Haskins. Op. cit., p. 50.

THE UNIVERSITIES AND THE EUROPEAN MIND

incessantly about the small profits of his archdeaconries, of which he held three, Bath, Wolverhampton, and London. But he was, as became a pupil of John of Salisbury, a fine classical scholar, and a voluminous writer too, and so was worthy of his place in the Canterbury circle. Vacarius, the great Italian legalist, was still more remarkable. He had been brought by Theobald from Bologna in 1149 in order to found a school of English law, and to be legal adviser to Theobald. The text-book that he wrote at Canterbury, *Liber Pauperum*, was confiscated by Stephen; but time justified Theobald's faith, for it was used as a text-book for many years. Under Henry II he was allowed to found his school, but he did not long preside over it, for he fell foul of the king and was banished from the country—a piece of provincial tyranny for which John never really forgave Henry. Herbert de Bosham, one of the many biographers of Thomas Becket, and another member of the circle, had studied under Peter Lombard, and first introduced to England his master's famous *Glosses* and *Sentences*. But the orthodoxy of these works had been questioned; and Herbert might be seen working at Canterbury on a task which demanded tact, and an ability to serve two masters at once. He must correct the offending passages without thereby seeming to agree that they offended, lest he should be disloyal to the memory of his great master. He remembered, however, that the great virtue of explanation is that it corrects inoffensively; and thus his marginal commentary on the *Sentences* resolved the problem of the contradictory passages which the Lombard delighted to quote by referring the reader to the passages which gave the solution. Thus, at one and the same time, Herbert increased the circulation and usefulness of the *Sentences* in England and averted from the author the suspicion of heterodoxy—an ingenious stroke. These, together with Gervaise and Nigel Wirecker, whom Stubbs mentions, were the most famous members of the Canterbury circle; but there were many others: John, Rector of Synesford, who went by the name De Belles Mains, the friend who had once shared with John of Salisbury a gargantuan banquet at Canossa, and "skilled in Hebrew, Greek, and Latin above any man that I have seen"; Baldwin, John's "most dear friend," who had been with him at the Papal Curia, and was to become Archbishop of Canterbury; Bartholomew the Archdeacon, whom John persuaded Becket to nominate to the king as Bishop of Exeter, who preached the sermon when Canterbury Cathedral was opened after the murder of Becket, and who was described by the Pope as "the great glory of the English Church"; Odo, Abbot of Battle; Gerard Pucelle, Bishop of Coventry; and many more.

Twelfth-century Canterbury, it is evident, was no mean city. If the claim of the Middle Ages to be regarded as bearing an essential part in the whole human striving after the perfected civilization rested on no other examples, it could not be lightly dismissed. In England alone, similar claims could be made for contemporary Exeter, Lincoln, London, and, a little later, for Oxford; and on the Continent, a little earlier, the names are legion, as this study has shown. If civilization fundamentally consists in the regard paid to Reason, to Æsthetic Awareness, the art of living richly and with grace, and the whole conception crowned by the passion for righteousness, the city of Canterbury which John of Salisbury knew lies in the same category as Periclean Athens, and in a far higher category than the Florence of the Medici or the Paris of Voltaire. And if its social grace was fleeting, so were theirs. To use the term

THE UNIVERSITIES AND THE EUROPEAN MIND

medieval to describe everything which is crude, brutal, and beastly is to display a most provincial ignorance.

3. *The Instruments of Authorship*

The history of human thought is the history of human life. What a man thinks is the most significant and influential thing about him, and in that sense every work of history forms one section of the whole colossal History of Human Thought. It is not difficult to trace the influence of the twelfth-century renaissance upon the developing forms of the social organism, or upon the work of the Church in presenting the challenge of Christ to the world. It is much more difficult to work out a thing so impalpable as the effect of the passion to be educated upon the moving current of European thought. Yet this is what is really significant and influential. There are, however, two stories which may be told, which, though they do not cover all the ground, at least provide the outlines of a map which will help us to trace our way through a very tangled piece of country. They are the stories of authorship and of heresy.

Thought achieves significance in speech or writing. The spoken thought becomes slowly, and the written thought swiftly effective. But before the written thought can become really effective there must be the means of circulating it, and a comparatively swift and vast circulation was made possible to authors first in the twelfth century, and as a result of the need of schools and universities to provide an adequate supply of the texts studied. This was naturally a great step forward in the history of thought, for it encouraged the art of authorship by enormously increasing the possible area of circulation. It is safe to say that no author, no matter in which century he wrote, has ever undergone the racking physical labour of writing a whole book with his own hands, to say nothing of the mental labour of composing it, unless he thought it at least possible that there would be someone to read it. But whereas a Sophocles or a Horace could count their readers in tens, an Abelard, a John of Salisbury, or a Gilbert Porée, could look forward to hundreds, and even thousands. A man as exciting and as popular as Abelard achieved so large a circulation for his work as to place him almost on the same level of ubiquity as any of the more famous novelists of to-day. "Peter Abelard is again teaching novelties," wrote the alarmed William of St. Thierry. "His books cross the sea, pass the Alps. His new notions and dogmas about the Faith are carried through kingdom and province." It is perhaps the only sentence in a long and hysterical letter which speaks the exact, unexaggerated truth. Abelard employed no literary or publicity agent, resorted to the good offices of no publisher, and was unassisted by woodpulp or linotype, but his books did cross seas and mountains and were carried throughout kingdoms and provinces. John of Salisbury's popularity was less extensive, but he too enjoyed a very considerable circulation all over Western Europe and in Italy. Not all the famous men of the century enjoyed so wide a circulation for their books. Gerald of Wales sent one of his books to King John, and suggested that the King might employ someone to translate it into French, so that "Gerald might reap the fruits of his toil which, under illiterate princes, had been lost, since there were so few to read his books. Poets and authors, indeed, crave after immortality, but do not reject any advantages that may offer."[1] It is

[1] *Autobiography*, Vol. II.

THE UNIVERSITIES AND THE EUROPEAN MIND

an interesting complaint, for it suggests that even then there was money in authorship. How was this money collected for the author?

When the twelfth-century author sat down to write, he had at least an hour's preliminary labour to prepare his materials. His chair was specially built with extended arms across which the writing-board could be securely placed. The board was covered with felt in order that the quire of parchment should not slip on the smooth wood, and he fixed across the top a thong of deerskin and inserted the quire under it as an additional and necessary means of ensuring the immobility of the parchment. That done, he took out his knife, and began to scrape away from the parchment the scales and incrustations and "superfluities of the parchment or membrane." Then came the pumice stone to rub away the traces of the knife, and smooth away the remaining roughness of the surface. Setting these on one side, the conscientious craftsman of letters took up his awl and marked out "in even measure" margins and lines, and then with a ruler joined with straight lines the points marked by the awl. Finally, Alexander Neckham's description of the process ends with the severe caution, "If any erasure or crossing-out occurs, the writing shall not be cancelled but scraped off." Neckham wrote from the fullness of his own experience, for he had a long list of books to his credit when he died. But did he, one wonders, never spoil his parchment by scraping incautiously with his knife, or rubbing too hard with his pumice stone, and so making a hole in his page? Perhaps not, for he was a very exacting judge of the appearance of a manuscript; and in any case parchment was too expensive a material to be lightly spoiled by careless handling, and the supply of membranes was less than the demand.

THE GOLDEN MIDDLE AGE

But parchment was not always expensive, and though for several hundred years its price had been so high that every scrap of it had had to be treasured, and words written on it had often been contracted out of all recognition to make it last, the eleventh century bequeathed to the twelfth one of the greatest of its legacies—cheap and plentiful parchment. In its last decades, the eleventh century had, moreover, bequeathed some important changes in the technique of book production. Vellum had become cheaper and there was not the old need of stinting economy in its use. For the first time in the Middle Ages MSS. were copied and written in one column to the page, rather than in three or even four; and words, paragraphs, and chapters were properly separated from each other. There were still many puzzling contractions, but they were retained as a concession to the weariness of the writer's fingers rather than as a means of saving space. It was also in the eleventh century that men learned to write more swiftly and freely than before by using the graceful Caroline Miniscule rather than the old Uncial characters. "Swiftly and freely," however, is a contentious phrase, when it is remembered that a Bible commonly took fifteen months to copy: six months was the record, but that must have been an endurance test. The combination of these circumstances makes the twelfth century the golden age of the palæographist, for it was the last century of the large folio volume. The next century is the opening of the era of the pocket volume, and hence the writing became more and more packed. The style of handwriting called Caroline Miniscule needs plenty of space to display its beauty.

It is clear that a system which can so multiply the works of an Abelard has already passed out of monastic hands, for few self-respecting abbots, and none over whom St. Bernard had

THE UNIVERSITIES AND THE EUROPEAN MIND

any influence, would allow such a suspected book as the *Sic et Non* to be copied in his abbey. Partly it was the twelfth-century renaissance, and partly the drop in the price of parchment which wrested the thousand-year-old monopoly of "publishing" from monastic hands. The one fact enormously increased the number of available copyists; the other put the material of their trade within their independent grasp.

For medieval publishing means copying—that and no more. The copying might be organized as a trade, or it might be subject to a purely individual caprice. By the fourteenth century, many manor houses were doing their own publishing, and in each manor of the Bishop of Durham were maintained "no small multitude of copyists and scribes"[1] John of Salisbury used both systems. His own *Policraticus* he sent to Peter of Celle, with the request that he would read it, censor anything which might give offence, and then send it to Becket. This was plainly the presentation copy—and it still remains. In course of time it drifted into Archbishop Parker's library at Lambeth, and was bequeathed by him to the library of Corpus College, Cambridge, where it is to-day. It is the identical copy which was sent to Peter, but it is not in John's handwriting. A copyist had been employed even at that early stage. We hear also of another copy of the same book which immediately bore fruit. John lent it—perhaps the rough draft, or perhaps another copy made by another copyist—to a friend at Canterbury, William Brito. In a letter written a little later, he calls him "that thief at Canterbury who got hold of the *Policraticus* and would not let it go until he had made a copy."

The casual and spasmodic system of taking a copy of a book one had borrowed certainly increased its circulation, but the

[1] *Philobiblon*, p. 63.

author was apt to regard such unregulated copying with more suspicion than gratitude, and John was more annoyed with Brito for making an unauthorized copy than for keeping his borrowed copy for too long a time. Authors often placed at the end of their books an injunction addressed to any who should copy the text:

> I adjure you who shall transcribe this book, by our Lord Jesus Christ and by His glorious coming, Who will come to judge the quick and the dead, that you compare what you transcribe and diligently correct it by the copy from which you transcribe it, and this adjuration also, and insert it in your copy.

Authors suffered much from the circulation of garbled copies of their works. Among the items in the indictment drawn up against Abelard at the Synod of Sens which condemned him are the following charges. His books, said his accusers, maintained these heretical propositions (among others):

1. That the Father is full power, the Son a certain power, and the Holy Spirit no power.
2. That diabolical suggestions are made to men through physic.
3. That sin is not committed by concupiscence and delectation and ignorance, and what is thus committed is not sin but nature.

William of St. Thierry, who drew up this indictment, may have been obscurantist, but he was not dishonest, and if he said that these remarks were made in Abelard's books that is sufficient evidence that they were certainly present in the particular copies which he read. But no one could seriously suggest that Abelard had really written anything so foolish. It had clearly happened that some hasty and careless copyists—very

THE UNIVERSITIES AND THE EUROPEAN MIND

likely enthusiastic disciples who had thought to make his meaning clearer—had been improving on their text. They unwittingly secured his condemnation. Even so unbending a pillar of orthodoxy as St. Bernard himself, whom no one would have dreamed of accusing of heresy, shows himself just as chary of unauthorized copying of his works as any other writer. He wrote to a friend:

> As regards the book you ask for, at the present moment I have not got it. For there is a certain friend of ours who has kept it a long time now, with the same eagerness with which you desire it. The book you shall have as soon as possible; but, although you may see and read it, I do not allow you to copy it. I did not give you leave to copy the other one I lent you, although you did so.

But perhaps St. Bernard feared chiefly that someone might tamper with his style, on which he greatly prided himself. He might approve heartily of the insertion of a clause in the Cistercian Rule forbidding any brother to be a poet; he might purposely write hymns which would not scan in order to remove the poetic impeachment from his own monastic reputation; but he was in fact as great a slave to the dictates of mere style in his writing as any of his less austere and more consciously literary contemporaries. He wrote to a friend, chiding him for having asked, nay demanded, an immediate answer to his letter which came in Lent:

> I ask you, where are peace and quietness if I am writing, dictating, and despatching you letters? But all this, you say, can be done in silence. It is strange if this be really your opinion. What a tumult invades the mind when in the act of composition—what a rushing multitude of words—what variety of language and diversity of expressions come upon one. Now the harmony of the words, now the clearness of

the expression, now the depth of the doctrine, now the ordering of the diction, and what shall follow and what shall precede are subjects necessarily of the most intense study.

Change the wording only a little, and the letter might easily be a part of the introduction to a novel by so careful a stylist as George Moore. St. Bernard, besides being a mighty and redoubtable saint, was also a man of letters though he gave less heed than many to the outward form if only the depth of doctrine were sufficient, and inspired John of Salisbury to declare of him, "Even if he held secular studies in small esteem, yet I have known no man pursue the art of poetry with so much grace."

Not, however, before the great days of the Cathedral Schools of Chartres and Paris, and the earliest days of the new Universities, was there a person in medieval Europe whose function can be said to correspond even remotely to a modern publisher. His office was created by the needs of these institutions. Among the most pressing of these needs was the very obvious one of keeping in stock enough copies of such standard works as the curriculum imposed upon the students. Before the scholastic revival in the twelfth century, when students were few, rough and ready methods, and small libraries were sufficient to meet the demand. But when the students increased so greatly in number that the old schools were so extended that they became universities it was urgently necessary to increase the scope and service of the libraries. Therefore, an official called a *stationarius* was appointed in each school, who had under him a reasonable staff of clerks. He was answerable to the school or university alone, and in those parts of Europe where military service was compulsory, he and his staff were exempt from it.

THE UNIVERSITIES AND THE EUROPEAN MIND

At about the same time that these stationers were coming into being, the needs of the times had created another new profession, that of the secular copyist, who, unlike the old monks, plied his trade, and made a reasonable living out of it. Secular copyists attached themselves to schools and universities, and to private patrons, and when the work was scarce, they made ends meet by writing letters for the illiterate. By 1150 no school was complete without its own copyists, and by 1250 there were 10,000 of them in Paris and Orleans alone. Their work broke the old monopoly of the monasteries in the multiplication of books, and in 1297 a complaint came even from the once famous writing school of St. Gall that very few monks "are competent copyists nowadays."

The university stationers took over and supervised the work of these university copyists, and it was their business to see that there was always a sufficient stock of authorized transcripts or copies of books regularly needed in the academic courses. These stationers were paid well, and out of their salaries they had to get the necessary manuscripts copied with meticulous accuracy. Books were not sold but hired to the student, and when he left the school they had to be returned intact and unsoiled to the stationer's office. "If this book of mine be defiled with dirt, the master will smite me in dire wrath upon the hinder parts,"[1] but perhaps the inscription was not accounted as dirt by the writer. One notices the same mentality among patrons of public libraries.

Every detail in the work of the stationer and his assistants and copyists was performed under the rigid scrutiny of the university officials, and was governed by unbreakable regulations. Even the size of the MSS. lent to the students and the

[1] G. G. Coulton. op. cit., Vol. II, p. 118.

THE GOLDEN MIDDLE AGE

manner of lending was regulated. MSS. were lent in specified portions of sixteen columns, which formed the unit upon which the lending fees were calculated. Each column had to contain sixty-two lines, and each line thirty-two letters, no more and no less. A book written to those dimensions was a good deal smaller than the average book produced in the monasteries, and it was owing to the sure demand for MSS. of this standardized size that in the thirteenth century books became so much smaller.

The monopoly enjoyed by the universities, and passed on to the stationers, endowed them with considerable powers, but in one way their powers were strangely limited. They had no control over private enterprise in the copying of MSS. which they lent. No student was prevented from copying any MS. which came into his hands; he was rather encouraged to do so. Many stories have been preserved of the students who lived together and sat up in watches all night along, that they might make for themselves a library by copying the books which they had borrowed from the stationer, and any other texts on which they could lay their hands. The common complaint that "my back is so bent that the ribs stick into the stomach, to its manifold discomfort and ill health" made but little difference to the eagerness with which the young student would copy the works of his favourite teachers. At least, it made none to the eagerness with which he began it. Carrying the task through to the finish was a less light-hearted business. "Three fingers write, and the whole body is in travail," groaned one student, and added the eternal complaint of the man who has a sedentary job, "yet they who know not how to write deem it no labour." And over and over again a triumphant flourish is hurled across the bottom of the last

THE UNIVERSITIES AND THE EUROPEAN MIND

page, *Expicit, Deo Gratias*, Thank God That's Done. The willingness of the twelfth-century scholar to labour at this monotonous task, and the presence in Paris and elsewhere of so many copyists easily accounts for the rapid way in which the books of teachers such as Peter Abelard and scholars such as John of Salisbury were multiplied in most parts of Europe.

Lending libraries were thus set up in all scholastic centres both by the authorities of the schools and by private enterprise. The books on their shelves, however, were mostly copies of the works in regular demand on account of their status as prescribed books for the courses studied. The monasteries, too, had their libraries, which they stocked by their own labour in copying, and by occasional recourse to barter. But their titles were primarily devotional and theological: nor were their libraries sufficiently extensive for it to be possible to say of them that they did much to create the demand for books of every kind which clearly existed in the twelfth century. It is indeed surprising how few books they possessed. The Abbey of Monte Cassino—the most famous and important in Europe, for it had been the home of St. Benedict himself—had seventy books in its library, theological, liturgical, classical, and historical. Bec, where "every other monk seemed a philosopher," had 164, and to these 113 were added by the Bishop of Bayeux in his will. The library of Clairvaux was extremely meagre and severely theological. Only Cluny possessed a library which could be called extensive. It consisted of 570 volumes of all kinds. This rather surprising poverty of the monastic library was no doubt due in part to the space which books occupied. Every Bible filled several large and fat volumes: the inevitable glosses and commentaries filled many more. Liturgical works were larger still; and the old Fathers, when they sat down to write, had always unpacked their hearts with many thousands of words. And the average library was not a large room with bookshelves all round it, but something much more like a wardrobe, kept in an alcove of the chapel or the cloister. The *Book of Customs for English Benedictines*, which was written at the end of the eleventh century, plainly assumes that the average monastery will possess enough books to be piled on a single rug without spilling over, that is, about the cubic capacity of a small wardrobe of to-day.

But bookshops already existed side by side with the libraries, and often under the same roof, for the modern bookseller who seeks to add to his precarious profits from the sale of books by lending them at a small fee has his medieval predecessor. We hear, for example, of a not-too-scrupulous Paris bookseller. In 1170 Peter of Blois walked into his shop, and became interested in a new volume on jurisprudence which the bookseller showed him. He agreed to buy it for his nephew, his own knowledge of the subject being already too extensive, he grandly said, for him to need to add to it. He paid his money, and ordered the volume to be sent round to his lodgings. Then a still greater notability entered, the Provost of Sexeburgh, and saw the same book lying on the counter. He was told that it was already sold, but he grandly put down a sum of money twice as large, and bore it off triumphantly in his arms. History does not relate the sequel. But the story seems to bear out Richard de Bury's assertion that booksellers are thievish folk, filled with malice.[1]

It is clear that books were a commodity in the commercial sense of the term, and that the day of the patiently illuminated manuscript, with every letter a separate work of art, was over,

[1] *Philobiblon*, p. 19.

THE UNIVERSITIES AND THE EUROPEAN MIND

except in so far as such volumes were still wanted for presentation purposes or show pieces. Standardization and mass production had begun with the suddenly increased demand. But it was not wholly a commercial matter. Charity still entered in, and so did barter. The founder of the Benedictine Abbey of Valmont gave in 1169 the hides of all the beasts caught in his park for book bindings; and about the same date we hear of someone exchanging a missal for a vineyard, and a Priscian for a house and a piece of land. The multiplication of books was still half a matter of disorganized barter, and half a matter of standardized trade. But at least they multiplied, every kind of them. No longer was the demand artificially limited to the Scriptures, the Fathers, the Commentaries, and the Classics. For works of all kinds of all contemporary writers there was an incessant demand, and many who could not afford to buy them paid the authors the greater compliment of thinking their works not only worth reading but also worth possessing, even though possession meant the labour of copying out every word. Had the twelfth-century author lived two hundred years earlier, his books would no doubt have found readers, but the circle of the influence would have been tiny in his own time. As it was he had no fear that they would not swiftly circulate: he feared only the cumulative errors of unauthorized and unchecked translation, for with people like St. Bernard, and his watchdog William of St. Thierry about, that might easily become a serious matter.

4. *Historians and Poets*

The books thus made generally available were of every kind, with theology and philosophy naturally predominating. But

THE GOLDEN MIDDLE AGE

what is remarkable is the great popularity of the historian; for him the twelfth century is almost as much of a heyday as the nineteenth. The histories and historians of the twelfth century form a study bewildering in its scope and variety. "In our times such great and memorable events have happened that the negligence of us moderns were justly to be reprehended, should they fail to be handed down to eternal memory in literary monuments," said William of Newburgh. There was hardly a monastery which did not keep a composite chronicle at some time, and at many centres, such as Westminster, St. Albans, and Winchester, chronicles were kept covering hundreds of years. The individual chronicler is a twelfth-century innovation, and he flourished nowhere more luxuriantly than in England. William of Malmesbury, William of Newburgh, Ralph de Diceto, Roger of Hoveden, Henry of Huntingdon, Florence of Worcester, Simeon of Durham, Jocelyn of Brakelond, and John of Salisbury, is a list of only English names among the century's historians, and it is not exhaustive. William of Malmesbury, the greatest of them all, who was offered the abbacy of Malmesbury but refused it lest he should be separated from his beloved work, put into words their common ambition:

It arose that not content with the writings of ancient times, I began myself to compose, not indeed to display my learning, which is comparatively nothing, but to bring to light events lying concealed in the confused mass of antiquity. In consequence, rejecting vague opinions, I have studiously sought for chronicles far and near, though I confess I have scarcely profited anything by this industry; for perusing them all I still remained poor in information, though I ceased not my researches as long as I could find anything to read.

THE UNIVERSITIES AND THE EUROPEAN MIND

The twelfth-century chronicle was of two kinds. Either it fulfilled the function of the modern history book, or that of the daily newspaper: it dealt with past or with present events. The chronicler as historian possessed something which went far to compensate him for mere inaccuracy, a philosophy of history, and a point of view. In the writing of history there is much to be said in favour of having an axe to grind. To start upon the task with a definite point of view the truth of which the narrative is undertaken to prove is to bring the mass of fragmentary material within manageable proportions. To be, for example, the victim of an invincible belief, as Macaulay was, that the facts of history were given by divine permission in order to demonstrate the fact that the Whigs were the chosen of God, may beg a good many questions, but at least it results in a readable narrative. For such a belief or obsession, as the case may be, does constitute a necessary fetter of coherence, without which no readable narrative can ever be written.

Christians, by their profession, enjoy such a point of view; and the angle from which they look at the enormous stage of human history gives them a majestic vision. For the Christian's vision of the drama of history is very much the same as Milton's was when he wrote *Paradise Lost*. The Christian sees the world as the stage whereon is set the eternal conflict between God and his angels and the Devil, and views history as the record of the long process by which the love of God, and all that doctrine implies, gradually becomes actual as well as potential among men. Such a vision of history is at least no petty one. Belief does not merely strengthen the hand of the universal historian, it gives him that without which he cannot even begin—a criterion of selection to apply to an otherwise overwhelming mountain of facts. He can begin happily at the

THE UNIVERSITIES AND THE EUROPEAN MIND

beginning—to be precise, at 6 p.m. on October 22nd, 5509 B.C. Nor need he worry over the possibility that he may never live to end so gigantic an undertaking. There are plenty of others, trained chroniclers all, and sharing all his preconceptions, and his ideas of the nature of existence. Thus chronicles are often passed on from hand to hand, written continuously for centuries, and it is hard, if not impossible, to say where one writer put down the monastery pen, and another took it up. At St. Albans, for example, the chronicle passed from one monk to another, and at least one novice was always being trained to carry on the work. In the end, the *St. Alban's Chronicle* ran without any break from Creation to A.D. 1440. The believer has also an ethic which again helps to reduce his material to manageable proportions. The Anglo-Saxon chronicler ended his account of the reign of William the Conqueror by saying, "We have written these things, both good and bad, that virtuous men might follow after the good, and wholly avoid the evil, and might go in that way that leadeth to the kingdom of Heaven."

"If I am not too partial to myself, a variety of anecdote cannot be displeasing to anyone," said William of Malmesbury, and it might be the *Apologia* of the twelfth-century chronicler who described the facts of his own day. They were all partial to the anecdote, and the taller the better, for they had a quite unmedieval standard of news values. The chief pre-occupation of the writers was no doubt political or ecclesiastical, but they were exactly like a good contributor to the modern *London Letter* of the provincial newspaper. Let anything strange happen in their own city, let the weather behave itself unseemly, and immediately the king was left to fight in France with his victories unsung and his defeats unbewailed, whilst

THE UNIVERSITIES AND THE EUROPEAN MIND

the chronicler turned avidly to these matters of more pressing and popular interest. The village pump was with them, as with us, the real centre of their interest, and anything which happened there was news above all else. They would use parchment without stint on royal weddings, on executions, on honours, and, above all, on the weather. Even the *Anglo-Saxon Chronicles*, as a rule heavily political, unbends when,

on the night of the third day before the Ides of December was the moon, during a long time of the night, as if covered with blood, and afterwards eclipsed.

and the *Chronicle of London* follows suit when,

In this same yere ... there were greete Reynes and eke Thundres. And also there ffylle grete hayles, ffor ther kome adovne with the Reyne out of the eyre hayle-Stones ffoure Squayre, as grete as any eyren.... And fferthermore ffoules were y-seyn ffleynge in the eyre, and berynge coles in her bylles, that weren cause off brennynge of many houses.... And also fyrye Dragons and Wykked Spyrites weren many seyn, merveyllously ffleynge in the eyre.

But to read the anecdotal chronicler at his best one should turn to the date of a royal wedding, or, better still, to the year of Jack Cade's rebellion:

And the same day at V at after none the Capteyne [Cade] came in to the Cite per force; and in his entry at the Brigge he hewe the Ropys of the drawe brigge asonder ... and at London Stone he strak upon it like a Conquerour.

Then he beheaded two citizens, and his followers

brought the hedis upon II stakes or polis, and in dyvers places of the Cite put theym togider, cawsying that oon to kysse that other.

THE GOLDEN MIDDLE AGE

The final indignity! But it was not hidden from the chronicler, and therefore it was revealed to those for whom he wrote, and to us also.

Speaking very generally, until the middle of the thirteenth century most chronicles were written by monks, and after that they began to lose their monopoly, which passed to trained laymen. But even before that there were lay chronicles of various kinds. The monks wrote because they were so ordered by their superiors; the laymen wrote for every possible kind of reason, because they scented money, because they were bored, or because they burned to glorify their city. Andrew Horn, Chamberlain of London and a fishmonger in Bridge Street, painfully wrote six volumes of civic annals, being actuated thereto by the purest of civic pride. Another London Alderman, of German extraction and industry, wrote the basic *London Chronicle.* Geoffrey Baker, a secular clerk, found an Oxfordshire parsonage too tame, and started a famous chronicle to while away his time. Adam Murimuth, Canon of St. Paul's, varied the duties of his canonry with the practice of ecclesiastical law, and the writing of a day-to-day chronicle of his times. Robert Avebury, a parson very much married, found that his defiance of the law of clerical celibacy decimated his income from ecclesiastical employment, and so set up as a chronicler. Whereas some of these men, such as the London Aldermen, wrote for love, most, no doubt, expected and received some payment.

The best of historians, like John of Salisbury and Otto of Friesingen, belonged to both schools. Their point of view, their criterion of selection, was exactly what Augustine's had been before them, that history is purposive, and the world the stage on which is enacted the most august and splendid of

THE UNIVERSITIES AND THE EUROPEAN MIND

dramas, the conflict between virtue and evil. John would have wholeheartedly echoed the prologue to the great history, *The Two Cities* written by his friend Otto, Bishop of Friesingen—the one twelfth-century philosophy of history which is worthy to be named in the company of St. Augustine's *City of God*—who began, he said,

> to compose a history whereby through God's favour I might display the miseries of the citizens of Babylon (the worldly city) and also the glory of the kingdom of Christ to which the citizens of Jerusalem are to look forward with hope, and of which they are to have a foretaste even in this life. I have undertaken, therefore, to bring down as far as our own time, according to the ability that God has given me, the record of the conflicts and miseries of the one city Babylon; and furthermore, not to be silent concerning our hopes regarding that other city. . . . We are to speak, then, concerning the sorrow-burdened insecurity of the one city and the blessed permanence of the other.

But though these words of Otto's form a first statement of the background of the *Historia Pontificalis*, John did not of course write it merely in order "to display the miseries of the citizens of Babylon" and "the glory of the Kingdom of Christ." On the contrary, he wrote the book because he had been for many years a constant witness of history in the making. It had been his business to be present at conferences and councils. There, he would listen quietly to all that was said, and, studiously preserving his detached, rather sceptical estimate of the proceedings and their value, would take notes of what passed. These notes he afterwards used as the rough draft of *Historia Pontificalis*, which, written at various times, was finished in 1164, and covers the period 1148 to 1152. The book is the main historical authority for the period it covers, but while its importance in that respect is naturally great, the manner of it, and the events chosen for emphasis as being of special importance, shed a good deal of light on his own mind. One chapter, for instance, is given to the Council of Rheims. The main business of this council was the trial of Gilbert Porée for heresy. John gives a full account of it, and drily adds to it the story of St. Bernard's discomfiture by Gilbert. It is a story after John's own heart, but it shows that his heart was hardly medieval, for it has too sardonic a flavour for a truly medieval mind to relish. As for the rest of his account of the council, he does not trouble to set down its decrees, and one can only suppose that it was because he thought them of small importance either way, but he takes pains to describe any little scene which caused a laugh.

Otto, the Cistercian Bishop of Friesingen, was perhaps the greatest historian of his age, and wrote, with equal dexterity and happiness of spirit, the vast universal history of the world, *The Two Cities*, the prologue of which has already been quoted, and the more local chronicle of the doings of his great master, the Emperor Frederick Barbarossa. In *The Two Cities*, he borrowed St. Augustine's terminology, as became a Cistercian Abbot and a Bishop, and viewed the whole cosmic drama of recorded history, from Adam to Frederick, as but an episode in the prolonged warfare between the Two Cities, the City of God, and the city of the world, between Jerusalem and Babylon. Thus no stretch of centuries was so enormous as to daunt his energies, and no little, trivial detail of an individual life was regarded as irrelevant or insignificant. The terms of reference which he set himself were thus such that nothing whatever in the world of nature, from the infinitely vast to the infinitely

THE UNIVERSITIES AND THE EUROPEAN MIND

small could be of no moment to a dramatic conflict of even such cosmic proportions of magnificence as this.

He began his task by setting out the stage. "Writers assert that there are three parts of the world, Asia, Africa, and Europe. The first of them they account equal in size to the other two. Yet some have declared that there are only two parts, that is Asia and Europe; Africa because of its small size they join to Europe." But let us not quote in ridicule. It is not to be expected that Otto's geography should be impeccable, or even that his historical assertions should be invariably correct. He was marvellously free from bias. It may be that the gigantic bias (as it may appear to some) of the general character of his work freed him from the little biases of detail which make most medieval ecclesiastical histories so tiresome. All facts are presented and interpreted as tending in two directions, to show the miseries of Babylon, and, in contradistinction, the blessedness and the gradual victory of Jerusalem. Such a thesis delivers him, for example, from being forced to deliver the Greek philosophers to the flames of hell. If it is true that he repeated the hoary rumour that Plato had met Jeremiah in Egypt and had been instructed by him; it is also true, and much more remarkable, that his account of Plato's inspiration is almost exactly the judgment which any modern Christian would deliver:

He and the other philosophers by natural keenness comprehended the invisible as it were by the means of the visible. For all things that could be discovered by human wisdom regarding the nature of God they found out, all except those matters on which ultimate salvation depends. These things are learned through the grace of Jesus Christ by the gentle of heart.

THE GOLDEN MIDDLE AGE

The Two Cities is naturally not an authority in the historian's sense of the word; and to follow the winding course which Otto charts through the seas of history is to throw light rather on Otto himself, and on the conventions of writing history in his day, than upon the worlds he seeks to uncover. The book is readily accessible in an English translation, and the casual reader would not find it uninteresting. Needless to say, Otto achieves his purpose, and shows quite clearly "How the divine wisdom, ever conquering evil, 'reacheth from one end of the world to the other with full strength.'" He is, too, splendidly thorough, not leaving his heavy task, which he wrote in considerable physical pain from illness, until he has thoroughly dealt with the geography of both Heaven and Hell, which he does with gusto and at length. *The Two Cities* is not without its importance for historians. That importance, however, lies more in the parentheses than in the main narrative. To provide an illustration of a point he is making, he includes in his main narrative, as it were between brackets, an excellent little biography of his predecessor in the see of Friesingen, Corbinian, of whom nothing would otherwise be known. And, redeeming his promise to speak of the foretaste of heavenly delights which the citizens of Jerusalem are to enjoy even in this life, he finds them naturally enough among those who, having forsaken the world, had embraced the life of religion in cloistered walls. At once his heart runs away with his sense of historic proportion. He seizes the chance he has deliberately manufactured, and writes a description of the daily round in a Cistercian Abbey so long that it is out of proportion in its length with the space given to the main theme of the book as a whole. But in all the book there are no pages so gravely beautiful as these, and when writing them his pen never once faltered or lost its

THE UNIVERSITIES AND THE EUROPEAN MIND

power to clothe the parchment with prose of grave and serene lyrical beauty.

Having completed his Essay on this high theme in 1147, Otto set to work to compile a chronicle of the reign of his nephew, the Emperor Frederick I. No man was more fitted for the task. Born in the purple, Otto had close blood relationships with four successive Emperors, and, besides that, he had had personal experience of both the vital movements of the century, for he had been a student at Paris University and Abbot of a Cistercian monastery. His facts, so far as they touched the Emperor himself, are vouched for by a letter which Frederick wrote him, in which he set down a brief record of the events and dates of his reign.

The *Gesta Friderici I Imperatoris*, to give it its full title, is a historical document of the utmost importance. It is filled with exactly the sort of information which most of all we want to know. All the worthies of the time flit across its pages— Abelard, Arnold of Brescia, Bernard of Clairvaux, Gilbert Porée. It is impossible to read a modern history of the times without finding Otto cited on almost every other page, and nearly always in terms of warm commendation. The historic events of the details of which he alone makes us aware are multitudinous. He, for instance, it is who alone states that Abelard was at one time the protesting pupil of John Roscelin; who sheds a flood of light on the famous trial for heresy of Gilbert Porée; who is the basic authority for the dramatic story of the unhappy Arnold of Brescia and the Roman Commune. The author of *The Two Cities* might certainly be accused of dragooning his facts to fit his thesis, and made no pretence of achieving what we could regard as a cool and impartial judgment. But the author of the *Gesta* is equally remarkable for the cool serenity of his poise. He was a Cistercian, tied and bound to St. Bernard by ties of great personal admiration, as well as by the unfailing loyalty the whole Order paid to its great saint. Yet he is able to view him sufficiently impartially to set down this admirable summary of his character:

> The aforesaid abbot was from the fervour of his Christian religion as jealous as, from his habitual meekness, he was in some measure credulous; so that he held in abhorrence those who trusted in the wisdom of this world and were too much attached to human reason, and if anything alien from the Christian faith were said to him in reference to them, he readily gave ear to it.

It is the perfect and the essentially just comment on the dealings of that redoubtable saint with Abelard and Gilbert. He seems to have been an exception among men. Few find it possible to be dispassionate about the men and events among which they are living, and which condition their lives. Few find it difficult to exercise a cool and lofty judgment about the remote past. Otto's reactions as a historian were exactly opposed to what is normal in modern times, perhaps because he was, after all, a child of medievalism, of which the characteristic trait was its love of thinking and working on the grand scale. Of all medieval bishops he is possibly the one who most worthily upheld in his own person the great traditions of the long succession of episcopal historians.

The historian, whether he compiled the local chronicle or had his being in the more ambitious fields of the philosophy of history, had in fact become a most useful member of medieval society, and was recognized as such. Here and there attempts were made to persuade him to prostitute his calling, to insert into his text grants of land and exemptions from taxation which had never in fact been made, in order to furnish evidence for a king, a magnate, or a corporation bent on legal marauding. Contrariwise, he might be bribed to omit uncomfortable truths, as poor Wace of Jersey found, who was commissioned by Henry II and Queen Eleanor to write a history of their reign and then was bilked of his fee because he had told the truth about one of their less creditable episodes, and hurt the royal feelings. But although some naturally fell into this trap, for historians in every age are human beings, prone to sin, we hear far more of temptations refused than of bribes accepted; and this again is perhaps what we should expect. To the historians was given the responsibility of getting new laws effectively promulgated up and down the kingdom and recorded in the histories. Copies of important laws were regularly despatched round the kingdom to the chroniclers from the twelfth century onwards. Page after page in Kingsford's admirable edition of the *Chronicles of London* is filled with exact copies of Acts of Parliament, or minutes of judgments and councils copied word for word, preambles included, with incredible industry. But apart from these written sources, the chronicler had to rely on what he saw and heard, or what was common gossip, or on what the actors in the events he recorded told him themselves. Some chroniclers were naturally well known, and all they had to do was to sit at home and wait for important people to come and say what was happening behind the scenes. Others relied on small talk, as witness the earlier parts of the *London Chronicles*, which mirror the small talk of the time with a fidelity which is highly entertaining.

The discussion has confined itself chiefly to the historians, and the theologians will come to be considered in their due place in this study. But enough has been said to show how

THE GOLDEN MIDDLE AGE

varied and how widespread was twelfth-century authorship. Few centuries have been more articulate. Biographies and dictionaries abound. Guide books to Paris, such as the Dictionary-cum-Guide Book of John of Garland, and to Rome, such as the anonymous *Mirabilia Urbis Romae*, and *Master Gregory on the Wonders of Rome*, are many. Professor C. H. Haskins has given an outline of the *Mirabilia*, which vividly shows the strength and the weakness of twelfth-century topographical writing:

This extraordinary combination of fact and fable, pagan and Christian, falls into three parts. The first, after describing the foundation of Rome on the Janiculum by Janus, son of Noah, lists its gates and arches, its baths, palaces, theatres, and bridges, its Christian cemeteries, and the places where the saints suffered martyrdom. The second comprises various legends of the saints and emperors, especially legends of statues, including the popular *Salvatio Rome*, a set of bells attached to the statues of the several provinces on the Capitol so as to give the alarm whenever the province revolted; the philosophers Phidias and Praxiteles in the time of Tiberias; the passion of the martyrs under Decius; and the foundation of the three great churches by Constantine. The third part takes the reader through the various quarters of the city and points out the striking monuments, and the ancient traditions connected with them.[1]

These, the author says, "we have read in old chronicles, and have seen with our eyes, and have heard tell of ancient men."

Above all, in the regard of posterity, the twelfth was a great century of lyric poetry, and the famous, easy Goliardic metre is brought to the perfection of its swift and pliant utterance.

[1] op. cit., pp. 121, 122.

THE UNIVERSITIES AND THE EUROPEAN MIND

> Fas et Nefas ambulant
> passu fere pari:
> prodigus non redimit
> vitrium avari:
> virtus temperantia
> guidam singulari
> debet medium
> ad utrumque vitium
> cante contemplari.

The poems are everywhere and of every kind, and vary from the hymns and the gravely passionate love lyrics of Abelard to the hard and modern confession of the arch-poet. But the most famous and comprehensive collection is that which has come to be known as the MS. of Benedictbeuren. When the abbey of Benedictbeuren was dissolved it somehow drifted to the Hof-Bibliothek at Munich, where it was discovered early in the last century. The MS. is a collection of students' poems of the twelfth century. They are of all kinds, love poems, drinking songs, satires on the failures of the age, and the outpourings of the poetic spirit passing through the "deep but dazzling darkness" of the immediate apprehension of God in the mystical vision. Its chief note is that of a youthful, carefree joy of the spirit, poem after poem saluting the spring sun shining, birds singing, girls dancing, leaves budding, and winter gone,

> Time's shut up and Spring
> Hath broken prison,
> Into clearer skies
> Hath the sun risen,
> Purple flowers the heath.
> Spring, put thy kingship on,
> Reborn to gleaming beauty
> From frozen earth.

THE GOLDEN MIDDLE AGE

Well might the chorus of one song be
>> Down in the greenwood sing the birds

and of another
>>> So short a day,
>>> And life so quickly hasting,
>>> And in study wasting
>>> Youth that would be gay.

And the gaiety, the imprisoned sap bursting through wintersluggish veins, led straight to an impassioned, sensuous delight in awakened Nature; and from there the spirits of the poems lightly turned to thoughts of love—"lightly," for even when denied or intensified through being temporarily withheld there is nothing pallid or self tormenting in the poems, and the Celias, Antheas, and Damarises of the Elizabethan lyric find no place in Benedictbeuren.

>> While summer on is stealing
>> And come the gracious prime,
>> And Phœbus high in heaven,
>> And fled the rime,

>> For love of one young maiden
>> My heart hath ta'en its wound,
>> And manifold the grief that I
>> In love have found.

"It seems not possible that poetry should be as gay as this," comments Miss Helen Waddell, whose translations have so aptly caught the spirit of "the youth of wavering branches and running water" which is buried in the Latin. "They do not look before and after, they make light of frozen thawings and ruined springs."[1] Perhaps some of these were the "Failed

All these translations are quoted from Helen Waddell: *Medieval Latin Lyrics* (Constable), pp. 185–273, and 341–3.

156

THE UNIVERSITIES AND THE EUROPEAN MIND

B.A.'s" and the unemployed graduates of which Europe was so full. Their lives were not wholly waste, and they take their place among the anonymous host in every articulate age who find praise because "they sought out musical tunes and set down verses in writing."

It was the poets who had in their keeping the authentic utterance of the spirit of freedom, for they alone among artists refused to hold themselves bound by the convention that because art is the handmaid of religion therefore the whole expression of art must be consciously religious. The rest of the arts were placed at the service of the Church, partly because convention demanded it, but more because the Church, by its very immensity, was the one universal patron and customer. In one sense it set them free, but in another it bound them. Prose, the sister art of poetry, unquestionably suffered from the guiding hand of the conception of the need of authority in the expression of religious thought. The authority was hardly questioned by any one, not even, in itself, by the notorious crusaders for the supremacy of Reason such as Roscelin and Abelard. In their time, and for centuries afterwards, one had to be careful what one said in writing either about religion, or about any of its collateral branches, such as sociology or political science. With people like St. Bernard about, one could be certain that any passage which did not follow rigidly the accepted lines of the orthodox statement would be expertly scrutinized for seeds of heresy. Hence the incessant "As Jerome saith," "And now mark what the Apostle saith," which is the bane of twelfth-century prose writing. When to the incessant need to take refuge behind the back of a recognized authority is added the eternal temptation of the newly learned to display the variety of their knowledge of the classics, it almost seems as

THE GOLDEN MIDDLE AGE

though the average twelfth-century prose document gave at least a third of its space to quotations. Not even John of Salisbury was exempt, though he quoted with far more grace than any other.

Take, for example, a few pages from so lively and vivid a document as the autobiography of Gerald of Wales. On one occasion he had to write to the Archbishop of Canterbury, and the letter occupies five pages of print. During its course he has quite substantial quotations from the following sources, the Psalmist; the Book of Wisdom, Ecclesiasticus, three times; Jerome, twice; Proverbs; Virgil; Ovid; and Horace, a great favourite, seven times. His editor, rather wearily, writes a footnote to tell us "Further quotations from Ecclesiasticus to the same effect omitted."[1] Even in so great a glory of prose as the Letters of Abelard and Heloise, the same habit prevails, in spite of the fact that at least the first four of these letters were concerned solely with their own personal and heartbreaking tragedy, and were meant for no other eyes than theirs. Heloise writes the first letter, which it is still difficult to read with dry eyes. She quotes but little. Abelard replies, and quotes over and over again from various parts of the Bible. There follow the two letters, which have no peer in the whole world, the supreme literary expression of tangled, hopeless love. If ever the authentic passion of the poets has been caught and expressed on paper, this is the place where we shall find it. Yet even so the habit of incessant quotation has become ingrained. Heloise cannot shake it off, for she is hardly conscious of it. In her letter she quotes from Seneca, Solomon, Job, St. Gregory, St. Ambrose, Ezekiel, Isaiah, and St. Jerome. Abelard's reply is one of the documents one reads

[1] *Autobiography*, pp. 131–6.

THE UNIVERSITIES AND THE EUROPEAN MIND

with reverence and a bared head; but quite a quarter of it is in quotation marks, and before he has finished there can be but few of the great Fathers who have not contributed to it.

Unstinted quotation is always the badge of a derivative art struggling to find expression within an artificially narrowed mould. In the hands of a great master, medieval prose can observe these limitations, and still remain a pleasure to read. But the great masters of prose were few, and most of them were among the historians, where the authoritarian conventions were more elastic.

5. The Battle for Freedom of Thought

"An army of dunces for the maintenance of theology."[1] It is the unkind judgment of John Addington Symonds on the achievement of the medieval university. But he wrote in 1884, and much has been discovered since then about medieval thought in its greatest centuries. To-day such a judgment could hardly be maintained. But one cannot simply reverse it, and write, "An army of educated and civilized men for the freeing of theology." The achievement of the twelfth century went nothing like so far as that. What actually happened was that theology in some of its modes and phases was partly set free from the crippling bonds of orthodox obscurantism by the labours of the scholars. But as the scholars were clerks, and so had a vested interest in keeping the Church alive, and because heresy was in actual practice as well as in ecclesiastical judgment an anti-social revolutionary activity, the battle for freedom of thought was never pushed to the point where it

[1] *Wine, Women and Song* (Chatto & Windus), p. 5.

might become socially disruptive. That was left for Luther three centuries later. None the less, real gains were made.

When the century began, religion was wholly in the keeping of the earlier medieval spirit, the spirit of the great abbots, of whom St. Bernard was chief, austere, heroic, tough, and obscurantist. It had been challenged but only by a few lone voices crying in the wilderness, and they had had but little effect. Berengar and Roscelin had both said things quite as violent as Abelard was presently to say, but their condemnation was almost perfunctory as compared with his, for nobody for a moment supposed that Christendom stood in any danger from them.

By 1175 the situation was entirely changed. St. Bernard was at the height of his power, and no one was ever so sensitive to the least suspicion of heresy as he. His nose was so keen that he could scent it from afar even when it was not really present at all. He had many jackals to help him, some honest, some less so, and all wildly credulous. They saw Christendom trembling on the edge of a desperately serious papal schism. They watched with troubled eyes the growth of heresy in southern France with its concomitant ethical squalor of the society typified in the Courts of Love, both men and women becoming as wanton as cats and living on a moral plane hardly higher. A social revolution of a most unpleasing kind seemed far from impossible, and only the unity of Christendom could hold medieval society together. How serious, then, was a threat to that unity; and since it was on a series of beliefs about God, man, and the world that this unity was built, the man who threatened doctrine was a much more serious danger than the man who threatened landlords. The language of St. Norbert, who rushed wildly round the country proclaiming hysterically

THE UNIVERSITIES AND THE EUROPEAN MIND

the imminence of Anti-Christ may have been extravagant, as St. Bernard said it was, but he gave voice to an apprehension present in many wisely judging minds.

What Abelard and others seemed to them to do was to attack that citadel at its most sensitive points, and under the guise of its friends and defenders. They would admit Greek philosophy to the company of the very elect, claiming for it a real inspiration of God. They would persist in questioning the classic form of the doctrine of the Atonement, refusing to believe that Jesus was the ransom for man paid by God to the devil and the Cross the trap in which the vaulting ambition of the devil was caught. Worse than either, they would insist on the supremacy for human beings of human reason, using as their motto Abelard's startling epigram, "A doctrine is not to be believed because God has said it, but because we are convinced by reason that it is so." "He, forsooth," said William of St. Thierry, "is a critic of the Faith, not a disciple; a reformer, not a learner." The indictment might have been childish but it was formidable.

You may not think or dispute on the Faith as you please; you may not wander here and there through the wastes of opinion, the byways of error. Something certain and fixed is placed before you; you are enclosed within certain boundaries, you are restrained within unchanging limits. For faith is not an opinion but a certitude.

That is St. Bernard writing to the Pope about Abelard's enormities. The first round of the battle was fought at the Council of Sens in 1140, and there Abelard was condemned, and his teaching pronounced "pernicious, manifestly damnable, opposed to the Faith, contrary to truth, openly heretical." As he had stood in the church of St. Etienne, where the Council was held, he had whispered to Gilbert Porée, who stood near, a prophecy that he would be the next to stand in his shoes. So it was, and it fell to Gilbert to fight the really decisive battle, and to win the crushing victory for freedom of thought.

In his youth Gilbert had been taught by Bernard of Chartres, and had passed from there to Anselm at Laon for his theological course. The fact that Anselm had taught him was counted to him for righteousness when he was arraigned for heresy, for Anselm was not only an unshakable rock of orthodoxy, but he was also, as John described him, "a man whose memory is in pleasantness and blessing." Leaving Anselm, he returned to Chartres as Chancellor of the Cathedral and the professor of theology in the school, and there he stayed for twenty years. His memory remained green at Chartres for many years for the special and devoted care he took of the books in the library. In 1142 he became Bishop of Poitiers; but before that he spent a few years in Paris, teaching dialectics and theology.

Of all the many distinguished men whom Bernard of Chartres taught, Gilbert stands first, and without a serious rival for that position. A contemporary called him, "the most illustrious master of our time, alike eminent in logic, ethics, theology, and philosophy. Of all the seven liberal arts he lacked only astronomy." His *Book of the Six Principles* he designed as a supplement to Aristotle's *Categories*. It was at once accepted as second only to its prototype, and was made the matter of heavy commentaries by Albertus Magnus and other schoolmen. Thus to Gilbert was given the honour of being "the first medieval writer who was at once taken as a recognized authority on logic, the immediate successor of Boethius and Isador."[1] But a higher honour still awaited him, for his logical writings were not only highly regarded and

[1] Lane Poole. op. cit., p. 113.

THE UNIVERSITIES AND THE EUROPEAN MIND

studied far into the sixteenth century, but one of them was included in the early printed editions of the Aristotelian *Organon*, and was for centuries accepted as Aristotle's own work.

Before Gilbert became a bishop, however, he was regarded with some suspicion for he belonged to that school of thought which would make of Plato, and of secular learning generally, an invaluable ally to Christian theology, and on which St. Bernard and his friends were never tired of heaping maledictions. The actual theological teaching of Gilbert and Abelard was different both in its approach and in its goal, but Gilbert was wholeheartedly at one with Abelard in that which made both alike obnoxious to all who drew the inspiration of their religious thinking from the abbot's cell at Clairvaux, and such obscurantists were still in command of the ecclesiastical situation.

Their real offence did not consist in the actual details of the heresies they were thought to propound. It lay rather in their whole approach to the perennial problems of theology. They were suspect because they refused to acknowledge and to perpetuate the ancient suspicion of St. Paul and Tertullian of secular learning in general and Platonic philosophy in particular. On the contrary, they, and a multitude of scholars whose inspiration they were, regarded Greek philosophy as but little if at all less authoritative for Christians than the Fathers. They held the characteristically modern idea that the Incarnation did not justify and crown Jewish religious history alone, but they proclaimed that Greek thought was also one of the means whereby mankind was prepared for the coming of the Saviour. These two were elements, comparable in importance and not unequal in influence, of the historic situation which Christ found and transformed. They were parallel lines of progress, which could only meet in their common appropriation by Jesus and His Gospel.

Now as Plato had passionately proclaimed that goodness was the vital and essential attribute of the Divine, as Aristotle had added to that the grace of energy, and as Plato, and all who followed him, had used language which distinctly and definitely fore-shadowed the doctrine of the Blessed Trinity, it is difficult to comprehend why sincere Christians of the type of Bernard of Clairvaux and his followers should have objected so violently to a grateful recognition of Plato's importance in Christian thought, and of an attribution to him of high authority in theological history. They did so for two reasons. First, they objected because such teaching seemed to imply a weakening on the question of St. Augustine's doctrine of predestinarianism. Throughout the Middle Ages Augustine enjoyed an authority scarcely less than that of the Bible itself, and though much of what he had written was not in the least inconsistent with the Platonic view of God and His attributes, nothing that Plato had taught could be squared with Augustinian predestinarianism. They objected in the second place because this insistence on the divine revelation in Greek thought was a novelty in the sense that there was nothing in the Scripture to warrant it. St. Paul had warned Timothy against the "profane and vain babblings, and oppositions of knowledge falsely so called," a prohibition which affected all novelties in matters of faith, and a text constantly on the lips of St. Bernard and his intimates, as they peered apprehensively at a company of educated churchmen, who, by daring to apply Reason to matters of Faith seemed to be, and indeed were, casting doubts on the fundamentalist interpretation of Scrip-

THE UNIVERSITIES AND THE EUROPEAN MIND

ture. Biblical fundamentalism was not an invention of the Reformation, but a vital medieval principle.

Gilbert's real offence was that he stood wholeheartedly by the new tradition, and was much the ablest and most influential exponent of it. His actual teaching was extremely difficult to follow, and nobody who was not a trained philosopher could hope to understand it. But the self-appointed censors of theology included no one who possessed any serious philosophic qualifications for their task, and to them it seemed that Gilbert's teaching, especially on the Trinity, approached the diffuse unprecision of mystical pantheism.

He began by so emphasizing the fundamental absoluteness of God as the basis of all creation that he denied that God could possess "substance." This must be so because substance cannot exist without its "accidents," and it cannot be held that the insubstantial Divine Spirit is compounded of "accidents." God is simply Being, an absolute beyond analysis or definition. "It is incorrect therefore to say that His substance, divinity, is God; we can speak only of the substance by virtue of which He is God."[1] But if this is so, the three Persons of the Trinity must be external to the Godhead, since if they were conceived of as being within It, they would become the very "accidents" which Gilbert begins by saying that the Godhead cannot of Itself possess. This is not to deny the being or the unity of the Trinity, but to make an extremely subtle distinction between Godhead in Its internal and external manifestation.

All this was written in his commentary on Boethius. When, however, he became Bishop of Poitiers, he began to give himself to the study of Hilary, much the most difficult of the Fathers and a predecessor of his in the see of Poitiers, and dis-

[1] R. Lane Poole. op. cit., p. 158.

covered there fresh confirmation of the Trinitarian views he had already set forward in his earlier work. He discussed the matter with his two embarrassed and alarmed archdeacons, Calo and Arnold "who laughs not"; and then, on their remonstrating with him, he summoned his clergy together and expounded the whole body of his thought in a charge to them. It is hardly likely that either the archdeacons or the diocesan clergy understood it, for distinctions and arguments so subtle as Gilbert's can only be grasped as the fruit of long and patient study of them, and only then by those who are accustomed to deal in abstractions. It is not possible to suppose that Gilbert wrote heresy in ignorance, and less possible still to imagine that he meant it. But that his works could be sincerely and not unreasonably construed as heretical by those who did not fully understand them is possible enough. Such, at any rate, was the effect on the two archdeacons and the clergy of the diocese. They appealed to the Pope to declare and to punish their bishop's heresy. Gilbert's letter followed theirs, in which he petitioned the Pope to appoint a day and place for trial in order that he might publicly vindicate his innocence of the charge. Swiftly the Pope's answer came back: he would personally hear the case, and would fix the place of the trial in France, where learned men competent to act as assessors would be more easy to find than in Italy.

In 1147 the synod met at Paris. The accusers had not previously been idle. When in doubt of the strength of your case, enlist St. Bernard—that was a very sound rule in those days, for the redoubtable abbot exercised an authority and prestige in Europe not again to be matched until the days of Napoleon. The two archdeacons, remembering that the mere presence of St. Bernard had been sufficient to ensure the pre-

THE UNIVERSITIES AND THE EUROPEAN MIND

judgment of Abelard's case, had themselves applied to him, and had had a ready response to their cry for help.

The prosecution was led by Adam of the Little Bridge; and, when he had finished speaking, Gilbert called an army of witnesses to speak for him from the ranks of those who had once been his pupils, and were now his fellow bishops. Then he elaborately refuted the charges against him, but that did not clarify matters much, for no one was able to understand the terms of his refutation. The Pope himself admitted that he was baffled. To escape from the impasse, the prosecution demanded that a copy of his Boethius *Commentary* should be given them; but Gilbert's clerks had carefully left the book at home, for they did not think that the members of the synod could understand it, and they emphatically did not trust the prosecution to refrain from tampering with it. All the written data which the prosecution possessed was a sheet of extracts from the book. This sheet was handed to an abbot present, with instructions that he was to annotate the propositions, and produce them at the next meeting of the synod, which was to take place at Rheims in the next year. With that the synod adjourned.

There was, however, a full year's grace before it was to meet again, and the zealous guardians of the Faith from the hideous dangers of secular learning were by no means well pleased with the inconclusive results of Paris. They therefore held a special private meeting in order to rehearse their tactics at Rheims. Of those present, several were English, and included Theobald, Archbishop of Canterbury, Roger, Archbishop of York, and Thomas Becket. John of Salisbury, though not present himself, heard what had passed at this secret meeting, and wrote it down. From his account, cool and objective as always, it appears that the French and English prelates regarded themselves as the champions of orthodoxy, not so much against Gilbert as against the Pope and his cardinals, and were determined to win the day by threatening to secede from the Catholic Church if Gilbert's condemnation were not granted them. St. Bernard himself arranged these more than dubious tactics, and, in addition, he had an unauthorized anthology of Gilbert's propositions circulated. It is interesting to see that the English ecclesiastical authority was solidly ranged on the side of obscurantism.

The adjourned synod met at Rheims in 1148. John of Salisbury was present, and to him we are indebted for the only impartial account of its proceedings. His impartiality was not studied, for he had friends in both camps. He was the pupil of Gilbert and the friend of St. Bernard. At Rheims Robert of Melun and, strangely, Peter Lombard led the prosecution. Gilbert entered, followed by a queue of his clerks staggering along under the heavy weight of the assembled Fathers. This struck consternation into the breasts of his accusers, for all the literature they had brought with them consisted of the single sheet of annotated extracts. There was a prompt adjournment while they raced to the nearest library, and marched proudly back again with a heavier weight of tomes than even Gilbert had. But Gilbert was too ready for them. He at once called out, "I am not to be called upon to agree with other men's works but my own." After this pleasant interlude business began in earnest. Gilbert settled down to a voluminous reading aloud from the books he had brought, and accused St. Bernard of wrenching propositions from their contexts. Question and answer followed. "Do you teach that Divine Essence is not God, but the form by which God is?" "I do not. The Form

THE UNIVERSITIES AND THE EUROPEAN MIND

of God, the divinity by which God is, is not itself God." After some hours of this illuminating backchat, the Pope intervened and threw out of the indictment the more absurd charges. As for the rest, the Pope said that he would erase from the Boethius *Commentary* anything which he found to be heretical. At once St. Bernard and his followers attempted to shift their ground, but in doing so created such a scene of confusion among the lay spectators that it was long before order could be restored. Then the Pope again intervened. He ordered the indictment to be destroyed, and pronounced Gilbert's acquittal in a judgment which must surely be a classic of unintended humour. "The essence of God," he said, "should be predicated not in the sense of the ablative case only, but also of the nominative." With that, Gilbert retired, made his peace with his archdeacons, and returned to his diocese filled with honour.

A little later John of Salisbury tried to effect a reconciliation between his two friends, Bernard and Gilbert. What came of it is told most neatly in Helen Waddell's words:

> Some time after the trial, comes a friendly overture from the Saint, suggesting a little informal conference on some points in the writings of St. Hilary, to which the Chancellor [Gilbert] replies that if the Abbot wishes to come to a full understanding of the subject, it would be well for him to submit for a year or two to the ordinary processes of a liberal education.[1]

The failure of this trial was thoroughly significant, for actually a better case could be brought against Gilbert than had been brought against Abelard. St. Bernard's own tactics had

[1] Helen Waddell. *The Wandering Scholars*, p. 125.

been partly responsible for his failure, and especially his conduct in arranging a secret meeting of his supporters after the abortive synod of Paris. The news quickly became known, and the cardinals protested to Pope Eugenius III against this unconstitutional behaviour. It is John himself who tells us this, and he was in a position to know. Moreover, in seeking to change the real purpose of the trial from the charge of heresy against a particular bishop to a challenge of strength between St. Bernard's followers and the Roman Curia, St. Bernard was flinging down a challenge which no Pope could hesitate to pick up, if he was to maintain even the semblance of his authority. There is no doubt that the Papacy was more than a little jealous of the overweening authority exercised from Clairvaux, and it is clear that Eugenius welcomed the opportunity that this trial gave him of asserting the supreme and overruling dignity of the office he held.

Gilbert's acquittal, however, was significant of more than the gradually increasing prestige of the Papal Chair, and the shifting of the vital centre of Christendom from Northern France to Rome. What it really signified was an advance in tolerance and diminution of the old credulity in religious matters. Abelard had been condemned and Gilbert had been arraigned for reinforcing St. John by Plato, and for interpreting Scripture by reference to the classics. But for John of Salisbury *Scriptura* really means all kinds of writing. "Whatsoever things were written aforetime were written for our learning"—that John understands as referring not to the Old Testament writings alone but to all kinds of pre-Christian literature, sacred and secular alike. In the things of the mind he ignores this distinction altogether, and in scholarship, Sacred and Secular are words which do not possess much

THE UNIVERSITIES AND THE EUROPEAN MIND

meaning for him. He does not argue much about the matter, as his immediate predecessors had found themselves forced to do. To study the classics as well as the Scriptures brings to fulfilment the old wish of Jerome, "Love the Scriptures and thou wilt not love the lusts of the flesh." "The classic authors do no violence to the mental faculty when it has been trained by Christianity: rather, they train them still further." But no one ever questioned the absoluteness of John's orthodoxy.

Scepticism, or, to speak more accurately, a diminution of credulity, was fast becoming a commonplace of clerical as well as of purely scholastic opinion. St. Bernard and his friends may have broken Abelard, but they themselves were defeated by the case of Gilbert Porée. Thereafter each separate innovation in theological method was indeed challenged, but hardly ever with much success. The Christian world had at last become a more suitable place for the speculations of scholarship. The change came slowly and with setbacks, as such changes always do. Peter Lombard, for example, was attacked after his death for the temerity of his Glosses and his *Sentences*. A suit for heresy was brought against the dead teacher on account of what he had written about Christ's human nature. Walter of St. Victor stormed against "the diabolical arguments of the Lombard, one of the labyrinths of France, who, inflated with the Aristotelian spirit, dare to apply their scholastic levity to the ineffable mysteries of the Trinity and the Incarnation." The Council of Tours in 1163 fatuously forbade any monk to study science or law. On Christmas Eve, 1164, the Pope presided over the synod of Sens, which did not explicitly condemn Peter Lombard's works, but anathematized any who treated theology "in artful words or undisciplined questions." There is, however, no doubt that Gilbert Porée's acquittal did

THE GOLDEN MIDDLE AGE

much to clear the atmosphere of scholarship. It was the last of the purely frivolous and framed charges of heresy in the twelfth century, and it was the final nail in the coffin of the earlier medieval obscurantism.

The change was most easily apparent in the field of the search for and veneration of the relics of the saints; and in this field its limitations are also most clearly perceived. It was not that anyone seriously doubted that relics were truly efficacious, but that the efficacious relics gradually ceased to be purely trivial. One of the most moving passages in the Chronicle of Jocelyn of Brakelond is that where Abbot Samson prostrates himself before the embalmed body of St. Edmund: the reader is unquestionably in the presence of genuine and authentic religious devotion. Gerald of Wales forgets all his perky boasting and his self-justification when he comes to describe the discovery of the relics of King Arthur at Glastonbury. John of Salisbury himself asked a friend in Rome to find him relics of the Three Kings, whose bodies had been removed there when Milan was captured by Frederick Barbarossa. He requested, further, that a relic of St. Ursula should be sent to him. He received them all, and bequeathed them to Chartres Cathedral. It was this sort of entry in an inventory of a church's treasures which gradually ceased to impress:

A piece of the Lord's Sign of the Cross, of His lance and His column. Of the manna which rained from heaven. Of the stone whereon Christ's blood was spilt. Item, another little cross of silvered wood, containing pieces of the Lord's sepulchre and of St. Margaret's veil. Of the Lord's cradle in a certain copper reliquary. In a certain crystal vessel, portions of the stone tables whereon God wrote the law for Moses with His finger. Item, in the same vessel of the stone whereupon St. James crossed the sea. Item, of the Lord's winding sheet.

THE UNIVERSITIES AND THE EUROPEAN MIND

Item, of Aaron's rod, of the altar whereon St. Peter sang mass, of St. Boniface: and all this in a glass tube.[1]

Of such nonsense and idolatry as this people began to ask questions. Guibert, Abbot of Nogent, for example, writing as early as 1119, had firm things to say on the subject. Had John the Baptist two heads? If not, why is one preserved at Constantinople and another at d'Angely? If the Abbey of St. Medard has what is truly a tooth of Christ, can He be said to have fully risen from the dead? How comes it that in France alone, no less than five churches claim to possess the authentic relic of the Lord's circumcision?

Here, as elsewhere, it is John of Salisbury who most completely illustrates the fundamental attitudes of the scholarly Christian mind. He was no sceptic, but he was thoroughly detached, and one of his books, the *Metalogicus*, is virtually a defence of philosophic doubt under the form of an examination of rival philosophies of the Christian life, and it illustrates the limits to which such a dubiety could then extend.

The fact that at bottom he was a churchman in the medieval sense of the term, as both the *Policraticus*, and his dealings with Henry II and Thomas Becket show, makes his view of the essential prerequisites of philosophic study the more remarkable. For the *Metalogicus* is virtually a defence of philosophic doubt, so long as—and the proviso is tremendous—the doubt does not extend to such matters upon which the correct belief has already been pronounced by authority. In other words, John held, and announced that he held, what was in effect a modified view of private judgment, and he found no man to say him nay. "There are many questions which every man has

[1] G. G. Coulton. op. cit. Vol. I, pp. 168-9.

a right to answer or leave unanswered for himself," and among them, "even those things which are reverently inquired about God Himself, who surpasses the examination of all rational nature and is exalted above all that the mind can conceive." But such an inquiry which might properly lead to the abeyance of judgment on the nature of God must plainly begin with an examination of the doctrine of the Incarnation, upon which authority had in fact pronounced. The list of the things "about which a wise man may doubt" is curious: Fate, Chance, Providence, Free Will, the Soul, Virtues, Fates. All of them are of such a nature that an inquiry into any one of them cannot be restricted to its subject alone, but must inevitably lead to a further inquiry about other matters which authority had already decided. Authority is therefore enlarged in its conception, and, by implication, narrowed in its range and effect. Reason is divine, but it can be exercised only by the virtuous.

The reasonable soul is the habitation of God, by participation in whom all things exist: the good man therefore . . . may be trusted to *know*. It is thus that John is able to declare that freedom is the most glorious of all things, because it is inseparable from, if not identical with, virtue.[1]

But that the hypothetical freedom of the future, which only virtue could confer, should proceed from the propriety and necessity of philosophic doubt in many matters of religion to be granted in the here and now to the wise is indeed a remarkable view for a medieval churchman to take and to "get away with." Abelard's defence of Reason had been more graphic and infectious, but it had not been anything like as sceptical.

[1] R. Lane Poole. op. cit., p. 196.

THE UNIVERSITIES AND THE EUROPEAN MIND

Yet he had been condemned, and John was never even challenged. It is surely not reading too much into the argument to say that John is trying to justify his innate scepticism. There is no evidence for the view that he doubted the truth of Christianity; but there is ample evidence that his was the essentially sceptical mind. The *Metalogicus* is a brilliant attempt at self-explanation and self-justification. What John doubted was not Christianity, but the usefulness of human effort; and the more one studies him the more one is reminded of so modern a figure as Arthur James Balfour.

This, of course, does not in the least imply that John ever doubted the fundamentals of Christian belief. His religion was absolute in theory and devout in practice. He expressed it in accordance with current medieval standards, with faith in the efficacy of relics, and all the rest. He strove ever to find the just philosophic and historical basis for the typically medieval and papal view of the relationships of Church and State. For that view he was as prepared to suffer exile as he was to espouse it in writing and speech. Yet he was at bottom a sceptic, applying his scepticism chiefly to human nature, and its achievements and aims. Because his scepticism was intuitive rather than rational it could exist side by side with his undoubted love of humanity, and his genius for personal friendship. His view even of his own friends was grave and steady, not in the least ebullient, a little sardonic, and tinged with remoteness. But scepticism never bred in him a trace of cynicism, and he never lost a friend. History affords few completer examples of the way in which scepticism and faith can co-exist within the same personality.

A society in which such a one as John could be held in high honour, be universally beloved, and die a bishop of Chartres, was plainly one in which obscurantism in things religious was in retreat. Learning was in process of defeating ignorance, and truth was triumphing over fear. A social structure at once truly civilized and truly medieval was a good deal more than an empty dream of the visionaries: it was a real goal, distant but plainly visible, and it was not irrational to hope and to work for it. Yet things did not so happen. Within three hundred years all that was base in the Christian medieval economy had triumphed over much of the good, and the progress that the striving of the twelfth-century scholastic movement had brought to birth. The twin revolutions of the Renaissance and the Reformation were the inevitable result. When they were over the medieval civilization had disappeared.

It was one of the great disappointments of history. Why did things happen so? There are a multitude of reasons, some profound and some apparently trivial. But one of them is that the battle for the freedom of theological speculation and for the supremacy of reason had been won too easily and too fast. The situation played straight into the hands of the heretics, and the heretics were much more than people who had odd ideas about religion: they were social revolutionaries without meaning to be anything of the sort, and their views about such matters as the creed were social even more than ecclesiastical dynamite. That is why they were universally detested.

Heresy was nothing new. In Northern Italy, for instance, heresy had always existed, and the worship of the old gods had lingered on here and there. In Ravenna in the year 1000 this subterranean paganism had issued forth in an open and widespread movement for the re-establishment of the old gods. Moving into the twelfth century, the old classic paganism

THE UNIVERSITIES AND THE EUROPEAN MIND

shows itself again at Orleans, where at least some of the students were worshipping the old gods again at various altars. But whereas paganism of the old kind was always cropping up, and was never more than a nuisance, Christian heresy began to be a serious menace. The particular heresy was generally some variant of Marischeeism, the gloomy faith which holds that all matter is essentially and radically evil. It was widespread in Lombardy, having been brought there from Bulgaria. In all the trading centres of northern France it existed. The Waldensian heresy was a form of it. But far more serious still was the situation in Provence, where the Albigensian heresy was soon to hold whole districts and provinces in its grip, and where its universality tempted the Popes to use the fatal weapon of the Crusade to root it out. From this crime the moral prestige of the Papacy never recovered and it has not fully recovered yet.

But all this is the short view only: it is merely to assert that the scholastic movement in the twelfth century did not achieve all its promise, suffered wounds in the house of its friends, and did not stave off, but even, from one point of view, accelerated the final breaking of the medieval civilization in the fifteenth century. On the longer view, however, it placed posterity eternally in its debt; and it made possible all the later victories of the mind. Cornificius ruined humanistic education, but the universities survived. Books were often unwise and harmful, but the means of their multiplication and distribution had been created. The ceaseless exaltation of Reason had effects not foreseen by the early heroes who fought its battles, but in spite of that its vindication was, until our own century, as final as it was public. Free speculation about the fundamentals of the Christian faith led weak minds to heresy, but never again would a reputable theologian cheapen God by speaking of the Atonement as a bargain, the Almighty as a cheat, and the Cross as a mousetrap. The twelfth-century scholar created an enormous bulk of capital value, and we are still drawing the mental and spiritual dividends.

CHAPTER V

THE SOCIAL BACKGROUND

1. *The Village*

OUR journey hitherto has been among the scholars. It was this class of the whole twelfth-century social structure which, far more than any other, held the future in its keeping: the anonymous host of students gave to this century its character and individuality. On them, moreover, ultimately rested the chief weight of the effort of medieval Europe to build a civilization distinctively its own. But they, in their turn, depended upon and their specialized labour was sustained by the broad masses of the people, living under the manorial system in villages, and under the guild system in towns. No state of highly civilized society can for long exist which does not share its benefits, and implant the desire for them, among such as these; and it was forgetfulness of this fundamental law which brought about the swift fall of Periclean Athens, Renaissance Italy, and Eighteenth-Century France. How, then, did the villein fare while the students were roistering in Paris taverns and the Goliards enriching literature by the freshness of their poems?

It is a question much easier to ask than to answer. The mind questing for evidence flies at once to John Langland's poem *Piers Plowman*. Its picture is grim indeed; and no civilization could hope to live long if it was contentedly sustained on the labour of such families as this.

THE GOLDEN MIDDLE AGE

As I went by the way, weeping for sorrow, I saw a poor man hanging on to the plough. His coat was of a coarse stuff which was called cary; his hood was full of holes and his hair stuck out of it. As he trod the soil his toes peered out of his worn shoes with their thick soles; his hose hung about his hocks on all sides, and he was all bedaubed with mud as he followed the plough. He had two mittens, made scantily of rough stuff, with worn-out fingers and thick with muck. This man bemired himself in the mud almost to the ancle, and drove four heifers before him that had become feeble, so that men might count their every rib so "sorry looking they were."

His wife walked beside him with a long goad in a shortened cote-hardy looped up full high and wrapped in a winnowing-sheet to protect her from the weather. She went barefoot on the ice so that the blood flowed. And at the end of the row lay a little crumb-bowl, and therein a little child covered with rags, and two two-year olds were on the other side, and they all sang one song that was pitiful to hear; they all cried the same cry—a miserable note. The poor man sighed sorely, and said, "Children, be still!"[1]

Langland lived nearly two hundred years later than our period, when the decline of medievalism had set in. The conditions of the twelfth century are likely to be better than the picture he paints, but in fact a good deal of the evidence supports his view. The peasant was a villein. He was not a slave in that he had the protection of law, and he might, and sometimes did, win a case against his own lord in the manorial court. None the less he was not a free man. He might not leave his village; and he must give the vast proportion of his labour to the farming of his lord's demesne, often using for the

[1] H. S. Bennett, *Life on the English Manor*, 1150–1400 (Cambridge University Press), pp. 185, 186.

THE SOCIAL BACKGROUND

purpose his own team of plough-oxen. His daughter could not marry without the lord's consent, and this consent had generally to be purchased. On the other hand, he could and did own land of his own, and from his ownership he could not legally be dispossessed. This land consisted not of a whole field, but of strips of various fields, for the Strip System of agriculture was in full swing. Many were the complaints of time wasted in walking from one strip to another at the far end of the village.

He had not a few rights at the lord's expense, food and drink from the manor's resources at times of extra work, and various odd customs might turn to his advantage. At harvest time on most manors the lord ceremonially turned a sheep loose in a field. Sometimes it belonged to the villeins as by right. Sometimes it was the property of whoever could catch it before it got out. At haymaking, a portion of the crop was often given to the villagers who had reaped, this portion being calculated more by the strength of arm and cunning craftiness of the villein than by exact measurements of cubic capacity. At Ramsey, for instance, the peasants could

> Carry home so much hay or straw as they can bind in a single bundle and lift upon their sickle or scythe handle, so that the handle touch not the ground. And if, perchance, the handle break, then he shall lose his straw or grass, and be at the lord's mercy, and pay a fine.[1]

And at Glastonbury, the measurement was even more elaborate:

> If any sheaf appear less than is right, it ought to be put in the mud, and the hayward should grasp his own hair above his

[1] Tr. H. S. Bennett, op. cit., pp. 111, 112.

ear, and the sheaf should be drawn midway through his arm; and if this can be done without defiling his garments or his hair, then it is adjudged to be less than is right.

He had also rights of grazing on the common land of the village, but whether that was really much of an advantage may be doubted. The pig was the universal stand-by, and pigs want more than pasture to fatten them. From time to time all the pigs of the village were led off by the communal swineherd to root up the fallen acorns in the lord's woods. But for the rest, the only feeding they got at human hands was waste, and they must scratch what they could from the fallow land. It is small wonder that these pigs yielded an average of but five pounds of lard apiece.

On the whole, and in spite of theoretical alleviations, it is difficult to avoid the impression that the lot of the village labourer was thoroughly wretched. That it had been worse in the past, and was presently to become worse again did not help him much. The lord had things all his own way. He farmed his demesne on free service, made freer still, so to speak, by the fact that his villein's tools and cattle were used as by right for his service. His financial resources were constantly augmented by the system of widespread fines. An extract from a typical Manor Court Record gives an idea of their ubiquity:

William Jordan in mercy for bad ploughing on the lord's land: pledge Arthur; fine 6d. Ragenhilda of Bec gives 2/- for having married without license: pledge, William of Primer. The Parson of the church is in mercy for his cow caught in the lord's meadow: pledges, Thomas Imer and William Cooke. From the whole township of Little Ogbourne, except 7, for not coming to wash the lord's sheep: 6/8.[1]

[1] André Maurois. *A History of England* (Cape), p. 85.

THE SOCIAL BACKGROUND

Then, to weight the scales still more unfairly, there was the system of Heriot and Mortuary. A peasant died. The lord at once stepped in and claimed his best piece of property, probably a beast of some kind, as his Heriot. Then the Church followed suit and claimed the second-best beast as a Mortuary. What was left for the widow and her brood of probably young children? It was true that a man might win his freedom, but what freedom worth calling by that name was then his? He would be most unlikely to possess more than two or three acres of land. This would only keep him and his family if he slaved on it day and night, and worked far harder than any villein. He was as tied as the villein he despised, and often enough he was forced by sheer economic pressure to work for a villein who had some land but whose lord did not leave him enough time to cultivate it. It is significant that the only freedom worth having was freedom of the illicit, runaway sort, when a man made his painful way to the nearest town important enough to be a Commune. If he could escape capture for a certain period, and by his craftsmanship win his way to membership of a guild he became a citizen and lay under the protection of the Commune, and woe betide the lord who tried to touch him then. All such towns were increasing their populations in this way at an enormous pace during the century, and this fact is the most eloquent comment on manorial conditions. A man does not leave the community wherein he was born and brought up, and face the company of strangers in an unknown land unless things are bad with him. It is only despair which prompts such journeys as these.

Such a journey would be also a great adventure, for very few peasants knew anything about any part of the country more distant than twenty miles from their village. Occasionally their isolation was broken by the sight of visitors to the Manor House, or by travelling pedlars and the like, but for all practical purposes a man's village was his world. From its resources must come all the things he needed to keep him alive, food, clothes, and shelter. The women and children could all weave coarse cloth—a village craft going back to prehistoric times and forwards to at least 1830 or thereabouts, when machinery at last killed handloom weaving. Crudely tanned hides, however, formed the staple of the peasants' working clothing. Masons from the nearest town were called in to build and repair the manor house, but the peasant's cottage, and his furniture too, were roughly knocked together by the village carpenter, often from untrimmed logs from the lord's wood, where the pigs rooted for acorns. Various pictures survive of life in these cottages. "Our fathers," said an Elizabethan writer, "yea and we ourselves also, have lain full oft upon straw pallets on rough mats covered only with a sheet, under coverlets made of dagswain or hopharlots, and a good round log under their heads instead of a bolster or pillow.... Pillows were thought meet only for women in child-bed."[1] There is a gruesome picture of the sick peasant in 1500. He lies in bed with a sheet and counterpane to cover him, and they are so tattered that both his legs have come through the holes. The thatched roof is so full of holes that they have suspended a rug to stop the rain from falling on the bed, the rest of the room having no protection from the weather. The walls are of unseasoned timber which has warped in many places, and the window, unglazed, has a broken wooden shutter, swinging by one hinge, to keep the rain out. This, of

[1] L. F. Salzmann. *English Life in the Middle Ages* (Oxford University Press), p. 89.

THE SOCIAL BACKGROUND

course, was in 1500, when village society had not recovered from the two devastating blows of the Black Death and the enclosures of common land.

In the twelfth century these blows had still to fall, and conditions were probably less appalling. But if the picture of the sick man would show a victim a little less of a skeleton, and a room a little more weather proof and less tattered, still there would be only a wooden shutter to cover the window, to keep the fresh air out and the smoke in, so that he and his family were always bleary eyed and coughing with the soot and smoke from the fire, built upon an iron plate placed in the middle of the room on the floor of beaten earth. The best the peasant could expect was the home Chaucer pictured, a cottage, of two rooms, the fowls running in and out at will, a "fully sooty life" from the fire. Perhaps the best of all pictures of the life of the village is that slowly gathered and pieced together from the old sermon-books. Mr. G. R. Owst has laid all students of humble folk under obligations to him for his research among piles of forgotten medieval sermons and has drawn from them this vivid picture of the daily life of the village:

Familiar sounds of the English countryside crowd in upon us from her ancient pulpits: cry of the "Wepynge babe" from a cottage door, presaging the endless sorrows of the race—"Welway." Why was I resceyved in anny womans barme?" Cry of the "cuckow that evere syngeth his owen name"; cry of the "carte-gweal, drye and ungreacid," that "cryeth lowdest of othere qwelys"; roar of the "smythes chymnye, in whiche chymnye is gret blowynge of belyes with wynde and gret brennynge of fyir"; flap of "the fleyl" that "puryth the corn out of the huske"; Gulp of the "gredy sowe in the chaff soke"; peal of the village tocsin, "bellis" that sometimes

THE GOLDEN MIDDLE AGE

"may not wele be yronge, for thei beth bounde so strongly to a tie that they may not be ymeved."[1]

Or here is the stone manor house, as multitudes of vicars have seen it:

A peep within the domestic hall, itself "blakyd wyth smoke," shows us the hall fire that now "brennyth fayr and lyzt togedyr," now "gwenchethe and smokethe"; the "catte, that sitteth nyhe the fyre," and "brenneth ofte hire hippes," the floor "with grene rusches and swete flowres strawed all aboute," each Eastertide, or straw-covered in winter. We learn there the mysteries of house cleaning—like "as a woman clenseth hur hous. She taketh a besom and dryveth togethur all the unclennes of the household; and lest that the duste ascende and encwmber the place, she spryineth with water; and when that she hath gadred all to-gethur, she casteth it with gret violence owte of the dore." As every modern housewife knows, it is a task that is never ended: "For on Saturday at afternone, the servauntes shal swepe the hous and caste all the donge and the filth be-hynde the dore on an hepe. But what than? Cometh the capons and the hennes and scrapeth it abrode, and maketh it as il as it was before."[2]

And, finally, a glimpse from the same most fertile source into a house of sickness, the sleepless night:

When "the sike man in bodi, that lizet in nizt [lieth in the night] gretli tormentid in his disese, herkeneth and desireth ever more after the crowynge of the cok; and as tyme he hereth hym, he is gretli confortid, for thanne he hopeth the dai be night." Then "the ffesicyan coming—and is in full purpose for gyfe hym medycyns, the whiche scholde be cawse of his helthe. Ffyrste he zevithe hym a preparatyffe,

[1] G. R. Owst. *Literature and Pulpit in Medieval England* (Cambridge University Press), p. 37.
[2] Ibid, p. 35.

THE SOCIAL BACKGROUND

secundary a purgatyfe, and aftyr that a proper sanatyff," washes the wound with a "leyghe" of ashes and water like that used by the "lawnder," or lets his blood as the case may be.[1]

"The whiche scholde be cawse of his helthe"—but it is very doubtful if it often was, and not merely because of the mad and horrid "cures" applied to various kinds of disease. There are of course no statistics, but it is impossible to avoid the impression that the twelfth-century village was a thoroughly unhealthy place, and that once a peasant had fallen ill of anything much more serious than a cold in the head there was not much likelihood of his getting better again. The death rate for young children was very high, partly because of the unhygienic conditions of life, and still more perhaps because of the chronic inbreeding which the policy of the lord to prevent marriages outside the manor involved. It is very doubtful whether the population of England even doubled itself between the Norman Conquest and the Black Death; and it has been computed that in the twelfth century it took a village community two years to add one soul to its population.

2. *The Town*

Whilst the population of the villages was growing very slowly, if at all, that of the towns was increasing at an altogether phenomenal pace. The frailty of the human flesh when money is scented in the distance is both ancient and modern, and in the Middle Ages, no less than to-day, the towns were the places where you had to live if you wanted to get rich quickly.

[1] G. R. Owst. *Literature and Pulpit in Medieval England* (Cambridge University Press), p. 36.

THE GOLDEN MIDDLE AGE

Ambition for money or for power thus filled the city streets, but not these two things only. The towns gained almost as much from the wretchedness of life in the country for all but the lord of the manor and the manorial officials.

There was a constant influx of runaway villeins. Freedom was of course to be had by more legal but also by far more expensive means, the winning of manumission from the lord. In the long run, however, it cost far less and was a good deal more certain avenue to the desired end, to steal out at night and bolt for the nearest town. Once within its walls, there was a really good chance that a recognized freedom would follow. For there were elaborate rules to govern this situation of the absconding villein. For four days after his departure, the runaway villein was virtually an outlaw. If the lord could catch him within that time he could bring him back whether he had gained the sanctuary of a town or no. After four days, the lord could still claim him, but would have to prove his claim in a court of law, which might well cost more than the villein's services were worth. But after the residence of a year and a day in a chartered town the villein acquired citizenship of a sort—not, probably, full citizenship—and could not then be claimed by his lord, provided he remained within the limits of the town. His status in the town was not necessarily satisfactory from a social point of view, but it was at any rate better and happier, and above all, freer, than the life from which he had escaped. Mr. H. S. Bennett, whose knowledge of this problem is probably unrivalled, cautiously concludes his picture of the runaway villein and his estimate of his chances of winning a happier life by saying:

The towns, on the whole, certainly gave a considerable measure of protection to the serf, so long as he exercised due

THE SOCIAL BACKGROUND

caution in leaving the town. In general, however, the towns' beneficent activities stopped here. The advancement of the serf was not particularly dear to the citizens' hearts. Indeed, we shall not be far wrong if we look at it in quite another light. To the majority of townsmen the landless serf was like the casual labourer is to the contractor to-day. He assumes little responsibility for him, but uses him if and when and where required, and then turns him adrift. In the medieval town there was great demand for casual labour; and the more highly organized the gilds became, the more they found it beneath their dignity to carry out the many necessary functions of day-to-day town life. We may imagine him employed on sporadic scavenging; on digging the foundations for buildings and doing navvy's work on the City walls; acting as porter and carrying heavy loads from river to warehouse, hanging about inns, and assisting carriers and ostlers; doing the rough work incident on the housing and feeding of a master's apprentices and journeymen.[1]

Not, of course, an idyllic life, but far preferable to anything the twelfth-century village could offer. Towns, moreover, though not health resorts, as the records of the plague show, were certainly more healthy than villages. A surprising amount of thought and care was given to sanitary regulations. At Oxford, for example, constant orders were issued that streets must be cleansed, and that cattle must not be slaughtered within the city walls. Every householder must regularly wash the stretch of pavement in front of his premises.

London was no more England then than it is to-day; but it was a microcosm of the kingdom, and, in some sense, an arbiter of its destinies by reason of its wealth and its position as the capital city.

Among the noble cities of the world that are celebrated by

[1] op. cit., p. 302.

THE GOLDEN MIDDLE AGE

Fame, the City of London, seat of the Monarchy of England, is one that spreads its fame wider, sends its wealth and wares further, and lifts its head higher than all others. It is blest in the wholesomeness of its air, in its reverence for the Christian faith, in the strength of its bulwarks, the nature of its situation, the honour of its citizens, and the chastity of its matrons.[1]

The panegyric is Fitzstephen's, who, writing in 1180 the biography of Thomas Becket, introduced his hero by providing a lyrical description of the city of his birth. His praise may sound hysterical, but it is not inaccurate in its details. In wealth and power London was what he claimed it to be; and if he exaggerated the surpassing virtue of its citizens, his description of its pleasant amenities was certainly true.

Peter of Blois estimated its population as 40,000; and research has corroborated his figure. Thus by sheer weight of numbers London was bound to be influential, and much the most important city. It had always been intelligently administered, and under the guidance of successive chief magistrates, by using its wealth and numbers as bargaining tokens, it had extracted from many occasions of political unrest a formidable list of privileges, which it had the power to guard. It had been one of the few cities in England which had escaped the evil effects of Stephen's anarchy. In the early years of his reign it had used its espousal of his interests to extort from him the grant and the privileges and independence of a Commune. Later in the reign, when Stephen was imprisoned, and the Empress Matilda entered London, she was cautiously welcomed. But when she at once began to levy additional taxes, and haughtily refused to confirm the grant of the Commune the citizens buckled on their arms and rushed in a body to the

---

[1] F. M. Stenton's edition (Bell), p. 26.

THE SOCIAL BACKGROUND

Palace of Westminster. Matilda heard the tumult as she was sitting down to dinner. She just contrived to escape before the mob broke in, and did not stop running until she reached Oxford. *The Great Chronicle of London* recorded the fears the Court entertained of the London crowd, "The flames of the mob alarms the realm," and when, at the end of the century, a citizen was banished the realm for asserting that London would have no king but its own Mayor, he did but give utterance to what was not far from being hard fact. The largest part of the population of any medieval town was what we should now call the artisan class, and it was largely recruited by runaway villeins, and their descendants. Such people had ample reason for holding revolutionary views, and throughout the twelfth century the town labourer was society's only militant revolutionary. The best and simplest path to social change seemed to lie in the vehement assertion of civic rights as against kings and feudal magnates.

In the second half of the century, it occurred to none to doubt London's pre-eminence and power. When Becket wrote to Gilbert Foliot, Bishop of Hereford, urging him to accept the offer of the see of London, he defined its position with absolute accuracy. "The city of London surpasses all other cities of this kingdom as is well known to us all, my brother: for the whole business of the realm is therein transacted. It is the residence of the king, and frequented more than any other by his nobles." Exactly similar arguments for acceptance were urged on Gilbert by the King himself. The city had the two great attributes of power, the possession of civic pride by all the citizens, and great wealth. This civic pride had its arrogant aspect. In 1135 the citizens had actually claimed that to them alone belonged the right to elect a king for England. When St. Edmundsbury held its annual fair the visiting London traders demanded to be quit of toll. "Having held a meeting about the matter, they sent word to Abbot Samson that they ought to be quit of toll throughout all England." This outrageous claim they succeeded in upholding, for they absented themselves from the fair for two years, which so impoverished it, that the Abbot made an agreement with them that though they should appear to men to pay toll, it should immediately and secretly be returned to them. By such thinly veiled blackmail, and other means more honourable, London succeeded in establishing itself even at this early date as the clearing house of English money and produce.

There is also plenty of independent evidence to support Fitzstephen's glowing description of the essential pleasantness of London. Except for the City itself, London still wore the air of an agricultural centre. During harvest time the Hustings Court suspended its sittings. All around it, not ten minutes' walk in any direction, were green fields and streams. The Walbrooke, the Bourne, the Oldbourne, and the Fleet were but a few of the streams running into the Thames; and the ponds and wells were many. Fitzstephen furnishes a description of Bloomsbury and the Borough of St. Pancras:

pasture lands and a pleasant space of flat meadows, intersected by running waters, which turn revolving mill-wheels with merry din. Hard by there stretches a great forest with wooded glades and lairs of wild beasts, deer both red and fallow, wild boars and bulls. The corn fields are not of barren gravel, but rich Asian plains such as "make glad the crops" and fill the barns of their farmers.[1]

[1] op. cit., p. 27.

THE SOCIAL BACKGROUND

The City and Westminster were both busy centres of a revolving life of their own, and were joined by a great highway, now the Strand, and already the slope running down from the Strand to the river was built over by the town houses of the notables. Of the great historic riverside mansions themselves, not many were built by 1150. None the less, distinguished people had already claimed for themselves the most splendid site in London. Their houses were mostly of the single-hall type, which had not as yet given way to the house of many rooms, each for its own purpose—kitchen, sollar, buttery, larder, wardrobe, oratory, and so on. Still, places had to be found in which the functions proper to such rooms might be discharged. Moreover, there had to be ample storage accommodation for the keeping until winter of the produce brought from the country estate. All the families who lived in them fed on what they produced on the premises, or carried from their estates in the country. They bought their sugar and wine at local shops and such of their cloth as they did not spin at home they purchased at fairs in the home counties. Butter, cheese, and candles were made on the premises; and daily, heavy mud-splashed waggons, filled with produce from their manors, lumbered up to the doors, and unloaded their freight. Their rooms were bright, painted a vivid green, spangled with stars, or covered by tapestries or mural paintings. Light came in through little windows, filtering through panes of white ox-horn shaved so thin as to be transparent.

Shops lined all the streets, in pattern like the stalls of the bazaar in an eastern town, with wares displayed for sale on open booths, and behind, the toiling apprentices making fresh goods for sale. London even boasted a restaurant, or, to be

THE GOLDEN MIDDLE AGE

pedantic, a row of cookshops, somewhere on the Embankment.

There daily according to season, you may find viands, dishes roast fried and boiled, fish great and small, the coarser flesh for the poor, the more delicate for the rich, such as venison and birds both big and little. If friends, weary with travel, should of a sudden come to any of the citizens, and it is not their pleasure to wait fasting till fresh food is brought and cooked, they hasten to the river bank, and there all things desirable are ready to their hand. However great the infinitude of knights or foreigners that enter the city or are about to leave it, at whatever hour of night or day . . . they turn aside thither . . . and refresh themselves, each according to his own manner. . . . Now this is a public cookshop, appropriate to a city and pertaining to the art of civic life.[1]

Passing eastward to Temple Bar, and by the bridge over the Fleet River, where there was a little wharf with barges tied up, unloading stone for the rebuilding of St. Paul's, the traveller left the countryside behind him, and came at last into the full swing of the crowded, tumultuous life of the city. He walked uncomfortably on cobbled streets, which smelt slightly from the pools of drainage and heaps of refuse thrown on to them from the windows above, the buildings overhanging on each side, so that while the surface of the streets was narrow, the sky above could be seen only through pale contracted slits. These houses were wooden, with thatched roofs, and at least every other one had an open booth on the ground floor, with wares displayed for sale. Most of these booths employed runners to beset casual passers-by with voluble and shrill importunities; and in rooms behind them, craftsmen were toiling for long hours making the goods for

[1] Fitzstephen. op. cit., p. 28.

THE SOCIAL BACKGROUND

sale. Before such shops as sold food, heavy waggons stood drawn up, unloading all the varieties of produce the English countryside provided. The streets were crowded by wayfarers and idlers, and also by a vast number of dogs, whose kennels were everywhere in evidence. One of the chief civic problems of the day was provided by bands of half-wild and homeless dogs, which infested the streets at night.

The crown of the city was the cathedral church of St. Paul, set on the top of its highest hill. In 1087 had occurred perhaps the most disastrous of all London's fires, in which the old St. Paul's had perished. With a spirit of truly medieval magnificence, the people and the bishop had then resolved that they would build the hugest cathedral in England, and had drawn up a set of plans so ambitious that all who saw them asked whether the building would ever be finished. The bishop began by purchasing and demolishing many houses in the neighbourhood in order to provide a close, which the earlier cathedral had lacked. The king allowed barges to land stone for the building free of duty at the wharf in the River Fleet, and also gave the stone from an ancient royal dwelling which was being demolished.

The work was delayed by further fires in 1132 and 1136, which damaged, but did not destroy, the new St. Paul's. As a result, the cathedral was not completed in 1150. It had no spire; but enough of the general structure was finished to show the wonder of London that it was destined to be. In contrast to Westminster Abbey, it was more sombre than gay, for the immense height and length of the nave, and the long line of straight pillars running the length of the nave, and stretching from floor to vaulted roof, gave to the whole the atmosphere of austerity, which was hardly dispelled by the customary

THE GOLDEN MIDDLE AGE

cheerfulness of the interior decorations. It was a cruciform church, and later a tall spire was to stand at the cross-over, supported at each corner by vast flying buttresses. And further flying buttresses ran right round the cathedral from the roof of the ambulatory to the top of the clerestory windows.

The people doubted whether such a church as this could ever be finished. The plans of it seemed so visionary and grandiose. But by the time that Becket became Archbishop it had been finished, and one of the "sights" of London was that most charming of Deans, Ralph Diceto, delighting to wander about the aisles of his great church, talking to chance visitors about it, and showing them round.

The life of the Church in the City was thus vigorous. In 1166 London contained no less than 126 parish churches and 13 monasteries, and though some were tiny, many were surprisingly large. During the century there was an enormous amount of church building, and the citizen of the twelfth century must have been as well accustomed to the sight of scaffolding as his modern successor.

The Church, was also responsible for London's two schools, St. Paul's and St. Martin's le Grand. Fitzstephen had more to say about their recreation than their work, and, as became so good a reporter, he described only the more exciting moments. A clear picture of boys at play emerges from his description. We can see them shying stones at a wretched cockerel, tied by one leg to the railings of St. Paul's churchyard; boar-baiting; cheering whilst bulls, bears, and dogs fought to the death in a wild melee: or, more civilized pastime, enjoying the twelfth-century equivalent of bumping races on the river; skating on it when it was frozen; and playing community football in the fields under the old wall.

THE SOCIAL BACKGROUND

Drunkenness and fires were named by Fitzstephen as the two blots on the fair escutcheon of London. But, in actuality, a plague more serious than either was crime. It was hardly safe to go out at night alone, and it was suicidal to carry money through those narrow, unlit streets during the hours of darkness. Henry I had done something to bring order and security to such citizens as wished to be abroad after dark by appointing a body of constables, and arming them with flaming torches. But it was common for large bodies of men, avoiding the constables, to raid wealthy houses, and to murder any wandering stranger they might find in the streets if he did not immediately hand over to them what he carried. Such wayfarers were indeed often murdered whether they parted with their money or not. Stowe takes from the author of the *Gesta Henrici Secundi* a vivid story which was a quite typical London scene:

It fortuned that, as a crew of young and wealthie citizens assembling together in the night, assaulted a stone house of a certaine rich man, and breaking through the wall, the good man of that house, having prepared himself with other in a corner, when hee perceyved one of the theeves named Andrew Bucquint to leade the way, with a burning brand in one hand, and a pot of coales in the other, which he assaied to kindle with the brand, he flew upon him, and smote off his right hand, and then with a loud voice cried Theeves: at the hearing whereof the theeves tooke their flight, all saving hee that had lost his hande, whom the goodman next morning delivered to Richard de Lucie, the King's Justice. This theefe, upon warrant of his life, appeached his confederates, of whom many were taken, and many were fled. Among the rest that were apprehended, a certaine citizen of great countenance, credit, and wealth, named John Senex, who, forasmuch as he could not acquit himself by the waterdome [Trial by ordeal of Fire and Water] offered to the King five hundred pounds of silver for his life: but forasmuch as he was condemned by the judgement of the water, the King would not take the offer, but commanded him to be hanged upon the gallows, which was done, and then the Citie became more quiet for a long time after.

As the reign wore on, the streets of London became noticeably safer for casual passers-by. Sermon books of a hundred years later disclose the presence of "cacchepolis" who, having caught a criminal, dragged him "upon the pavement at the tailles of hors til tyme that the pavement have i-frett the fleshe fro the bones".[1] But the small beer of crime was not diminished by such horrid punishments, which in any case were too gruesome for twelfth-century taste. Tradesmen continued to show an almost praiseworthy ingenuity in cheating the housewife. The turbulent citizen could not refrain himself from uttering outcries and insults against his civic rulers—an offence with extremely severe penalties attaching to it. Punishments were heavy, but not savage. Humiliations, whether in the stocks or by public penance or public ridicule, were the favourite medieval weapons for dealing with minor offences. For worse crimes, death was the penalty.

The twelfth was an articulate century, prolific in written records; and so many are the references to London and the manner of life of its citizens that a quite large volume could be written on twelfth-century London. It would have gloomy as well as great things to note, but when all had been said, it would be a justification of and a commentary upon Fitzstephen's words, "In truth, a Good City."

[1] Owst. op. cit., p. 33.

THE SOCIAL BACKGROUND

3. *The English at Home*

Perhaps the most significant of all facts about medieval London, as about medieval Europe, was the passion of its people for vivid colour, in their houses, in their churches, and on their clothes. It reveals much that is essential in the twelfth-century English spirit, and most strange to us, their successors, who live to-day.

Where there is a love of colour for its own sake, there will also be an air of exuberant gaiety. Every competent observer of the life of England in this period was impressed by it. Alexander Neckham, Walter Map, John of Salisbury, Fitzstephen, all of them very different writers, speak of it; and they are corroborated by the accounts of visiting strangers from the Continent. These last, indeed, looked somewhat sourly on the cheerful gaiety all around them. Contrasting the Englishman's smiling demeanour with the essential *gravitas* of the French, they supposed it to be mere light frivolity, and a symptom of incompetent irresponsibility. "But for their levity," said Pope Eugenius III, "the English are by nature better fitted than the men of any other nation for any enterprise they might undertake." They were, he thought, lazy. They took too many holidays—every single saint's day—and on their holidays they loved too greatly the noisy buffoonery of travelling clowns and jongleurs, of which there were innumerable companies always passing from village to village. The graver, more serious Frenchman was apt to be scandalized by the boisterous mirth he saw everywhere in England; and the medieval apostle of "Life is Earnest: Life is Real" found in every English town and village an apt text on which to base a denunciation.

THE GOLDEN MIDDLE AGE

He found still graver matter of complaint in the staggering amount of food the Englishman seemed to require—the perennial astonishment of the foreigner over the British breakfast. In those days even more than now, the English liked their food, and were not ashamed to show it. Every village had its holiday banquet in the local guildhall on every saint's day, and, as a hearty monk of St. Alban's Abbey said, "nowhere are faces more joyous than at the board, or hosts more eager to please, or entertainments more sumptuous." Even so refined a scholar as John of Salisbury liked to savour over and over again his memory of a great feast he had once enjoyed at Canossa with his friend John de Belles Mains, Rector of Synesford, when they had eaten without pause from nine o'clock in the morning until midnight, and Constantinople, Babylon, Palestine, Tripoli, Barbary, Syria and Phoenicia, all combined to furnish the table. A foreign archdeacon came one day to an abbey at Canterbury. He was a little shocked to find that there were to be no less than sixteen courses for dinner that day, and that the drinks included claret, cider, mead, and mulberry wine. It reminded him, he said, of a similar experience at St. Swithin's Abbey at Winchester, when he found that the monks had made insurrection when their dinner was cut down from thirteen courses to ten.

The generality of men and women of twelfth-century England were thus renowned for their bucolic gaiety and exuberant life. John of Salisbury himself sketched their composite portrait: "In conversation he claps his hands, waves his arms, gesticulates, or, for variety, talks upon his fingers. At one moment he struts like a peacock; at the next he blusters like a gamecock." The nineteenth-century Englishman's portrait of the Frenchman is here almost exactly reversed.

THE SOCIAL BACKGROUND

Except for his clothes and his appetite, the countryman of John of Salisbury might well have sat for the *Punch* drawings of the 'eighties of "Moosoo the Froggie."

To espouse extremes for their own sake, and to gain a reputation for bucolic gaiety can be done on little more than an economic pittance. In the higher reaches of the social order, the court, the nobility, and the wealthier London traders, this reputation was tinged by the affectation of a bizarre exoticism. They had the wealth for it, for England was rich. John of Salisbury looked a little askance on the general luxuriance, and laid the blame on William the Conqueror, who sent abroad for everything which was unusual and luxurious, so that "there flowed into this island, which was already wealthy and almost the only one in the world which is self-sufficing, whatever could be found magnificent, not to say luxurious." At a court banquet the food and drink was as exotic as possible; and while the guests ate it they were entertained by companies of harpers a hundred strong. This splendid and careful exoticism in food does not however seem to have been very usual, if we can trust Peter of Blois, who had much to do with courts in his time:

Court chaplains and knights are served with bread hastily made, without leaven, from the dregs of the ale tub. The wine is turned sour or mouldy; thick, greasy, stale, flat, and smacking of pitch from the cask. . . . There also (such is the concourse of the people) sick and whole beasts are sold at random, with fishes even four days old; yet shall not all this corruption and stench abate one penny of the price; for the servants reck not whether an unhappy guest fall sick or die, so that their lord's tables be served with a multitude of dishes: we who sit at meat must needs fill our bellies with carrion, and become graves, as it were for sundry corpses.[1]

[1] G. G. Coulton. op. cit., Vol. III, pp. 2, 3.

THE GOLDEN MIDDLE AGE

It does not sound very inviting, and clearly there was a considerable difference between the Royal Banquet and the Court Supper. The king himself liked to have strange Eastern beasts about him, and was never more delighted than when the Saracen king of Valencia sent him a gift of camels. As Matthew Paris commented, "the King sat gloriously on his throne clad in a golden garment of the most precious brocade of Baghdhad." Thomas Becket, when Chancellor, was hardly less oriental. When he went on a diplomatic mission to France, he and his attendants rode at the head of a long train of painted waggons. To each waggon a dog was chained, "great, strong, and terrible, which seemed fit to subdue a lion." Every baggage horse carried a monkey. Boys led the way, singing English ballads. Becket at home was no less magnificent.

The house and table of the chancellor [says his admiring biographer, Fitzstephen] were common to all of every rank who came to the king's court, and needed hospitality: whether they were honourable men in reality, or at least appeared to be such. Hardly any day did he dine without the company of earls and barons, whom he had invited. He ordered his hall to be strewed every day with fresh straw or hay in winter, and with green branches in summer, that the numerous knights, for whom the benches were insufficient, might find the floor clean and neat for their reception, and that their rich garments and beautiful linen might not take harm from its being dirty. His board shone with vessels of gold and silver, and abounded with rich dishes and precious wines, so that whatever there might be either for eating and drinking was recommended by its rarity: no price was great enough to deter his agents from purchasing them.[1]

[1] Tr. W. H. Hutton. *Thomas Becket* (Cambridge University Press), p. 29.

THE SOCIAL BACKGROUND

The fact is that the breaking down of barriers between England and the Continent which the Norman Conquest had effected, had exposed the traditional and native character of the wealthier sections of the population to certain influences, which, while more oriental than European, were at the time influencing the Continent, and had not yet been assimilated. Knightly chivalry was a European ideal: its degenerate parody, "The Courts of Love," was Arabic in origin. Many of the heretical ideas of Provence were similarly African; and the works of Aristotle were not the only commodities exported from Arabia to Europe *via* Spain. The very architecture and craftsmanship of England at this time showed unmistakable traces of a Moorish inspiration. The technique of much of the carving on Rochester Cathedral, where Solomon and the Queen of Sheba were the subjects, and on the cloisters of Westminster Abbey is plainly the orientalized Romanesque of Provence; and the scribe who illuminated the Winchester Bible, greatly admired by Henry II, was certainly imitating Cufic writing.

4. *The Struggle for Civilization*

All of these facets of English life, its gaiety, its colour, its love of learning, and its exoticism were together symptoms and instruments of the great struggle which was all the time proceeding; the struggle for civilization and the liquidation of brutality. This is the deep underlying motive of the many-sided English effort of the twelfth century, and the key of interpretation which explains events so various as the controversy between Becket and the King, and the foundation of the monastic Order of St. Gilbert of Sempringham. The soldiers in this unwarlike crusade were the whole people of

THE GOLDEN MIDDLE AGE

England, and almost all of them were only half conscious of the goal they were trying to reach; but it is this struggle to create a civilization, which should be truly civilized, truly Christian, truly medieval, and truly English, which gives point and purpose to the whole tract of English history which lies between the Norman Conquest and the death of Henry II. The dream was never fully realized, but in the lifetime of John of Salisbury its realization did not seem at all impossible.

To redeem brutality was the first and most pressing need. The earlier feudalism had been brutal almost by necessity. When life is one long succession of Danish invasions, baronial marauders, rival monarchies, and civil wars, society can only maintain itself by resort to brutalities of all kinds. The most important effect of the Norman Conquest was to set an end to that state of chronic political insecurity. When we read of Harold's last stand at Senlac and Hereward's in the Isle of Ely our hearts instinctively thrill, and our resentment flames against the foreign invader. But without the Conquest no medieval civilization would have been possible—even as a dream. It opened the gate to the Continent, at that time in the throes of a great creative movement of all the materials which go to make a civilization. By providing a stable and secure England, it tore away brutality's justification and excuse. By bringing with them the current ideals of chivalry on the Continent, the invaders imported a code of honour which, for all its Quixotry and artificial self-consciousness, at least held up courtesy to the social inferior and generous assistance to the weak and oppressed as a high ideal.

During the consolidation of the kingdom in the reign of Henry I, "the Lion of Righteousness," brutality seemed everywhere banished, and the struggle for civilization already half

THE SOCIAL BACKGROUND

won. The anarchy of Stephen's reign meant that all must be again begun: that is why the note of the chroniclers' accounts is resentment rather than mourning. It is a grisly story which the *Anglo-Saxon Chronicle* has to tell of the nineteen years. One sentence of it—"They said openly that Christ slept, and His saints"—is quoted in every child's history of England; but the rest is hardly quotable for children, for the chronicler's description of the ways in which marauding barons, like Geoffrey de Mandeville in the Fens and Robert Fitzhugh in Wessex, paid and fed their private armies, spares neither himself nor his readers. The tortures and ravages are described in detail, and epitomized in the phrase, "all was dissention, and evil, and rapine."

Though other chronicles corroborated the *Anglo-Saxon Chronicle's* account, it was at one time charged with exaggerating the gloom, and in recent years a careful investigation of the charge has been conducted in the pages of learned journals. As a result, the substantial accuracy of the *Anglo-Saxon Chronicle* has been vindicated. Though there were certain parts of the country, such as Kent and Sussex, which suffered little, and one or two great cities, such as London, which suffered hardly at all, it is clear that, with the exception of the Black Death, at no time in the Middle Ages did England suffer so bitterly as in the years of Stephen's titular reign.

The greatness of the suffering was due to the large number of private armies. Most of them were so nearly equal in strength that a pitched battle rarely paid either side, and was usually avoided. Only siege was left as a method of gaining a military decision; and as defensive had outstripped offensive engineering, a siege was a particularly long and grim business. Both armies must maintain themselves by raiding the adjacent countryside, and as the siege wore on, the raids were spread over a greater, and still greater area. In the end every castle which had been besieged—and they were many—stood at the centre of a circle of ravished and deserted country.

When, therefore, Henry II was crowned in Westminster Abbey on December 19th, 1154, it was as though an intolerable burden had at last slipped from the shoulders of the English people. On that day hope was reborn and the seers descried the dawning of a golden age. The general emotion was symbolized by the gesture of the chronicler, Henry of Huntingdon, who solemnly closed the book in which he had written the evils of Stephen's reign, and for Henry II opened a new book.

With Henry II the struggle against brutality began again and was intensified. On paper, the chances of a Golden Age seemed real, and to hope for it was not absurd. The native English character was then, as it is to-day, tolerant and kindly. "By nature the Englishman is liberal, his hand is never weary of giving," as a twelfth-century observer said. An acute modern historian, H. W. C. Davis, describes "the general buoyancy and good fellowship" of the English, and ascribes it to medieval Christianity working upon fundamentally kindly natures. "The conviction that good and bad fortune were in no way due to human causes, but to the working of an inscrutable providence, made them at once less solicitous for their own earthly ambitions, and more compassionate to those who had dropped out of the race." All the civilized arts flourished luxuriantly in twelfth-century England, and particularly scholarship and architecture. The Normans themselves, though stern and grave, ornamented their strength with graces, as their buildings showed. They were no less anxious than the

THE SOCIAL BACKGROUND

native English to redeem the ancient brutalities and to create a civilization.

There were many factors standing in the way of success. Chief among them was the existence of the royal forests, covering a third of the area of the country, administered by a special code of law. It prescribed a heavy, crippling fine for the first poaching offence, and thereafter mutilation and blinding; and it was administered by magistrates in comparison with whom "Minos was merciful, Rhadamanthus reasonable, and Æacus long-suffering." The words are those of Walter Map who had been an itinerant justice in his time, and knew of what he spoke. Against these forest laws incessant protests were made. John of Salisbury's denunciations are typical:

> They are not afraid for the sake of a brute beast to destroy a human being whom the Son of God redeemed with His own blood. They dare, in God's sight, to claim as their own property the wild creatures which are by natural law the property of the first comer. And it is often held a crime to snare a bird.

The passion for hunting was indeed one of the traits of English life which mitigated against civilization. When Samson was made Abbot of St. Edmundsbury, though he himself was no huntsman he thought it only consonant with his position to make a game forest. "He made many parks which he filled with beasts, and had a huntsman and dogs. And whenever any important guest arrived, he used to sit with his monks in some retired grove, and watch the coursing for a while; but I never saw him interested in hunting."[1] John himself devoted a chapter of the *Policraticus* to the practice of hunting, which he calls one of the Toys or Idle Pleasures of Courtiers. He

[1] *Jocelyn of Brakelond*, p. 44.

denounced it because to the craze for hunting was due the severity of the Game Laws, and because the huntsmen loved their sport to so prodigal an extent that for its sake they neglected their families and their estates.

The *Policraticus* of John of Salisbury, might well be called *The Civilizer's Handbook*. Its full title is *Policraticus: de Nugis Curialium et Vestigiis Philosophorum* (The Statesman's Book: Dealing with the Toys, or Idle Pleasures, of Courtiers and the Traditions of the Philosophers). It is partly satirical and partly constructive. He begins with a list of the hindrances to good government, and though he draws his examples almost wholly from the Bible or the classics, and rigidly avoids the mention of any contemporary notabilities, his comments shed a deal of light on the social customs of the England of his time. The worst of all evils is hunting. The Game Laws make it so. Classical always, he calls the huntsmen centaurs, "seldom modest or serious, seldom self-controlled, never, I believe, sober." Gambling is almost as bad, and music but little better, because it is notoriously softening. There must be no "*melica pronunciatio*." To believe in omens is lengthily condemned. It is unlucky to meet a hare which runs away—unlucky for a much more obvious reason, comments John. "Omens are fulfilled in so far as they are believed." Nothing happens without legitimate cause, and the interpretation of any event must clearly depend on the particular bent of the beholder's mind. Diseases are cured by medicine, not by magic. He goes into a riot of classical images in his discussion of omens and dreams—Dido and Æneas, Scipio, Alexander's vision of his assassination are all instanced—and he is soon led into a discussion of astrology, of God's foreknowledge and ours, and of miracles. His conclusion is that all divination and

THE SOCIAL BACKGROUND

astrology is useless and therefore wicked. To flatterers a whole book is given, for the prince could have no deadlier enemy about him than a flatterer. John discussed the question with originality, observing that as the world is a stage, when one actor is deprived of his part another's automatically goes with it, and instancing the inevitable suicide of Cleopatra when Antony would not speak Cæsar's lines.

But these are minor ills when they are compared with the fundamental error of misconceiving the purpose of the State, and the source and nature of its power. The end of the State is security, and life is secure only to those citizens who can perceive truth and practise virtue. Thus the immediate aim of the State, rather than its ultimate end, is to bring into being a society in which the perception of truth and the practice of virtue shall be helped and not hindered by the environment of the citizen. The condition of this attainment is the close co-ordination and harmony of spiritual and temporal power, which, in turn, cannot be achieved without a true understanding of the nature of both.

The State is a functional organism. It can thus be compared with the human body. In a lengthy commentary on the *Institutio Trajani*, eked out by a sentence by sentence commentary of Deuteronomy, John proceeds to make the comparison in considerable detail. The soul is the priesthood, the head is the prince, the heart is the senate, the eyes, ears, and tongue are the judges, the hands are soldiers, the sides are courtiers, and the feet are husbandmen. Pages and pages of discussion follow, illustrated profusely from Scripture, mythology, ancient history, but also contemporary events. But if the soul is the priesthood and the head is the prince the superiority of the priesthood follows. In the body the soul guides and the brain rules; but it rules *under* that guidance. Divine law transcends human law, as witness the part played in the coronation of a prince by the Church. Or the metaphor may be varied to that of the Two Swords; or again, so that the *Georgics* can be brought in, to a hive of bees. But whatever metaphor employed, the result is the same. All authority is derived from the Church, and must be used in accordance with the Church's direction and will. "Vain is the authority of all laws except it bear the image of the divine law; and useless is the decree of a prince unless it be conformable to the discipline of the Church."

The political state of the *Policraticus* is thus a triangle. At its apex stands the ecclesiastical authority. One of its corners is the prince, "the minister of the priesthood to perform functions which it is below the dignity of priests to perform themselves." The other corner of the triangle is the law. For, according to John's view, the prince is neither above nor below the law, but stands on a level with it. John's whole conception of political equity lies in the perfect adjustment and balance between prince and law. "His pleasure has the force of law because his sentence differs not from the mind of equity."

But supposing the prince's pleasure is not equitable, what then? Then, of course, he becomes a tyrant and ceases to be the prince, for by overthrowing the law he had already committed the supreme betrayal and denied his title. John is really savage about tyrants. Everything goes so ill under a tyranny that to slay the tyrant is not merely something to be excused under the circumstances: it is a positive duty. "Any citizen who fails to avenge the tyranny when he can is thereby proved false to himself, and therefore to the commonwealth."

THE SOCIAL BACKGROUND

No trick is too vile to lure him to his death, with one exception —poison. He may not be poisoned, but, in any other way he must be killed.

When he had finished the book he sent it to Peter of Celle, whom he asked to remove anything in it which might give offence at court, and to Becket and Henry, who were then besieging Toulouse. John was curiously ingenuous at times. Did he really imagine that a single word of such an argument would not be the worst form of *lèse majesté* in the eyes of such a monarch as Henry? Small wonder that his income was sequestrated. He was lucky to escape with so slight a penalty.

But Henry II was not simply a tyrant and nothing more, though one could hardly expect John to see that. Actually, in the conflict with Becket, in which it is hard indeed to resist the impression that Becket asked for what he got, it was Becket who stood on the side of barbarism in that he was upholding the most uncivilized principle that clergy and laity should not be equal before the law. But, for all that, Henry failed, and ultimately his failure was due to the fact that he was an incompetent father. When allowances have been made for the existence of the Game Laws, and even for the fact that the punishment of hanging, drawing, and quartering dates from Henry II's reign, it remains true that during the twelfth century immense strides were taken towards the day when brutalities should be no more. Had Henry been succeeded by monarchs as able as himself, or even by monarchs who had some sort of feeling for the country they ruled and the civilization they represented, the dreams and visions of the far-sighted might well have been realized. But in that day in England everything hung on the Crown, and the failure of the Crown involved the failure of the infant civilization, trembling to be born. No tragedy in medieval England was sadder in its consequences than the failure of Henry II to manage his sons as well as he managed his country.

Reason, Æsthetic Awareness, and the Art of Living Gracefully—without each of these no real civilization is possible. The medieval struggle for civilization, which came to its height in the twelfth century, achieved at least two of these three goals, and, within the limits of certain rather isolated individuals, achieved the third as well. Abelard, Gilbert Porée and the Scholars fought Reason's battle, and won her right to arbitrate in the fields of religious practice: after them, Peter Lombard, Thomas Aquinas, and Duns Scotus wrote never a line without invoking Reason's aid and benediction. No era can be dismissed as irrational and superstitious which can point to a *Summa Theologia*; and although that monumental work was written in the thirteenth century, it rests upon the achievements of the twelfth, and would be inconceivable without them. If Æsthetic Awareness consists in the ability to handle and to create the masterpiece, the twelfth century passes this test also. It widely spread the general appreciation of the old classic masterpieces of literature, and it produced one or two documents, the Abelard—Heloise Letters, and a very few of the Goliardic poems, which are not unworthy to stand in the temple of fame beside the classic sources of their inspiration. Not, however, in literature but in architecture did the century find the real field of its artistic self-expression. The great medieval cathedrals were nearly all building during the century, and these were expressions of the æsthetic consciousness which not even Greece in all her glory could rival. As for the civilized way of life, the life that is gracious, urbane,

THE SOCIAL BACKGROUND

serene, and detached, the attitude towards experience of a Pericles, a Thomas More, or an Asquith, it is a temper which the twelfth century hardly knew. St. Bernard had it in certain moods, but in others as violently denied its value. Perhaps John of Salisbury comes nearest to it, but he was medieval only in parts of his nature. Yet the Middle Ages had not been left unaware of this gracious serenity, expressed within the limits and through the terms and symbols of its own characteristic consciousness, for it was precisely the attitude of mind for which the school of Chartres in its great days had stood.

But as all history shows, while these three qualities are essential to the growth of a civilization they cannot by themselves create one. It takes more than them to redeem the squalor of a rudimentary society. They must conceive from without, and there must be a fourth quality to which they aspire and which gives them their sanctions. This quality is the hunger for that goodness which is the fruit of the spiritual interpretation of life, grounded in the supernatural religion of Christianity, and, for the Middle Ages, expressed in and through the Catholic Church. This study must therefore turn to examine the ordinary, everyday life of the Church.

CHAPTER VI

THE CHURCH OF GOD

1. *Rome and the Curia*

IF Paris was a siren who sang to the scholars, Rome, the common memory, the inspiration, and the mother of a whole continental civilization, was a name which called forth a reverence passionate in its intensity. The medieval faculty for wonder and worship is unsurpassed in history, and Rome, far more than any other city, drew the rays of this love to itself as through a prism.

> What wert thou, Rome, unbroken, when thy ruin
> Is greater than the whole world else beside?

asked Hildebert of Le Mans, as he gazed with awe at the eternal city, after Robert Guiscard and his Normans had sacked it. *Roma Magna* was its most staid designation. When pilgrims came to praise, all the resources of heraldry, all the adjectives in Latin were not enough. Rome, often conquered, eternally unconquerable, was the Lion, the Eagle, the Star, the storehouse of fabled, unimaginable wealth, the mother of France and Germany, and all their fair cities, the apex and the settled glory of the world. Lord Bryce expresses this devotion in a noble passage, not a word of which is too strong.

By the extension of her citizenship to all her subjects heathen Rome had become the common home, and, figuratively,

THE CHURCH OF GOD

even the local dwelling-place of the civilized races of man. By the theology of the time Christian Rome had been made the mystical type of humanity, the one flock of the faithful scattered over the whole earth, the holy city, whither, as to the temple on Mosiah, all the Israel of God should come up to worship. She was not merely an image of the mighty world, she was the mighty world itself in miniature. The pastor of her local church is also the universal bishop; the seven suffragan bishops who consecrate him are overseers of petty sees in Ostia, Antium, and the like, towns lying close round Rome: the cardinal priests and deacons who join these seven in electing him derive their title to be princes of the Church, the supreme spiritual council of the Christian world, from the incumbency of a parochial cure within the precincts of the city. Similarly, her ruler, the Emperor, is ruler of mankind; he is deemed to be chosen by the acclamations of her people: he must be duly crowned in one of her basilicas. She is, like Jerusalem of old, the mother of us all.[1]

Midway through the twelfth century, however, the actual state of Rome corresponded as little as the manners of her citizens with the mystic ideals held of her by the medieval world. In 1084 the city had been sacked and burned by Guiscard and the Normans, a blow from which whole districts never recovered. The Romans might proudly stamp the ancient letters S.P.Q.R. on their coins in Arnold of Brescia's time, but that flourish did not encourage them to take any active steps to preserve their ancient and irreplaceable monuments. Many became the spoil of the lime-burners. Other statues and columns were exported for gain. Some went to Italian cathedrals, others to the famous abbey of Monte Cassino, and others again to Westminster Abbey. Henry, Bishop of Winchester, visited Rome in 1151, seeking to be

[1] *The Holy Roman Empire* (Macmillan), pp. 312, 313.

made Archbishop of Wessex. He assuaged his disappointment by buying and exporting a large number of ancient statues. Suger, Abbot of St. Denis in Paris—the same Suger who had ousted Heloise and her nuns from Argenteuil—even sought to bring the columns in Diocletian's baths to his abbey, but he was frustrated. With Suger, the despoilers evidently overreached themselves, for in 1162 the Urban Senate decreed that the Column of Trajan should not be destroyed or mutilated, but "remain as it stands to the honour of the Roman people as long as the world endures." But although the Rome of Augustus Cæsar was fast disappearing, many fragments remained—the ceremonial arches of a pagan culture, through which the Popes delighted to pass in festal procession, symbolically claiming the kingdoms of that old world for the greater kingdom of Our Lord and of His Christ—the Maidens' Fountain, of which Gerald of Wales gives so charming an account in his gossip, "a most beautiful fountain, pouring forth cold clear water, and enclosed by man's art in Parian marble, whence it sent forth a pleasant and ample stream to water the fields." There the Pope delighted to rest, "sitting by the bubbling waters of the fountain as it were in a room beside a narrow path and shut in on all sides by waves and waters."[1]

The Pope needed all such retreats: he had the Roman citizens to deal with, the most emptily turbulent of all city mobs in history, drunk with dim memories of their city's past imperial greatness and majesty, and thinking to revive it by the simple process of riot and murder. There was but little Roman trade to employ them, and they would never suffer the discipline of municipal organization, which had given such strength and power to their Lombard rivals.

[1] *Autobiography*, pp. 279, 280.

THE CHURCH OF GOD

Their composite portrait was drawn by St. Bernard with his customary incisiveness. "What," he wrote to Pope Eugenius,

> am I to say of the populace? It is the Roman people! I could neither more briefly nor yet more exactly give you my opinion of your parishioners. What for centuries has been so notorious as the shamelessness and arrogance of the Romans? A race quarrelsome and turbulent; a race up to this very day untamed and intractable, that knows not to submit save only when it is not strong enough to resist. That is the misfortune! And upon you falls the duty of dealing with it.[1]

St. Bernard did but write the common medieval opinion. The reverence which universally greeted the name of Rome was matched only by the universality of the contempt which all Europe had for the Roman people.

Had Rome been utterly blotted out in the raids of the Visigoths, and her memory destroyed, it would have been necessary to invent her. For the Church was the state-universal, and a state must have both a centre and a titular head. It was not for nothing that the medieval imagination feasted upon memories of imperial Rome and left the republic severely alone, that Dante could not find it in his heart to award Brutus any higher place than the jaws of very Satan in the last and deepest of the seven concentric pits of hell, a place so awful that of all sinful humanity only Judas Iscariot was found evil enough to share it. To be a Roman was to be a Christian, and the opposite was as true, to be a Christian was to be a Roman—such is Bryce's famous aphorism. But to be a Roman Christian in the Middle Ages, was to be heir of the shade of imperial not of republican Rome, and thus to assert the

[1] *St. Bernard of Clairvaux.* Watkin Williams (Manchester University Press), p. 249.

authority of a supreme ruler and the glory of his earthly seat. But it was also to deliver oneself captive to the *Curia*, the heir of the old Roman international civil service. And all this was necessary because the Church was a state, unlike others in its ethos, but profoundly like them in its practice, save that its vision was less cramped and its authority wider. This ecclesiastical state was not merely necessary to medieval Europe; it was the lynch pin of its whole social structure. That it was universally beloved was not by any means merely due to superstitious fears of hell: it was far more due to the fact that the medieval Church was the only great human society which has yet existed in which a real equality of opportunity was practised. This practice was both steady and consistent. The ploughman's son did not hold an equal chance with a prince's son in theory: he had it in actual practice. At least half of the medieval Popes were humbly born, and the two most powerful of all priests in the twelfth century, Suger, Abbot of St. Denis and the greatest of all the French King's administrators, and Adrian IV, the English Pope, were the sons of peasants. These were but extreme examples of what was constantly happening all over Europe.

Because the Church was a state, with all the governing apparatus of any secular state, and because it was universal both in its claims of authority and in the range of its daily action, it could not hope to escape the centralizing tendency of the century. The twelfth was thus a great century for Popes. In this statement a paradox lurks, for the earlier Popes of the century were all bullied by St. Bernard whose power was greater than theirs; and during the course of the century there were no less than five Papal schisms, at least two of which were extremely serious. But in spite of this, a century which can produce two Popes as great as Eugenius III and Adrian IV, a papacy more than capable of holding its own against an emperor as formidable as Frederick Barbarossa, and which can end by enthroning in Innocent III, probably the greatest and most powerful Pope who has ever lived, must plainly be regarded as a century in which the office of the papacy flourished exceedingly, and came to the very apex of its power.

And yet contemporary documents always draw portraits of this Pope or that as a pleasant, even a good man, but not as a happy man, for they were imprisoned in the impalpable but very tough net of the machinery of their own *Curia*, or civil service. Why any sane man should covet the Throne of Peter is more than John of Salisbury can understand:

> If he is the servant of covetousness that is death to him; if he is not he will not escape the hands and tongues of the Romans. If he have not the wherewithal to stop their mouths and bind their hands, he must harden his ears, eyes, and heart to endure reproaches and sacrilegious crimes. It is no empty title of his, as some suppose, that of *Servus Servorum Dei*.[1]

Here, as almost everywhere, John of Salisbury is the best witness to call, for he spent many years, 1146 to 1154, as a clerk in the *Curia*, and was a close personal friend of at least two Popes. The first was Eugenius III, a holy man of God, and a man of tireless industry. But it is not the impression of happiness, or even effectiveness at all commensurate with his merits, that one receives from John's picture. Few Popes can have travelled more widely; none can have been more free from personal suspicion. He had been a novice under Bernard of Clairvaux, and in the Papal Chair he remained what Bernard

[1] Tr. Clement Webb. *John of Salisbury* (Methuen), p. 71.

had taught him to be, a simple-minded monk, whose elevation to the most exalted of human dignities awoke in him not pride, but a resolute sense of sacrificial duty. Such men in high office are very futile or very strong. Eugenius was strong. He allowed himself uncommon freedom in retracting the decrees of his predecessors, and he had the courage to make an adamant stand against the heresy hunting of St. Bernard at the trial of Gilbert Porée at Rheims. He laboured always under the disadvantage of physical infirmity, and this, suggested John, bred in him a certain suspiciousness of temperament. But he judged men wisely, and pursued his ends, even as against the united voices of his counsellors, with uncommon pertinacity. No Pope laboured more incessantly than he to remove the stain of rapacity from his *Curia*, but his councillors and servants were too much for him.

Of Adrian IV John spoke still more directly, and the impression is the same.

Adrian asked his friend what men said of him and of the Roman Church of which he was the head; and John freely told him how he had heard it complained that the mother of all Churches was rather a stepmother than a true mother, that there sat in it Scribes and Pharisees who bound on others' shoulders grievous burdens which they would not touch themselves with one of their fingers, lords over the clergy rather than patterns to their flock.... The Roman Pontiffs themselves, it was said, were unbearably oppressive; they went clad in purple and gold, neglecting the Churches and altars which their predecessors' devotion had founded, in order to build new palaces for themselves.

"This, father, is what the people say, since you wish me to repeat their opinion...."

But on the present occasion Adrian only laughed, bade John always tell him as freely as now what people were saying of him, and repeated as his own apology the ancient fable of the belly and the members.[1]

The centuries have left but few glimpses of John's life during his period of service in the *Curia*. But these glimpses are, significantly, those of a great Christian living a rather trivial life far from the scene of the real battle. We see him very ill in Sicily after drinking too much Greek wine; helping the Pope to prepare for an attack—which was unsuccessful and costly—on the unruly Romans; reading the letter of his lifelong friend Peter, Prior of Celle, who begs him to use his influence to persuade the *Curia* to uphold the rights of his priory over a cemetery, which a local abbot violently impugned, thus violating a grant of Anastasius IV, "which you yourself have seen and had a hand in drawing up." He bears with dignity the noisy attack of a cardinal on the *Curia* clerks in general and himself in particular; and he witnesses the pageantry when envoys from Germany come to announce the election of Frederick Barbarossa as Emperor, the said envoys so behaving themselves as to give John a marked distaste for Germans of all kinds. He was never for long without the sight and society of his own countrymen, who, despite their strong aversion to the employment of foreigners in England, are themselves to be found in high office everywhere in twelfth-century Europe. His great friend, Nicholas Breakspear, was Cardinal Bishop of Albano—"a man most kind, mild, and patient, skilled in the English and Latin tongues, a master of polished eloquence, eminent in both song and sermon, slow to anger and quick to forgive, a cheerful and generous giver, and distinguished for the whole disposition of his character." It is John's tribute to his friend, soon to become, as Adrian IV, the

[1] Clement Webb. op. cit., pp. 49, 51.

first and the only English Pope. Boso, Breakspear's biographer, was chamberlain of the *Curia*. Hilary, dean of Christ Church, Twynham, in Hampshire, was the *Curia's* expert in affairs of litigation, till he became Bishop of Chichester and returned home to England. All these John saw day by day. But in addition, various English prelates flit to and fro across the scene, Archbishop Theobald of Canterbury, and Henry, Bishop of Winchester, striving hard and unsuccessfully to prevent his supercession by Theobald as English Legate, or, if that might not be, to add to himself a new title, Archbishop of Wessex. Another Englishman, Robert of Salesby, appears momentarily as Chancellor of the Norman Kingdom of Sicily, who has specially intricate business to transact with Eugenius.

The *Curia* was the seat of the trouble; and yet it was absolutely necessary to the existence of medieval Christendom, and Professor F. M. Powicke goes so far as to call it "the most technical and also the most efficient administrative machine which had ever existed."[1] That it might be, and it certainly did not occur to any twelfth-century thinker to deny it. But how they hated it! Of all human institutions, there is probably none which has suffered as much abuse as the Roman *Curia*. Nor is its bad name merely a result of the rantings of the fifteenth-century German reformers. Luther, Melancthon, and the authors of the *Epistolae Obscurorum Virorum* used pretty violent language about the *Curia*, but the denunciations of medieval writers, whose fidelity to the Pope was beyond question, was more incessant and more violent still.

Money is the root of all evil, said Walter Map, especially when it is written thus:

[1] In *Legacy of the Middle Ages*, p. 54.

THE CHURCH OF GOD

Radix
Omnium
Malorum
Avaricia

Map's accusation was put more neatly than most, and spoke for all. There is hardly an end to the denunciations of the *Curia's* rapacity, and in the indictment, satire, rhetoric, and sheer abuse all take their place. John, who as an official in the *Curia* was in a position to know, had no doubt of the justness of the charges. Petitioners expected to be fleeced and bribed accordingly. A priest, with a case pending, approached John's patron, Pope Eugenius III, with a golden mark, and was honestly insulted when the Pope said, "You have not yet entered the house, and do you already wish to corrupt its master?" Most petitioners John described as coming under one or the other of these headings, "One trusting in the multitude of his riches has entered in with Simon Magus as his guide, finding none to bid him and his money depart to perdition. Another shuns approaching Peter openly with gifts, but creeps into the Church's lap secretly like Jupiter stealing into Danae in a shower of gold." This he reinforces with a denunciation of the cardinals, whose stranglehold of Papal policy he regarded as the root of the trouble, in the person of Giordono, who officially visited Germany, and France in 1131, "making purses shake and innocence quake," and that in direct defiance of Papal orders. The actual extent of the bribery cannot be estimated. Gerald of Wales and the Archbishop of Canterbury entered upon litigation which lasted for years. Eventually the Archbishop won, but he said that it cost him "eleven thousand marks not to mention the loss of his good clerks and servants

THE GOLDEN MIDDLE AGE

who died in Rome." This he admits, was in bribery alone.[1] Gerald himself was considerably more virtuous. He gave the Pope not money but books—not *libras* but *libros*—the books being six of his own writing, and the Pope "who was most learned and loved literature kept all these books together by his bedside for about a month, and used to display their elegant and pithy phrases to the cardinals who visited him."[2] But of all denunciations none was so wickedly clever as the famous Goliard parody of the Gospel according to St. Mark:

Here beginneth the Holy Gospel according to Marks of Silver. At that time the Pope said unto the Romans, "When the Son of Man shall come to the throne of our Majesty, say unto him first, 'Friend, wherefor art thou come?' But if he shall continue knocking without giving you anything, cast him into outer darkness." And it came to pass that a certain poor clerk came to the court of the Lord Pope and cried out, saying, "Have pity upon me, O doorkeepers of the Pope, for the hand of poverty hath touched me. I am poor and needy, and therefore I beseech you to succour my misfortune and my misery." But when they heard him they were filled with indignation and said, "Friend, thy poverty perish with thee! Get thee behind me, Satan, because thou savourest not what the pieces of money savour. Verily, verily, I say unto thee, thou shalt not enter into the joy of thy Lord till thou hast paid the uttermost farthing."

So the poor man departed and sold his cloak and his tunic and all that he had, and gave unto the cardinals and the doorkeepers and the chamberlains. But they said, "What is this among so many?" and they cast him out, and he went out and wept bitterly and would not be comforted.

Then there came into the curia a certain rich clerk, who had waxed fat and grown thick, and had committed murder in an insurrection. He gave, first to the doorkeepers, then to

[1] *Autobiography*, p. 293. [2] Ibid., 164.

the chamberlain, then to the cardinals. But they thought among themselves that they should have received more. Then the Lord Pope, hearing that the cardinals and servants had received many gifts from the clergyman, fell sick unto death; but the rich man sent him a medicine of gold and silver, and straightway he was healed. Then the Lord Pope called unto him the cardinals and the servants and said to them, "Brethren, see to it that no man deceive you with vain words; for, lo! I give you an example that even as I receive, so receive ye also."[1]

As satire, and for sheer verbal dexterity, that is worth an honoured place in any anthology. Its effect, however, was small, for Golias, even in his palmiest day, was never an influential personage.

Had the *Curia*, however, been merely a bribe-taking machine, it would never have survived; and its survival was due to the fact that it was indispensable to medieval society. It was the centre of the whole mechanism of law-making for the Church. As such, it not merely issued all Papal decretals and enactments, but it kept copies of them all, and many clerks were continually employed simply upon the copying and indexing of such documents. The whole of the Pope's personal correspondence was written in and despatched from the *Curia*. To work out an accurate average is impossible, but to suppose that in an average year the Pope issued through the *Curia* some fifteen hundred letters, as apart from official documents, is probably an understatement. Every letter had to be copied and indexed.

There was hardly an end to the extent or variety of the work the *Curia* was called upon to transact. There were innumerable applications to nullify marriages within the prohibited decrees, and for permission to contract such marriages.

[1] C. H. Haskins. op. cit., pp. 185, 186.

THE GOLDEN MIDDLE AGE

Permission to hold benefices in plurality, or to deprive such as held them, passed through the *Curia*, and also all testamentary disputes and dispositions. All grants of assent for the founding of new religious orders, or for the addition of a new house to existing orders were dealt with by the same body. The Archbishop of Canterbury proposed to use his legatine authority and visit the Abbey of St. Edmundsbury. The abbot objected, and sent to the *Curia* to uphold him. On this occasion the bribe was insufficient "unless in the circumstances use might be made of the cross which was above the high altar, and of a Mary, and a John, which images Archbishop Stigand had adorned with much weight of gold and silver, and given to the blessed Edmund[1]." Every time a monk wished to transfer his allegiance from one order to another, or a friar wished to use a travelling altar, the *Curia* had to be called in. A village called Berlin had entertained not angels but excommunicates unawares, and lay under the displeasure of its diocesan. Would the *Curia* deal with its bishop? An abbey wanted an exclusive patent for a special breed of sheep and pigs. A Shropshire rector had lost some of the grants which showed him to hold his benefice from a certain abbey, and the abbot demanded their replacement. Would the *Curia* issue new documents, and what would it cost? In addition, a clerk in the *Curia* had to possess the gifts of a literary detective, and by a special knowledge of seals and handwriting decide whether a particular document was forged or genuine. Lanfranc, when Archbishop of Canterbury, forged no less than nine documents to prove his pre-eminence over his brother of York.[2] The *Curia* rejected them on the ground that there were no seals and "did not at all savour of the Roman style." The

[1] *Jocelyn of Brakelond.* op. cit., p. 7.   [2] Haskins. op. cit., p. 90.

clerks had to learn and use a special and privileged handwriting, called the *Cursos Romanæ Curiæ*, which was extremely difficult to imitate. In fact, the *Curia* was the first great Civil Service of the medieval world, and the only truly international court. Everything which is now done for the subjects of a country by government departments was done, or at least supervised, by the one Papal *Curia* for the whole of the Western world. Small wonder there were so many delays in its transaction of business.

Such delays, moreover, were at least sometimes due to the fullness of the care that was taken to do strict justice in a day when justice often demanded that the Church's officers in a distant country must first make a full investigation and send a report. In Devonshire there was an obscure village called Waplam whose vicar complained to the Pope that the Abbey of Lenton was trying to dispossess him of his church. The circumstances were tedious and extremely complicated. It was claimed, for example, that the vicar was the son of a priest and so incapable of holding a vicarage. This turned on whether the decree of 1163, on which Lenton rested its case, could be regarded as retrospective. The *Curia* waited the results of a long investigation by the Bishop of Winchester and Exeter, and eventually decided for the vicar in a judgment which any judge in any age might be proud to give.[1] But it naturally took time.

The incessant complaints against the *Curia*, however, as a cumbersome and slow-moving machine for the taking of bribes and the perverting of justice also had truth behind them. When Thomas Becket was in exile his party bribed incessantly,

[1] Adrian Morey. *Bartholomew of Exeter* (Cambridge University Press), p. 56.

which was of little avail since the King's party gave the *Curia* bribes still heavier and still more often. Such a man as St. Bernard could not be expected to regard the *Curia* with any great favour, and he knew the extreme irritation caused by the stranglehold which lawyers always seem to get on the life and work of the Church. But he was in a position to know also the necessity of the *Curia*, and the good which it often did. Yet, on balance, it seems impossible to resist his judgment expressed to Pope Eugenius as a warning: "I do not think that even were I to keep quiet and to say nothing, the murmuring of the churches would cease unless the Roman *Curia* ceased to give judgment in untried cases and in the absence of the accused, simply as its members happened to wish[1]." The *Curia* in fact was a gigantic machine for the purpose of keeping the existing wheels turning round. As such it was quite indispensable. But in an age of vast creative experiments, of religious revival, of supreme crisis when civilization and barbarism trembled in the balance, much more than this was needed of the central headquarters of the Church of Christ. It embarrassed the Popes, infuriated the diocesan bishops, scandalized the faithful laity, kept most of the best and ablest churchmen of the day occupied in lengthy and incessant journeys to Rome for the purposes of litigation, and seriously impoverished the financial resources of the Church as a whole by its members' habits of bribe-taking. To the extent to which the whole Church failed in its mission in the twelfth century, the failure was due to the worldly lack of vision displayed in Rome.

[1] Williams. op. cit., p. 249.

THE CHURCH OF GOD

2. *The State of Religion in England*

The state of everyday religion in the twelfth century, the question of whether on the whole dioceses were well administered and parishes faithfully served, and whether the parochial clergy were of a high or low standard, fit or unfit for their office—to attempt any decision upon such questions as these is to enter upon a sea of trouble. Rashdall's modern editors, in one of those bracketed footnotes which tactfully correct and sometimes gently chide the sacred text of the master, draw attention to a more than usually wild remark of his on this subject, and comment, "Rashdall here expressed himself (in most uncomplimentary terms) about the most difficult problem in the history of the medieval Church . . . the problem is insoluble."[1] What Professor Powicke pronounces insoluble, let not the amateur pretend to solve. This study makes no attempt to solve such a riddle, but contents itself in producing a little of the evidence relating to one corner of the European field, religion in England; and even here the evidence will be far from clear. But if it was, and is, a part of the function of religion to provide the civilizer with the ground of his advance; and if, as has been contended throughout, the fundamental significance of the twelfth century for human history lies in its struggle to bring into existence a social structure at once truly medieval and truly civilized, then plainly something must be said about the way in which religion was presented to the ordinary people, and of the everyday life of the Church. The English field is chosen because the contemporary evidence about it is most easily accessible, and because the life of the Church in England was unquestionably of a higher

[1] Rashdall. op. cit., Vol. III, p. 448.

standard than anywhere else in Europe. Here, if anywhere, the Church could become the soul of a great civilizing effort.

In England, a great religious revival had begun. The religious inspiration which, a few years earlier had resulted in the foundation of the two purest of the great medieval monastic Orders, the Cistercians and Carthusians, had crossed the English Channel. "It was as though the very world had shaken herself and cast off her old age, and were clothing herself everywhere in a white garment of churches." The words refer to the achievements of the millenary year, 1000, but they might well have been written to describe the England of Henry II. More than a hundred new foundations date from Stephen's reign, and a hundred more from Henry II's. There was hardly a wealthy merchant or nobleman who did not give of his plenty for the endowment and building of monastic houses; and the people in town and country, who had little wealth to give, formed themselves into voluntary auxiliary bands, and helped to dig foundations, to pull carts, to drag boulders to the masons' benches and all to the accompaniment of the communal chanting of psalms.

The capacity for asceticism which lies behind all this tumult of Church life, however, had softened in subtle ways by the time it reached these shores. It was not less heroic, but much of the obscurantism and harsh unreason which marred the activities of a St. Bernard were charmed away by the milder English air. There was no baiting of scholarship in England, no heresy hunting. The Cistercians brought with them their rather spectacular austerities, and did not raise their reputation in England thereby. "They are proud of their pale faces, and sighing is with them a fine art. At any moment they are prepared to shed a flood of tears. They walk about with

THE CHURCH OF GOD

downcast heads and half-closed eyes. They move at a snail's pace, muttering prayers the while. They cultivate a ragged and dirty appearance; humbling themselves that they may be exalted."[1] The striking judgment is John of Salisbury's; and it is the more remarkable in that John himself was thoroughly austere. He had no doubt, for example, that virginity is a higher state than marriage; but he added the thoroughly English qualification, "Still, some married persons are holier than many virgins," a remark which Matthew Parker, the first officially married Archbishop of Canterbury, approvingly scored in red in his copy of the *Policraticus*. He approved St. Bernard's strictures on music, and thought it softening. He agreed absolutely with Gilbert of Sempringham, his contemporary, "a venerable man and the father of seven hundred nuns," who "forbade them to sing at all." They might "intelligently recite the Psalms" but there must be no *Melica Pronunciatio*.

There was a real English ascetic achievement in that generation, and it was none the less remarkable for being purged of its Continental extravagances. Beyond doubt the purging force was the almost universal hatred of the Cistercians. Walter Map, an itinerant justice amongst almost everything else (for he was the Pooh Bah of his age) used to boast that he made a mental reservation in the case of the Cistercians when he took his oath to do justice to all men since "it is absurd to do justice to those who are just to none." Gerald of Wales was much more violent, but to Cluniacs, not Cistercians. There was a suggestion of making a Cluniac monk Bishop of St. David's, which at once brought Gerald tempestuously into the

---

[1] Tr. H. W. C. Davis. *England Under the Normans and Angevins* (Methuen), p. 197.

THE GOLDEN MIDDLE AGE

fray. Let anyone be bishop—or almost anyone. "But I make an exception of all wild beasts in black cowls. For from all monks and more especially Black monks and all-devouring plagues of that sort may God henceforth and for ever defend our miserable church, lest from being miserable, it become most miserable and perish utterly of starvation."[1] Monks, and nuns as well, suffered much hatred and abuse in England from their fellow Christians. So far as the Cistercians are concerned, it was in part because they were far too successful as sheep farmers to be popular. But the incessant complaint is of their outward parade of holiness. John of Salisbury lashes them continually for their "hypocrisy," but exempts two Orders of Chartreuse and Grammont, in neither of which are hypocrites tolerated a moment. As for the others, they are whited sepulchres. Still, he adds with characteristic honesty, "the least holy monk leads of necessity a life which would be considered most religious if lived by a secular priest such as I myself am."

Cistercians might be unpopular but they had come to stay, and the social and economic structure of the Church had to make room for them, as for their predecessors of older Orders. One result of the sudden increase of monastic Orders in England, to which reference has already been made, was to make very acute the difficulties involved in the means of maintaining them by granting them all, or part, of the revenues of various benefices. Thus an abbey became the Rector of a benefice, and if it could not be served by the monks themselves —a practice dubious in canon law and often impossible in practice—they hired a curate or vicar to perform the charge in their place. The dangers of abuse were obvious; and since Christianity then, as always, had to be mediated to the mass of

[1] *Autobiography*, p. 147.

THE CHURCH OF GOD

the people by the parochial clergy, the real sufferer would be the Christian religion. In 1102 the Council of Westminster ordained that "monks do not accept churches without the bishop's consent, nor so rob the revenues of those that are given them that the priests who serve them lack that which they need for themselves and their churches."[1] The proper share of the vicar was reckoned to be one-third of the value of the benefice. But abuses occur throughout the century. Occasional reformers, like St. Bernard, strive to put things right. He once accepted and re-colonized as a Cistercian house the Abbey of Alne, and his first act was to give back to the vicars the things which the abbey had wrongfully usurped. "Since that same church possessed certain altars, tithes, serfs, and handmaids, which men of that Order cannot regularly hold, the aforesaid abbot returned all of them into my hand,"[2] wrote the bishop of the diocese. But this generosity and justice did not survive St. Bernard's death even among Cistercians; and among other Orders it was hardly known at all. On one occasion, John of Salisbury, when acting as Archbishop Theobald's secretary and *alter ego* was enmeshed in a long correspondence, involving the preparations of writs, sequestrations, and mandates without number when the monks of St.-Omer claim the church of Culham, and, on that being given against them, they lay unabashed claim to Throwley, and get it. Councils and Synods constantly strove to regulate this practice and to purge it of its scandals, but with little effect. So far as English parish life in the twelfth century is concerned, the judgment of Mr. R. A. R. Hartridge, the

[1] R. A. R. Hartridge. *A History of Vicarages in the Middle Ages* (Cambridge University Press), p. 19.
[2] Hartridge. op. cit., p. 16.

authority on this question, is that the system worked wholly for ill:

The abuse most frequently dealt with by the twelfth-century councils is not the service of churches by monks but the inadequate service of them by the underpaid clerks hired by the monks. In England it is specially doubtful whether monks often served the churches themselves. The opinion of the present writer, which the sources are inadequate to prove, is that in the appropriated churches of eleventh- and twelfth-century England, the "mercenary" priest, removable at pleasure and without a settled benefice in endowments, was the rule and the monk incumbent the rare exception.[1]

Moreover, there were many pluralists other than monks. Walter Map was made a Prebend of St. Paul's. At that time he was already Canon and Precentor of Lincoln and Rector of Westbury, and he saw no reason for resigning them. Later he was appointed Archdeacon of Oxford, whereupon he resigned the precentorship of Lincoln, but none of his other cures. Gerald of Wales also had firm things to say about Welsh bishops who "aspire continually to the rich benefices of England, whether by means of translation or by adding them to that which he already has."[2]

It is clear that the parish priest had no parson's freehold to protect him, and that his income was likely to be minute, variable, and insecure. Yet the contemporary documents give on the whole an impression of a body of hard-pressed men honestly struggling to give of their best to their people amid social and economic conditions which constantly hamper their fulfilling of their charge. They seem to have had faithfulness, the rudimentary virtue of the English priesthood in every age.

[1] Hartridge. op. cit., p. 25.   [2] *Autobiography*, p. 147.

THE CHURCH OF GOD

They were constantly charged with ignorance, and horrifying evidence of it can be plentifully produced. In 1222 a visitation was held in the deanery of Sonning. Five of the clergy were unable to translate the prayer of oblation in the mass; and when the Vicar of Sonning himself was questioned, it was found that he knew nothing of the Gospel for the day. But then visitations always find out things like this: that is what they are for. They describe the bad and say nothing about the good, and the unwary in subsequent generations jump to the totally erroneous conclusion that a visitation return reveals the average. Every parish parson must at the least be able to read: canon law requires of him first and foremost that he should teach the boys of the parish their letters, and introduce the likelier ones to the mysteries of reading and singing. The majority, no doubt, had passed far beyond this elementary stage of education. But it is very doubtful if more than a small proportion of the parochial clergy had been to the universities during the twelfth century. Accurate figures are impossible to get. But in the diocese of Exeter in Bishop Bartholomew's time, 1154-84, the majority of those priests who had been to the university were either canons of the cathedral or among its innumerable clerical hangers-on. "At the beginning of his period," says Mr. Adrian Morey's biography, "six out of twenty-three canons bear the title of *magister*, and in one of the charters belonging to his later years, that belonging to the leper hospital of St. Mary Magdalen, the title is used by seven out of thirteen witnesses."[1] Exeter was perhaps the best-administered of English dioceses in that generation, and would be likely to show the most favourable figures. Priests with a university degree were plainly increasing in Devonshire. It did not, of

[1] op. cit., p. 87.

course, follow that a man who had not been to the schools knew nothing, or that he cared little for learning. Nor was the possession of a degree any guarantee that a man would continue scholarly pursuits when he settled down to discharge a parochial ministry. The pressure of his social and economic life told against it. There is constant complaint, coming mostly from monks whose profession relieved them from the temptation, that the secular clergy quickly became rustics again once they were buried in a remote parish: "all here studie is granges, shepe, nete, and rentes, and to gadre gold and sylver," said Master Rypon. Rusticity was always an enemy to learning, and the parish priest could hardly help acquiring the mind of a rustic when his living so often depended on his knowledge of country way and life.

In the majority of villages the priest strove with the serf to win a living from the products of the earth. He was priest first, but agriculturalist after; or, as an early Parson Trulliber, he might even be primarily an agriculturalist. His beasts fed side by side with those of his parishioners on the commons, and he bargained at the neighbouring market against his fellows in the hope of making a good purchase, or effecting a profitable exchange.[1]

But even if all the implications of such a statement are granted, they do not amount to a charge of faithlessness and sloth, and from another source comes evidence which suggests that in many parishes a real and consistent effort was made to discharge the ministry faithfully. The congregations most certainly heard sermons, and the parochial clergy preached them, though there was constant bickering as to whether they or wandering friars were the more apt to preach the Word

[1] H. S. Bennett. op. cit., p. 31.

in the village church. Towards the end of the century there was almost a revolution in the art and extent of preaching, and the people of most parishes definitely demanded that their parson should regularly preach to them, and if he did not, then they would quickly find some friar who would be only too glad to do it for him. That the parish priest did respond to this demand, and took real pains over it, is suggested by the widespread discussion there was on the art of preaching.

It centred for the most part on the problem of whether the classical allusion was permissible and meritorious or not. The ancient monastic tradition of the Church had striven to keep itself unspotted from the classics, generally with marked lack of success. In the twelfth century so liberal a man as Abbot Samson of St. Edmund's could describe the ideal sermon as one which avoided "rhetorical colouring and elaborate verbiage and neatly turned sentences" for it should be "delivered in French, or rather in English, for the securing of the improvement of manners, and not as a literary exercise."[1] But some preachers had other views and liked to air their classical knowledge within reason. One in the diocese of Worcester had actually quoted poetry, and his people had held an indignation meeting after church. Next Sunday the offended preacher began thus:

Crysten peple, thies wordes that I af take to speke of, at this tyem, thay er the wordis of seynt Powl, wryten in the pystell of this day. I rede in haly wryte: I sey noght as I rede in Ovidie, noyther in Oras. Vor the last tyme that I was her, ich was blamyd of som mens word, because that I began my sermon with a poysy. And therfore I say that I red in haly wryt, in the secund book of haly wryth, that I suppoise be sufficiant inowgh of autorite.[2]

[1] *Jocelyn of Brakelond*, p. 200.   [2] Owst. op. cit., p. 179.

THE GOLDEN MIDDLE AGE

One hopes that congregation felt properly crushed, though much more likely there was a second indignation meeting afterwards. This particular priest lived later than the twelfth century, but his problems were the same as theirs. He could at any rate claim the support of the Dominicans, the really expert preachers of the world. Bromyard, a prelate of that Order, wrote a manual on preaching, and came down heavily on the side of using the classical allusion:

From the moralization of Gentile fables a form of instruction is sometimes derived; and it is right to be taught by the enemy, and to enrich the Hebrews with the spoils of the Egyptians. It is to be noticed in this work that the Gentiles and their works are frequently introduced as witnesses of the truth. And if anyone asks what these things, which are without, have to do with us in the doctrine of the Christian Faith, the blessed Gregory replies in his *Moralia* to refute our shamelessness.[1]

Both Bromyard and the anonymous but injured preacher could claim much authority. Gratian had debated this very point, assembling the evidence on either side, as became a lawyer. He had been clear that the classical allusion was justified, and in giving his judgment, he leaned mostly on no less stout a pillar of austerity than Bede; while Bishop de Bury sums up the matter in his usual common-sensible way by saying, "If he have found a profit in poetry, as the great Virgil related that he had done in Ennius, he will not have done amiss."[2] The classics undoubtedly carry off the victory. A discussion which rages so vehemently and lasts so long suggests that the twelfth-century pulpit was undoubtedly used. The comparatively free-and-easy posture adopted by the twelfth-century preacher was

[1] Owst. op. cit., p. 180. [2] *Philobiblon:* p. 87.

THE CHURCH OF GOD

reflected in his discourse, whereat he came in for both praise and blame from his successors. For the sermon rapidly developed a technique and set forms for its delivery; and later practitioners of the sermon, considered as a means of artistic expression, condemned the twelfth-century preachers for their lack of set forms and constraint. They liked to hear sermons which conformed to the rules of the preaching text-books, and the preaching which later became the vogue has been described by Professor Haskins as consisting of "elaborate subdivisions, piling of text on text, senses literal and allegorical, tropological and anagogical." It sounds wearisome, and there were many who found it so, among them a fifteenth-century Oxford Chancellor, who regretfully recalled the preaching of the twelfth century, contrasting it with the arid formalism of his own times.

But it takes two to make a sermon, the preacher and the congregation. "After mete loke thou go to the prechynge," and in spite of the bitter complaint of Bromyard, "there is not a Christian people which so rarely or so unwillingly hears the word of God as the English,"[1] the weight of evidence is against him. People certainly went to the "prechynge," partly, as one of them said, because "we understand every word of the sermon, but the Mass we understand not." The fact is that Bromyard was rather jaundiced on this point, having visited just before he wrote, a surfeit of villages where

most people rise late and come to church later. They only want to be there a short time, and say to the priest, "Get it (meaning the Mass) over quickly, because we have a friend coming to dinner and must hurry back." If there is supposed

[1] R. F. Bennett. *The Early Dominicans* (Cambridge University Press), p. 97.

THE GOLDEN MIDDLE AGE

to be a sermon about the soul's health, they either try to prevent it by various excuses, saying, "It's getting late," or something of the sort, or at least make a burden of it. If they cannot get away altogether, but do stay a short while in church, they pass the time with absurd stories or in useless gossip, not remembering that the house of God is the house of prayer. Afterwards they go home and then to the tavern, and there they do not hurry away, but some of them spend the rest of the day, and until late at night, eating and drinking and having a great celebration.[1]

The material is not lacking from which can be drawn pictures of congregations listening with eager concentration as they sit or squat round the preacher, who stands, with hand uplifted, in his little portable pulpit, set up on the Gospel side of the altar. There are more women than men; and all the feudal classes are represented. The great ladies are there, dressed in their best, wearing their high conical headdresses and long flowing veils. They have probably arrived late, being of the quality, as the preacher bitterly remarked, and have swaggered up the aisle with mincing step, consciously the cynosure of all eyes, "stirring the dust with their trains." In front of them are the commonalty, squatting stiffly on heaped beds of rushes; and behind them stand several men, leaning against a pillar, gravely listening. Their attitude seems to suggest that they are the amateur theologians of the assembly, the deacons of the chapel, satisfying themselves of the preacher's orthodoxy.

The ages of faith were considerably less well behaved in church than are our own times. The people talked, and the preacher had to endure a hum of conversation, unless he could gain their lost attention with a tall story or an apt cautionary tale. Worse than talking, they slept. Many stories there are

[1] Bennett. op. cit., p. 99.

THE CHURCH OF GOD

of preachers dealing painfully with slumberers. Jacques de Vitry, for example, once broke off in the middle of his discourse to exclaim, "Do you want me now to talk to you about worthy womanhood? I am going to say something instead about that old dame whom I see asleep over there. For God's sake, if anyone has a pin let him wake her up." Sometimes there were people who even diced or played chess during the sermon, and others who indulged in "myche jangling and japynge and many other vanytees, settynge nought bi prechinge and teachinge of Goddis word." Others occasionally annoyed the preacher by ostentatiously leaving the church before the sermon began, or no less ostentatiously arriving only when they were sure it would be over. Such tactics, for all their boorishness, are not unheard of to-day. Finally, the people were accustomed to cheer and clap when their approval was won. It seems irreverent, but there was good precedent. St. Wilfrid preached a magnificent sermon on the occasion of the consecration of his great cathedral at Ripon in the seventh century. His every sentence was greeted by cheers; thereupon he promptly invited his congregation to a great feast which lasted three days and three nights. But in the Middle Ages, though cheering was not uncommon, there is no record of similar wholesale episcopal hospitality. That fine custom died young.

After the lesser came the greater lights, archdeacons for instance, who, in spite of the fact that there among them were men so plainly attractive as Walter Map and Gerald of Wales, were universally detested. Their sign manual was reckoned to be the heraldic eagle who seeth his prey afar off. These were the real dignitaries: bishops supported far less pomp; and, what is more, did not, like the archdeacons, expect the parish

THE GOLDEN MIDDLE AGE

priest to support it for them. Their trains of servants and horses which they took on visitation journeys were enormous and the unfortunate vicar had to provide quarters and sustenance for them all. They had a bad reputation for keeping parish churches vacant for long periods and pocketing the revenues. As legal officials they had the lucrative office of proving wills —a practice which survives to this day in the Channel Isles where the Deans of Jersey and Guernsey prove all wills. Whether the possibilities of an archdeacon's eternal salvation were ever seriously debated is open to doubt; but certainly John of Salisbury asked the question. "Is it possible for an archdeacon to be saved?—there are some few exceptions," he wrote to a friend, who had just become Archdeacon of Huntingdon. Archdeacons gave John a lot of trouble. The Archdeacon of York was charged with poisoning his Archbishop. John had to try the case, and acquitted the archdeacon. A citizen of Scarborough complained that an archdeacon was blackmailing him by threatening to prosecute his wife for adultery, for which there was no evidence. He expresses his horror over the conduct of one Walkelin, Archdeacon of Suffolk, who had a mistress and an illegitimate son. When Pope Adrian IV issued mandates against him, he cheerfully replied that he was going to call the boy Adrian after the Pope. Worse than that, he hoped that his mistress would before long give him another child, and should it be a girl he would call her Adriana, or if a boy, Beneventus, for he was about to wait on the Lord Pope at Benevento. "A crying scandal and a conspicuous liar," John called him, but it does not appear that he was dealt with according to his deserts. It is small wonder that archdeacons as a class were unpopular. The chief qualification for an archdeacon was legal knowledge, and so Bologna was filled by young potential archdeacons; and to their wildness they added, it was commonly said, an unholy proficiency in mastering all the Italian subtleties in the art of administering poison.

Of bishops, John was equally critical. Simony, aggrandisement, and hypocrisy were the three evils which he most denounced in the Church of his day; and of these the greatest was hypocrisy. Bishops were peculiarly guilty of it. They compass sea and land to get the offer of a bishopric, rarely disdaining bribery, and more seldom still the small but potent voice of influence. Then, when at last the bishopric is offered, they make a great show of pretending to refuse it on the ground of unworthiness, and crying *noli episcopari*, are with difficulty dragged to the place of consecration by applauding crowds and singing choirs, whose presence they have previously arranged. If, on the other hand, the offer of the bishopric seems like to be denied on the ground of unworthiness, none so prompt or ready as they to turn even their failings into reasons why the offer should be made to them:

> ... If he is of low birth, so was St. Peter; if under age, so were Jeremiah and St. John the Baptist, when first set apart for their ministry; if a youth, so was Daniel when he defended Susanna against her accusers; if unlearned, so were the Apostles; if married, so were the bishops who St. Paul said were to be chosen ... if he is of a slow tongue like Moses, an Aaron can be found to speak for him. ... St. Peter's assault on the high priest's servant will serve as an excuse for violence, the timidity of Jonah and St. Thomas for cowardice, the tax-gathering of St. Matthew for entanglement in public business. If he is accused of gluttony and wine-bibbing, so was our Lord; if of insubordination, St. Paul withstood St. Peter to the face. ... St. Peter foreswore himself; Zacharias, though dumb, dis-

charged the office of a priest; St. Paul was blind when Ananias laid his hands upon him; ... Christ Himself was, according to the prophet, like a leper, "without form or comeliness". The objection that he was of despicable condition was brought against St. Martin, St. Cyprian erred in doctrine, St. Gregory the Great was an invalid, St. Brice was proud and vain, the confessor Paphnutius was mutilated, the sons of Zebedee canvassed for the first places in the kingdom of heaven, St. Augustine had been a Manichee, Pope Marcellinus had committed idolatry, St. Ambrose was not yet baptized when chosen to be bishop, St. Paul had been a persecutor, the Apostles themselves were not canonically elected by the people.[1]

John was in a position to know of what he spoke, and his evidence could be supported by a mass of quotations from Gerald of Wales, though for the most part Gerald's acid observations were directed towards the bishops in Ireland. Yet in spite of this impressive testimony, it may be doubted whether the picture of the English bishop as simoniacal, ambitious, greedy, and hypocritical, is either just or accurate. In actual fact, the English bishops in the middle years of the century were a most distinguished set of men, and set a remarkably high standard to Christendom. At Canterbury Theobald was followed by Becket. At Hereford there was Robert of Melun, and at London Gilbert Foliot, both considerable figures in the Schools. Exeter had Bartholomew, the canonist, and author of the famous *Penitential*.

Bartholomew was a great diocesan bishop, but not wholly untypical. His biographer draws a pleasant and impressive picture of him at work in the Devonshire villages. We see him taking the place of the parish priest and hearing the con-

[1] Clement Webb. op. cit., pp. 56, 57.

THE CHURCH OF GOD

fessions of those who have grave crimes to tell, sleeping in a village vicarage and waking at midnight to recite Matins, appointing a chaplain for a cemetery and setting aside a moiety for him to live on, preaching innumerable sermons—*exhortatio* in the villages and *doctrina* in the monasteries, organizing the common life of the new Exeter Cathedral and finding an income for its priests, sleepless for six days and nights and hard at death's door with pneumonia and all his household down at the same time with influenza, ordaining, confirming, holding synods, issuing charters, stamping on simony, and disciplining archdeacons. He was among the company of bishops who grudgingly undertook central church work in London, giving the first place of his time to his own diocese, and the second to writing his *Penitential*.[1] Probably he was the best diocesan bishop of his generation, but the fact that his high standards caused but little remark suggests that others too served faithfully.

But when all is said which can be said, it remains the fact that the twelfth-century Church failed in its most vital function. Many things it did admirably, especially in England. It was the home of scholars, preachers, pastors, priests, laboriously performing unexciting tasks, and not a few saints. But the primary duty which history laid upon it, it did not fulfil. The thing needed most was that the Church should make the civilizer invincible by its redemption of highly placed tyranny and brutality, and set the poets and scholars free to make their contribution effective in terms of the common life of the age. And this it did not do.

To do it meant to justify a theory. The instinct of the medieval ecclesiastic to argue for the Two Cities, or the Sun

---

[1] Morey. op. cit. See Chapter V, *passim*.

THE GOLDEN MIDDLE AGE

and Moon theory, of political science was wholly justified by the facts. In the conflict of Church and State, whether fought out between Pope and Emperor, or more locally between Henry II and Thomas Becket, the triumph of the secular view led straight to barbarism. But before the Church could triumph, it had to be shown worthy to sustain so colossal a task, and this it never was.

John of Salisbury's *Policraticus* sets out the terms of the problem, and indicates the reasons why the Church as he knew it could never solve it in practice.

The pressure of political events is the generating force of the *Policraticus*. When John began it we do not know, but it can hardly have been earlier than the date of his return to England from the service of the Papal *Curia*; and he finished it a year or two before Theobald died. The book is thus the product of his Canterbury years. It reflects the pressure of the primary problem of his time, the relationship between Church and State. In England, the events of Stephen's reign had raised it, though not in an acute form since the evils which then fell upon the Church were due rather to the weakness and division than to the strength and unity of the secular authority. When Henry II had come to the throne and quickly proved himself to be a strong, autocratic monarch, it required no great perspicacity of judgment to foresee trouble between the lay and ecclesiastical arms if Theobald were succeeded by a primate as strong and resolute as Henry II himself was. Already, before Theobald's death, trouble had begun to rear its head when the Church was taxed to provide funds for the siege of Toulouse, and John himself had suffered the royal displeasure for permitting and forwarding unlicensed appeals to Rome. On the Continent the same trouble was showing itself

THE CHURCH OF GOD

in an even acuter form in the controversy between Pope Adrian IV and the Emperor Frederick Barbarossa; and John was far too close an intimate of Adrian's, and met him far too frequently, not to have been told the full details of the story as they were seen from the Papal point of view. The rival claims of Church and State were in fact a first-class controversial issue, and it was natural for one of the first scholars of his time to set down in writing the political principles on which, as it seemed to him, good government depended. There is no doubt that one of the motives which guided him was the desire to spare England—his own *Patria*—precisely such a conflict as developed immediately upon Theobald's death.

The book's foundations are buried deep in history. Everything in the Middle Ages seems to have its roots somewhere in Augustine, and he is certainly the father of medieval political science, in that he first states the terms of its primary problem, the relationship which should subsist between the ecclesiastical and the lay authorities, between the Prince and the Church. In the *City of God* Augustine had suggested that the problem existed and was difficult because of the lamentable confusion in this world between the two Cities, the City whose builder and maker is God and whose citizens are moved to belong to it by their love for God, and the Temporal City, made with hands, doomed to perish, and peopled by citizens whose prevailing characteristic is the love of self. In the sight of God they are distinct, and therefore they are distinct in fact, but owing to the dullness of our blinded sight their distinction does not become apparent in this world. In the next world we shall no doubt clearly perceive the distinction but in this world the two cities are in practice too confused and mingled to be exactly severed and docketed under the titles Church and State. Yet the very fact that efforts are continually being made to save souls, an occupation clearly divine both in inspiration and in origin, suggests the existence in the here-and-now world of at least a province of the City of God. Hence, whenever the Church is at work on its primary task of saving souls, that is of persuading the citizens of the earthly city to become citizens of the heavenly, it automatically constitutes a part of the *Civitas Dei*.

This was a theory which made history, and there is no medieval thinker in the field of political science who does not sooner or later revert to it. Hildebrand seized on it as a buttress for his claim that the hierarchy was more honourable and more filled with authority than the earthly monarchy. Pope Gregory VII went further still. He claimed for the humblest priest a higher authority than monarchs and emperors possessed. Yet the society he envisaged was functional, and he did not for a moment demand any measure of clerical omnicompetence. His aim was so to assert the inherent priority and privileges of his order that the prevalent *superbia* of the lay monarchs should become *justitia*. And to this end his aim was twofold: to press the temporal power to acknowledge that its authority was derived from the spiritual power, and then so to reform the spiritual power as to make it in fact what it claimed to be in theory, the redeeming agency by which men transfer their citizenship from the earthly to the heavenly city.

Such are the arguments and the aims which underlie the *Policraticus*. John, too, used the metaphor of the Two Swords, claiming that both are derived from the Church. "From the Church the Prince received the material sword, since both weapons were originally hers. The material sword the prince wields for her use and advantage, and is consequently her minister."

The essential premiss of the whole argument is the theory of the Fall of Man. To believe the Fall of Man, and all that must logically follow from it, is already to be committed to some form of the "Social Contract" theory of the basis and purpose of society. By this, men are held to contract into a society and out of their previous state of isolated and chaotic brutishness; and the basis of such a state is therefore aptly described as springing from an essential evil. Gregory VII was by no means illogical in suggesting that the real founder of the temporal power was Cain, who shed the blood of righteous Abel. But the Fall of Man involves a state of righteousness in the past, and sanity demands belief in a state of righteousness in the future, towards which men gradually struggle. Into the midst of this not ignoble conception of social evolution is thrust the redeeming life and death of Christ, for which its theory must find a place in its statement. Hence Augustine's Two Cities theory, and the later improvements and variations upon it. But John was at one with his political predecessor, Gregory VII, who saw clearly that it was useless in practice to suggest the theory, the pre-eminence of the clerical order, if that order did not so behave as fitly to bear the burden of eminence which his theory thrust upon it. The main concern of Gregory's life had been the reform of the Church, and, in the same spirit, John followed his analysis of the respective powers and spheres of Church and State, by a thorough-going and unsparing account of such current evils of the Church as made the ecclesiastical arm unfit to wield the sword which his political theory handed to it.

THE GOLDEN MIDDLE AGE

The picture John drew of the Church of his day was certainly blacker than the facts warranted, and no one would guess from it that a great religious revival was in full swing as he wrote, nor that the greatest saints were then plentiful on the earth. But it was useless to claim for the Church the position of the fount of all earthly authority and power, and to shirk the manifest unfitness of the Church to wield *de facto* the power this theory claimed *de jure*. The medieval theory of Church and State, which John stated in its completest and most uncompromising form, has everywhere vanished from the modern world; and to attempt to revive it would be to court amused and even irritated laughter. If we can still read with pleasure and sympathy the classic statements of the medieval theory, it is because the writers save themselves from the charge of arrogance by never shirking or cloaking the evils which made the Church —their own clerical order—so sorry an instrument to bear the terrific responsibility they would theoretically thrust upon it, and also because, in medieval conditions, what was really at stake was the idea of civilization.

As it was, the twelfth century which opened so gloriously and has laid mankind so heavily in its debt, ended by being betrayed in the house of its friends. It brought the universities to birth, fought the battles of Reason in the field of theology, and gave to the cause of Reason the apt instrument of its perpetual growth: and then the scholars themselves struck Reason a deadly blow by admitting Cornificius in Paris, and starving Chartres to death. For the first time for centuries, grace and gaiety of living were made widely possible and the fruit of it is seen in the sudden outburst of joy in the goliardic poems: and then the goliards themselves, the wandering scholars, betrayed their cause by allowing their order to be justly regarded as synonymous with every kind of undisciplined futility, and even beastliness of life. The century even seemed to promise the redemption of appalling rural social conditions by the rapid growth of towns, the guild system of industry, and the accumulation for the first time for centuries of surplus wealth; and then it dissipated that wealth in essentially squalid international forays like the Crusades, or in civil wars of every kind. And the Church which preached the Crusades, which benefited by the villeins' labour, and was fatally tied to the manorial system, which made the universities and then turned the arts and humanities out of them, for all its faithfulness in lesser fields wholly failed to establish the theory it had evolved and which contained the one condition of real civilizing progress in the conditions of the medieval world.

Yet the century had given much. It had redeemed the slurs of medievalism and given a great treasure to the world. Medieval Europe could thereafter take its place with Ancient Greece: it had given a dazzling century to history, filled with hope, promise, and achievement, when life for a larger proportion of the people than had ever been the case in Athens seemed new every morning. Its glory was fleet and passing, but it was real.

INDEX

There is hardly a page in this book in which the name of John of Salisbury does not occur. I have therefore refrained from listing him in this index.

A

Abbo, Abbot of Fleury, 27
Abelard, Peter, 9, 25, 39, 41, 44, 45, 55, 68, 69, 76, 80–2, 93, 96, 121, 130, 134, 151, 155, 158, 161, 174
Absolom of St. Victor, 72, 111, 112
Adam du Petit Pont, 94–6, 167
Adrian IV, Pope, 104, 218, 219, 220, 221, 242
Alberic of Rheims, 84
Albertus Magnus, 151, 215
Alcuin, 17
Anselm of Laon, 41, 67, 121, 162
Aquinas, St. Thomas, 49
"Archpoet," the, 66
Aristotle, 37, 38, 74, 120, 163, 164
Arnold of Brescia, 151, 215
Arnoul, Bishop of Orleans, 26
Augustine, St., 3, 147, 164, 247
Averrhoes, 37, 120

B

Bartholomew, Bishop of Exeter, 235, 244, 245
Becket, St. Thomas, 34, 104, 118, 126, 167, 173, 191, 211, 227, 244
Benedict of Clusa, 39
Bennett, H. S., 188
Berengar, 8, 160
Bernard of Chartres, 70, 83, 84, 88–92, 162

Bernard, St., of Clairvaux, 55, 61, 121, 132, 134, 135, 148, 151, 157, 160, 161, 162–71, 217, 219, 230
Boethius, 72, 74, 121, 167
Boniface, St., 10–12, 15
Bryce, Viscount, 13, 14, 214, 217
Buoncompagno, 108
Bury, Richard de, Bishop of Durham, 52, 60, 94, 101, 133, 140, 238

C

Cæsarius of Heisterbach, 114
Capet, Robert, 27
Carlyle, Thomas, 1, 116
Cassiodorus, 21
Charlemagne, 4, 10, 12–23, 122
Chesterton, G. K., 51
"Cornificius", 88, 92–7, 122

D

Donatus, 92

E

Erasmus, 58
Eugenius III, Pope, 100, 170, 199, 217, 219, 223

F

Fitzstephen, 79, 80, 190, 192, 196
Florence of Worcester, 142
Foliot, Gilbert, 191, 244
Francis, St., of Assisi, 116
Frederick I, Emperor, 34, 148, 151, 172, 219, 221
Fulbert of Chartres, 27, 28–32, 70, 83

INDEX

G

Gerald of Wales, 46, 65, 109–11, 124, 130, 158, 172, 216, 223, 231, 234
Gerbert of Aurillac, 23–31, 70
Giraldus Cambrensis. (*See* Gerald of Wales.)
Gratian, 121
Gregory II, Pope, 11
Guibert de Nogent, 8, 121
Guiscard, Robert, 214
Guitmund of Aversa, 27

H

Haskins, C. H., 63, 154, 239
Heloise, 68, 158
Henri d'Andeli, 99
Henry II, King of England, 34, 35, 118, 119, 123, 124, 127, 153, 173, 204, 206, 211, 230
Henry of Huntingdon, 142
Henry, Bishop of Winchester, 215, 222
Herbert of Bosham, 127
Hermann of Dalmatia, 120
Hildebert of Le Mans, 214

I

Isadore of Seville, 111
Ivo, Bishop of Chartres, 83

J

James of Venice, 78
Jocelyn of Brakelond, 1, 76, 77, 142, 172
John, King of England, 130
John of Celle, 69
John of Cornwall, 55, 97
John of Garland, 57, 59, 64, 154
John of Synesford, 128
Jusserand, 32

K

Kingsford, Charles, 153

L

Lane Poole, R., 25, 29, 94, 101
Langland, 179, 180
Leo III, Pope, 16
Louis, St., King of France, 49

M

Map, Walter, 106, 124, 199, 222, 231, 234
Martel, Charles, 15
Milton, 143
Moore, George, 136

N

Neckham, Alexander, 130, 199

O

Odericus Vitalis, 28
Odilo, St., 29
Otric, 24
Otto II, Emperor, 24, 26, 27
Otto, Bishop of Friesingen, 83, 121, 146–52
Owst, G. R., 185

P

Paris, Matthew, 34, 202
Parker, Matthew, 133, 231
Pepin, 12, 15
Peter of Blois, 57, 93, 123, 124, 126, 140
Peter of Celle, 52, 125, 133, 211, 221
Peter Lombard, 121, 127, 168, 171
Philip the Fair, 35
Plato, 72, 74, 120, 149, 164, 170
Porrée, Gilbert, 55, 130, 148, 151, 162–71
Powicke, Professor F. M., 222, 227
Priscian, 71, 121

Q

Quiller-Couch, Sir Arthur, 43

INDEX

R
Ralph de Diceto, 142
Rashdall, Hastings, 8, 42, 69, 74, 75, 229
Reade, Charles, 33
Rémusat, Charles de, 81
Robert of Cricklade, 123
Robert of Melun, 55, 168, 244
Robert de Sourbon, 61, 72, 73
Roger of Hoveden, 142

S
Samson, Abbot of St. Edmunds, 1, 34, 46, 108, 172, 192, 207, 237
Simeon of Durham, 142
Stephen, King of England, 35, 40, 118, 119, 190, 205
Stubbs, Bishop, 124, 125
Suger, Abbot of St. Denis, 216, 218
Sylvester II, Pope. (*See* Gerbert of Aurillac.)
Symonds, John Addington, 159

T
Theobald, Archbishop of Canterbury, 104, 124–9, 167, 222, 244
Thierry of Chartres, 70, 83
Traherne, Thomas, 102

V
Vacarius, 127
Vitry, Jacques de, 56

W
Waddell, Helen, 63, 113, 156, 169
Walkelin, Archdeacon of Suffolk, 242
William of Champeau, 67, 80–2, 84
William of Conches, 123
William of Malmesbury, 23, 26, 142, 144
William of Newburgh, 142
William of St. Thierry, 130, 161
- Wirecker, Nigel, 125